文化发展论丛（世界卷）

Culture Development Review: World (2015)

2015 年第3期 总第9期

湖北大学高等人文研究院 中华文化发展湖北省协同创新中心 ◎ 编

主 编 ◎ 江 畅

执行主编 ◎ 强以华

副主编 ◎ 李家莲

社会科学文献出版社

SOCIAL SCIENCES ACADEMIC PRESS (CHINA)

"亚洲价值和人类未来"研究专辑

《文化发展论丛》编辑委员会

文化发展论丛（世界卷）2015
卷首语

若说自然是人类共同的物质家园的话，那么，文化则是人类共同的精神家园。在全球化的今天，在不同国家、不同民族让各自的精神家园逐渐融入人类共同的精神家园的时候，其间既包含了共建人类共同精神家园的喜悦，也包含了各种不同的国家和民族的精神家园因其所含价值观的差异所引起的冲突的苦恼。因此，从文化的角度探讨人类的共同的精神家园的建构问题，特别是从文化之核心亦即价值观的角度探讨如何消除人类共同精神家园建构中的各种不同的价值观的冲突问题，便是相关学者的重要的历史使命。

湖北大学高等人文研究院和中华文化发展湖北省协同创新中心正是本着这一使命感与校内外、省内外、国内外的学人探讨世界文化，思考如何共建人类共同的精神家园。为了更好地承担自己肩负的历史使命，湖北大学高等人文研究院在成立中国文化研究中心和湖北文化研究中心的同时，也成立了世界文化研究中心，定期举办世界文化发展论坛。论坛每年选定一个主题从一个侧面探讨世界文化，并且每年围绕所选主题举办一次大型的国际会议，以期取得实质性的突破。20 世纪末 21 世纪初以来，在全球化的进程中，一个历史性的重大事件就是亚洲的崛起。这次亚洲的崛起与此前的亚洲"四小龙"的崛起有所区别，这一区别不仅表现在这次有更多的亚洲国家的崛起，更表现在这一次崛起中，还包含了诸如中国和印度这样的大国的崛起，它表明这一次崛起不是哪个亚洲"国家"的崛起而是整个"亚洲"的崛起。亚洲的崛起首先表现为亚洲经济的崛起，亚洲经济的崛起必将推动亚洲价值的崛起。但是，何谓亚洲价值，亚洲价值如何崛起，它应该以什么样的方式融入世界，以及在建构人类共同的精神家园中应该起什么样的作用，如此等等，都是急迫需要解决但又无现成答案的问题。

因此，湖北大学高等人文研究院把 2015 年世界文化论坛的主题定为"亚洲价值和人类未来"，并且联合印度古瓦哈蒂大学召集来自亚洲、欧洲、南美洲、北美洲的专家学者齐聚一堂，共同深入讨论亚洲价值以及它对人类未来发展的影响问题，它的最终成果集中体现在本卷亦即《文化发展论丛·世界卷》（2015）之中。这些成果分别围绕"理论前沿"、"论坛专题"、"问题探讨"和"比较研究"等四个领域细致探讨了有关亚洲价值及其影响的诸多方面的重要问题。我们真诚地期待本卷论文能够引起相关学者和关心亚洲价值崛起的人士，以及那些关心人类共同的精神家园建设的人士的关注，激发他们对于这些问题的探讨兴趣，并且期待我们的研究对于他们的探讨能够有所启发。

International Conference on "Asian Values and Human Future"

This international seminar, "World Culture Development Forum" on "Asian Values and Human Future" has been two years in the making. Bringing together seminal thinkers from 20 universities and 8 other institutions from 11 countries of the world to deliberate on various facets of this timely theme has been the achievement of team that gave it all they had. This Book Abstracts is a testimonial to the divergence of outcomes when "Asian Values" and "Human Future" are put through the viewing glasses of scholars and thinkers from right round the world.

The idea of holding this conference emerged from the recent debates that have been continuously reminding us that all our cultures are under pressure from modern and postmodern trends, more so in the developed countries. But in our part of the world, this trend is shaking today the very foundations of ancient Asian civilizations.

Great social movements that have freed the human spirit and lifted people out of dead-ends have required heroic effort by those who have imagined a better world and done something about it. This sort of imagination is once again central to fashioning and securing the moorings of our civilizational and cultural riches. A profound reflection on Asian values that have stood the test of time could be instrumental in fashioning such a world.

Traditions are invaluable. But change is inevitable. The path to a better future may not always be through a throw-back to the ways of old. The imperative today is for creative and critical thinking to break new grounds and take humanity forward. Though traditionalists often tend to grow over-defensive and their sense of insecurity leads them to take rigid stands, what is required instead is to integrate the old and the new. This Conference aims at making a fresh synthesis of ideals, values, ethical norms, and philosophical principles drawn from different Asian cultures to address this emerging situation.

An acceptance of human embeddedness in multiple cultural experiences forms the basis of this re-examination. The willingness to contemplate a different self/other and to draw from the cultural assets and ethical principles of a variety of communities is the guiding principle of this debate.

This debate is necessitated by a globalized economic agenda that has been pulling younger people from their homes, their families, their religious beliefs, their cultural roots, their community identities, their familiar terrain, and throwing them into the rough seas of uncertainties. They are adrift with but little sense of security and even less of belongingness. With the weakening of family and community bonds, they are often unable to develop a clear vision of the future or depend on their convictions. Everything is under threat.

Increasingly, the trends are clear-trends that undermine our moral fibre, social bonds, sense of common belonging and commitment to shared values and ideals leading to corruption, unabashed egotism and closed-minded sectarian thinking. As individuals and communities grow uprooted and materialistic, people become self-centred and lose sight of the sources of their moral vitality: family, religion, local traditions and cultural roots. They fail to draw energy and motivation from the organic and life-giving dimensions of culture and lose the ability to see the sublime in the simple dimensions of their tradition. It is in such situations of helplessness that people, especially the youth, develop attitudes that are aggressive and contentious, and grow stubborn and unbending. They do not realize how, while they fight their way forward against real and imagined enemies, they are developing a counter culture that cannot sustain them in the long run.

Asian thinkers down the centuries have been the promoters of the unifying vision of reality behind every civilization. This conference is an attempt to take a long, hard look at present day realities in the light of Asian values that have stood the test of time, possibly offering a fresh vision for the future of humanity.

It gives me great pleasure in acknowledging here the admirable job put in by the two Secretaries to the Conference: Prof. Joy Thomas from Assam Don Bosco University and Dr. Li Jialian from Hubei University. Their dedication has been outstanding. Let me acknowledge also the tenacity and commitment of the members of the Organizing Committee from our University: Dr. Basil Koikara, Dr. Paul Pudussery, Dr. Dominic Meyieho, Dr. Francis Fernandez, Dr. Riju Sharma, Dr. Peter Paul Hauhnar, Ms. Juhi Baruah, Ms. Nabamita Das, Mr. James Thafamkima, Fr. CM Paul, Fr. Joseph Nellanatt, Dr. Prasanta Kumar Choudhury, Mr Bikramjit Goswami, Ms Hemashree Bordoloi, Ms Gitu Das, Mr Utpal Gogoi and Ms Irina Barua.

Dr. Stephen Mavely
Vice Chancellor, Assam Don Bosco University

目录
CONTENTS

比较研究

序　亚洲价值的崛起

强以华

随着亚洲经济在当今世界的崛起，亚洲价值也正在随之崛起。

从经济和价值观念关系的角度说，经济的发展通常会先于并且快于作为一种精神现象的价值观念的发展，因此，在当今的亚洲世界中，经济首先发展起来。在最近 30 多年的时间里，在日本经济崛起之后，亚洲很多国家的经济随之先后崛起，其中包括中国、印度、韩国和新加坡等国经济的崛起。中国和印度作为当今世界人口最多的两个国家，它们经济的崛起具有特别重要的意义，它使得亚洲经济在世界经济中所占的比重大为增加。当前，中国已被誉为"世界工厂"，它的经济规模逐渐超越法国、英国、德国、日本等发达国家而成了当今世界仅次于美国的第二大经济体。随着亚洲特别是中国、印度经济的增长，亚洲的价值观念不仅在客观上大大地增强了自己的影响力，而且它在主观上也需要在世界上拥有更大的话语权。所以，在亚洲经济崛起之后，学界开始积极探讨亚洲价值崛起的问题，包含何谓亚洲价值，它有什么特征，如何对它做出价值判断，它如何崛起，以及它对未来世界将会产生什么影响，等等。正是在这样的背景之下，印度阿萨姆邦博斯科（Assam Don Bosco）大学和湖北大学高等人文研究院于 2015 年 7 月 7~9 日在印度古瓦哈蒂联合主办了以"亚洲价值和人类未来"为主题的国际学术会议，让来自亚洲、欧洲、南美洲、北美洲的专家学者齐聚一堂，共同讨论亚洲价值以及它对人类未来发展的影响问题。这次会议是湖北大学高等人文研究院举办的系列"世界文化发展论坛"国际会议的一个有机组成部分，此次论坛是继 2013 年 9 月在中国湖北大学举行的以"当代世界主流文化的现状与未来"为主题的首届"世界文化发展论坛"（2013）和 2014 年 7 月在美国圣托马斯大学举行的以"经济不平等与世界公正"为主题的第二届"世界文化发展论坛"（2014）之后的第三届"世界文化发展论坛"。会议共收到 50 多篇具有重要学术价值的论文，这里，我们围绕"理论前沿"、"论坛专题"、"问题探讨"和"比较研究"四个领域收录了一批论文公开发表，以期引起国际学界的进一步重视和讨论。

在"理论前沿"之中，我们收录了《构建超越西方价值观的亚洲价值观》、《核心价值观教育与终极美德实践研究》（A Study on the Education of Core Value & A Practice of Ultimate Virtue）、《倡导确保安全未来的价值观：指向世界未来的亚洲价值观》（Encouraging Values to Ensure A Future：Asian Values for the Future of the World）、《和谐与和平视域中的宗教多元化》（Religious Pluralism as A Proper Ideology for Harmony and Peace）等数篇学术论文。这些论文分别探讨了价值、中西方的价值、亚洲价值，以及核心价值观、伦理、宗教方面的理论前沿问题，特别是探讨了如何构建亚洲价值的理论问题。

在《构建超越西方价值观的亚洲价值观》中，江畅教授认为现代西方价值观"伴随着强大的现代西方文明逐渐流行到全世界，深刻影响着世界发展的进程，导致整个人类价值观日益一体化和趋同化。然而，西方价值观存在着一些不可克服的根本缺陷和弊端，西方价值观假如世界化就会加速人类的毁灭"。基于这样的理解，他说："……整个人类特别是具有丰富历史资源和诸多独特优势的古老亚洲，应该努力构建超越西方价值观的更先进的价值观，从根本上改变今天西方价值观日渐全球化的世界格局。"为此，他探讨了试图超越西方价值观的亚洲价值观的构建问题，指出"在非西方世界中，亚洲具有诸多构建先进人类价值观的独特优势"，这些优势除了人口数量的优势之外，更是包括了下述四个方面的优势，即：其一，亚洲有悠久的历史、文化传统和丰富的历史文化资源；其二，亚洲人都是土生土长的本地居民，他们祖祖辈辈生活在这里，这里是他们的家园，因而亚洲人有强烈的民族认同感和独特的民族性格，很难全盘西化；其三，近代以来，亚洲思想家和政治家对构建具有本民族特色的发展模式做出了艰难的探索，积累了丰富的思想理论和实践经验；其四，亚洲意识正在觉醒，亚洲迅速崛起，亚洲命运共同体正在形成之中。在这篇论文中，江畅教授从一个新的角度提出了问题，并且给出了自己的观点，他的文章将会引起进一步的思考。

在《倡导确保未来安全的价值观：指向世界未来的亚洲价值观》中，印度的托马斯·梅纳帕拉皮尔（Thomas Menamparampil）教授探讨了指向世界未来的价值观问题。该论文的触角十分广泛，在它十分广泛的触角中，作者表达的是一种综合、和谐的思想，他想要通过综合亚洲文化中的各种价值乃至西方价值中的各种各样的合理因素，追求亚洲以及全球的团结与和谐。首先，他提出了全球化影响下的弱势社区如何对待全球化的立场问题。他说，在全球化的影响下，弱势社区（例如亚洲）通常采取两种相反但又都很极端的立场，即：或者是对自己的文化感到自卑，特别是在分析自己的文化不能帮助自己在这个善变的世界中解决任何问题的时候更是如此，因此，他们简单地认为传统价值已经过时，直接拒绝传统并且如饥似渴地吸收新型文化；或者对自己的文化极度自信，对传统文化表现出前所未有的迷恋，甚至对传统文化中的糟粕也是如此，因此，他们拒绝接受任何他们不熟悉的对象或者异质文化的内容。作者认为，这两种立场都是错误的立场。在他看来，正确的立场应是这样的立场，即：既对自己的文化具有信心，又以开放的态度学习和吸收对自己有益的新的文化。只有这样，我们才能让各种不同的思想融合并取长补短，从而形成新的观念世界，为我们的后代找到希望。因此，作者基于这样的立场对亚洲价值观进行了反思和共享。在论文中，作者广泛地讨论了市场问题、腐败问题、经济中的不平衡问题、后殖民的焦虑问题、暴力抗议问题等一系列重要问题，在这些讨论的基础上，作者反思了中国传统文化和印度传统文化中的合理价值，并且以宽容的态度吸收西方的文化，探讨指向未来的亚洲价值观，作者进一步认为，这才是确保未来安全的价值观。此篇论文的思路开阔，观点开放，值得推荐。

　　韩国的金英硕（Kim Young Suk）教授在《核心价值观教育与终极美德实践研究》中探讨了为什么要改进教育，特别是在教育中如何培养核心价值观从而实践终极美德的问题。在他看来，从根本上说，学习的目的是"格物致知"，也就是说，掌握事物的原理。宗教的目的是追求不变的真理并使其成为现实。因此，哲学和神学一样，源自揭示人类的起源和基础，并寻求上天的智慧来回答"什么是正义的生活？"然而，在众多教育学派中，却没有人能够发现真相和幸福。迄今为止，无知的学习与教育固定了所有人的思维模式。人们想挣脱意识的精神牢笼，但却被自身错误的意识所束缚，被欲望牢牢捆绑住，最终缓缓消亡。他说："我已经在学校教学 29 年，但从来没有见到过公共教育体系能使学生满意或使他们幸福。"在他看来，这是因为学校没有优先教授学生共同利益的伦理观、共存共荣的道德观，也没有教会学生尊重生命。这样的教育使学生把别人视为对手而未将其视为爱的对象，它使人们之间的关系变得冷漠和无情……"换句话说，学校并没有去教那使学生在自身内部认识到无限的快乐并在自己的自我意识中解放出来的真正的哲学和核心价值。这就是学校教育的现状。现在，学校应该避免会培养自私主义的竞争性的教育，而要教育如何促进人类的共同利益。此外，教育还迫切需要专注于培养正直的人乃至圣人，从而在地球村中开启一个新的和平年代。"作者认为，现在正是学校通过教育帮助学生获得重生成为正直的人乃至圣人的时刻，它应开导学生走向真理，并且实践终极的美德，而这种终极的美德就是公共利益。因此，在本文中，作者集中讨论了核心价值的重要性，并且认为这是全人类走向和平、真正幸福的选择。论文充满了浓浓的向善的情意和深切的对于世界和平的渴望，它大大地增加了论文的意义。

　　在"论坛专题"中，我们收录了《亚洲价值观和伦理秩序探微》、《大学外拓项目对区域发展及亚洲价值的现实意义》（Relevance of University Outreach Programmes for Regional Development and Asian Values）、《亚洲精神传统：孕育一种跨文化精神》（Asian Spiritual Traditions：Birthing A Trans-Cultural Spirituality）、《儒家伦理的情感特征

及其作用》、《中国诚信价值观的过去、现在与未来》、《以家庭为纽带的可持续发展》（Sustainable Development Vie the Family）等数篇学术论文。这些论文主要围绕亚洲价值、中国伦理和家庭伦理探讨了一个共同的专题，即：亚洲价值及其作用。

在《亚洲价值观和伦理秩序探微》中，刘可风教授指出，从纯粹学术的意义上说，亚洲价值观的提法似乎有些偏颇，也就是说，用洲际、国别来界定价值观其实没有根据。不过，他说，我们现在讨论亚洲价值观时已经超越了纯粹学术的范围，它与亚洲人讨论洲际的命运和未来密切相关，所以就此而言，我们还是可以把亚洲价值观作为一个有意义的问题来进行探讨。在此意义上，刘可风教授认为，"亚洲价值观不是所有亚洲人和亚洲国家一致认同的价值观，而是起源于亚洲的并且可能对亚洲的未来发展有益的价值观。"尽管我们十分需要一种亚洲价值观，但是，"我们必须明确，以国家为本的亚洲价值观是否已经完成了由传统身份制国家观向现代契约论国家观的转变；亚洲价值观中与威权主义的肯定的国家观相反相成的无政府主义的否定的价值观的强大作用力是否被我们认识；在儒家传统伦理所维护的'三纲'秩序被打破以后，我们能否建立起不同于'丛林法则'的'园林法则'伦理新秩序"。在他看来，只有"认清和解决这些问题，亚洲价值观才能成为亚洲发展的未来价值目标，反之则可能成为亚洲发展的障碍"。刘可风教授在指出了人们在探讨价值观时通常忽略的三个方面的问题之后强调，我们应该跳出纯亚洲人的视角来客观地看待问题，从而解决相关的问题。

强以华教授在《儒家伦理的情感特征及其作用》中分析了儒家伦理的情感特征以及这一特征的积极作用和消极作用。在他看来，儒家伦理学的情感特点是它区别于西方伦理学的一个根本特征。尽管西方伦理学中也包含了情感主义伦理学，但是，从其主流观点而言，西方伦理学主要还是一种理性主义伦理学，因此，若要正确地把握儒家伦理，重要的是把握它的情感特征，尤其是基于亲情的家庭情感特征。论文指出，在作用伦理对象的时候，由于情感伦理与理性伦理之间存在着作用范围狭小和作用范围广大、内容比较丰富和内容比较贫乏的不同甚至对立的特色，所以，儒家伦理作用于对象的方式也有自己的特色，即：它更加适用于私人领域但却更少适用于公共领域。在当年日本的经济奇迹中，儒家伦理就曾经起过十分重要的作用，它构成了日本企业文化的重要价值基础，增强了企业的凝聚力，并且随着日本经济的崛起，带有儒家情感色彩的文化也对国际社会起着越来越大的作用，并且是正面的积极作用。"这种情况就与当今整个亚洲，特别是中国的情形十分相似，即：中国的经济腾飞毫无疑问也有着中国儒家情感伦理在其中起的推动作用，同时，随着中国经济的崛起，中国儒家的情感伦理也必将会对国际社会起着越来越大的积极作用。"但是，由于儒家带有情感特征的伦理广延不大从而更少适用于公共领域的特色，我们也不能无限地夸大它的作用，在公共领域中，它只能起到辅助性的作用。

吴成国教授和曹林的文章《中国诚信价值观的过去、现在与未来》考察了中国传统文化中的诚信价值观，分析了它的过去、现在与未来。他们在对于"诚"、"信"两个概念释诂的基础上考察了诚信的起源和历史演变，指出中国古代"对诚信观念的推崇和引导，其道德价值是远远大于其他任何一种价值的"，"即使今天看来，这种将诚信的表现本身与著名历史人物进行叠加的组合也是宣导价值观的有效方式。它表达了对一种美好品格的肯定，并希冀未来的人们能够效仿"。总之，"两千年来儒家思想的发展，将诚信理念由一种实际操作上升为道德标榜"，它与逐渐道德化的儒家思想史的演化历程是息息相关的。作者进一步指出，在当代社会中，中国传统的诚信价值观遇到了困境，这种困境主要表现为中国传统诚信价值观赖以生存的土壤发生了变化，这种土壤由农业社会转向了现代化的工业社会。作者强调："儒家传统的诚信伦理主要是基于地缘、血缘的人与人交往过程中的诚实守信，主要依靠个人良心和无字无据的'君子协定'来约束各自的行为，缺乏相应的制度的保障。……这种基于血缘、亲缘、地缘的信用，其约束力、约束范围都极为有限。如果说在传统社会由于交换范围的有限性，社会在缺乏公共生活伦理和制度伦理层面的信用伦理的条件下依然可以维持下去的话，那么，在市场经济条件下，人们的交往日益普遍和复杂，交往的范围日益扩大，不再局限于有限的范围和熟人的圈子，非人情的交易也越来越多，传统的人伦信用已经无法满足市场秩序的需要，必须借助于以法律为保障的契约信用来维持。"正是由于诚信价值观在当代中国社会中存在着这样的困境，所以，作者在文章的最后对当代的诚信提出了反思和展望，试图找到消解诚信价值观当代困境的办法。我们认为，该论文对于儒家诚信价值观当代困境的分析十分到位，因此，我们相信该论文所提出的消解儒家诚信价值观当代困境的方法也一定会具有某种启发性。

在"问题探讨"中，我们收录了《以新人类文化和未来学为核心的一体化新生命文化运动研究》（A Study on New Life-Culture Movements for Oneness Focused on Neohumans' Culture & Futurology）、《网络舆情事件传播与社会公平正义的实现》、《国际法视域下的中国法律文化发展》（The Development of China's Legal Culture in the Perspective of International Rule of Law）、《人类未来的传统"希望"》（The "Hope" of Traditions for Human Future）、《〈泰凯尔〉知识分子关于中国的想象》（The Maoism of *Tel Quel* around May 1968）、《理性机巧与人类自由关系辩证》、《杰文斯悖论的价值论根源》等数篇学术论文。在这些论文中，学者们根据自己的研究领域和面对的现实情况探讨了各种不同的问题。这些问题的探讨扩展了关于亚洲价值和人类未来问题的讨论视野。

曾丽洁教授在《国际法视域下的中国法律文化发展》中分析了中国的法律文化如何在国际法视域下发展的问题。在她看来，人类历史的发展其实就是人类交往的发展，并首先是经济交往的发展；其中，法律作为规范交往秩序、保护交往安全的工具在人类交往和经济交往中起着关键的作用，从而导致了法律文化的交流并且进一步促进了法律的发展。在此基础上，作者继续分析法律文化以及中国如何在国际法视野下发展自己的法律的问题。她说，法律文化作为文化系统的一个分支，它像文化系统中的其他分支例如宗教文化、道德文化和政治文化一样具有文化的一般本性、特征和功能，这使得它与它们之间相互作用、相互补充；但是另一方面，法律文化作为一种特殊的文化现象，它又具有自己的不可替代的内容。一般来说，法律文化由一套观念和价值系统构成，它们通常会内化在法律思想和法律体系之中，成为人们的行为模式，制约人的发展。根据上述法律文化与其他分支文化，以及法律文化与法律、人的思想和行为之间的关系的理论，作者指出，在全球化的今天，在不同的文化，特别是法律文化交互作用之中，正处于伟大的社会转型和法律系统变革之中的中国应该在全球化的背景下注重法律文化的相互影响，让自己的法律文化的发展能够与国际法律文化以及其他国家法律文化的发展相互同步。

在"比较研究"中，我们收录了《东西方伦理文化差异比较》、《东西方经典著作中的不同处世方法之比较》（Different Methodologies of Life Indicated in Eastern and Western Classical Works）、《东方智慧和西方文化可以回答"何谓人类尊严"这一问题吗?》（Does Wisdom of Eastern and Western Cultures Respond to the Question：What is Human Dignity?）等数篇学术论文。这些论文从不同的角度比较了东西方文化、伦理，以及蕴含于其中的东西方的价值观念。

在《东西方伦理文化差异比较》中，葛晨虹教授分析探讨了东西方伦理文化的差异，并且揭示了造成这些差异背后的深层的历史原因和现实理由，她试图通过这种探讨更好地理解中西方文化，并且融通东方伦理文化和西方伦理文化，从而促进人类伦理文化的发展。论文首先对于东西方不同的历史道路进行了比较，指出西方的以古希腊为代表的"古典的古代"和以古代东方国家为代表的"亚细亚的古代"是两条存在着巨大差异的历史道路，前者是"从氏族到私产再到国家，个体私有制冲破了氏族组织，国家代替了氏族"，后者则是"在没有摧毁原始氏族组织的情况下直接进入奴隶制国家，血缘氏族制同国家的组织形式相结合"。正是在不同的历史道路的基础上，才造成了中国宗法（氏族）国家的特点，并且由之"引发出一整套天人合德、德性天赋，以及仁礼治世的思想，形成了儒家独特的以仁义道德为价值核心的德性思想体系"。这套思想体系就是儒家的伦理文化。在此基础上，论文进一步分析了东西方关于理性文化的两种取向，以及东西方关于社会治理的两种模式。就前者说，论文认为，西方文化更加重视"科学理性"，东方文化更加重视"价值理性",前者主要回答世界"是什么"的问题,后者则主要回答世界"应当是什么"的问题。其实,西方早期的科学理性和价值理性也是结合在一起的,但是,它在从古代走向现代的历史中,逐渐过分注重科学理性而忽视了价值理性,所以,唤醒东方的价值理性在当前具有重要意义。就后者说,"相对来说,西方社会治理传统具有比较独立的法制特点,而东方社会治理传统则具有德主刑辅的特点"。其实,人类历史都是由道德走向法律的,东方社会长期没有像西方那样由伦理法走向成熟的独立法,就其原因来看,主要有两个历史因素,即:第一个因素是东方社会缺少深植于西方传统中的"契约精神";第二个因素是"平等"观念的历史差异。所以,东方社会应该随着人类文明向工业社会的发展以及商品经济社会的发展,逐渐建立更加独立、更加完善的法律体系。该论文具有深厚的历史基础,具有重要的启发意义。

此外,李家莲教授的论文《东西方经典著作中的不同处世方法之比较》也值得一读。该论文通过中国传统文化中的《道德经》和西方传统文化中的《创世纪》比较了东西方社会两种不同的处世方式。李家莲指出,《道德经》与《创世纪》作为中西方道德哲学的经典著作,阐述了两种截然不同的处世方式,《道德经》重视"知常",而《创世纪》强调"谦卑"。不同的文化经典演绎了不同的文化内涵并奠定了不同的文化底蕴,前者孕育了中国文化中的乐感成分,而后者孕育了西方文化中的罪感成分。作者试图通过这样的比较研究给予读者某种启示。

理论前沿

构建超越西方价值观的亚洲价值观

江　畅[*]

摘　要：现代西方价值观深刻地影响着世界发展进程，直接导致整个人类价值观日益一体化和趋同化。本文探析了西方价值观的形成、优势与问题，为了克服西方价值观的弊端，寻求非西方价值观具有现实必然性和历史紧迫性。在这个过程中，亚洲肩负着构建超越西方价值观的先进价值观的特殊使命。

关键词：西方价值观　非西方价值观　亚洲价值观

Building Asian Values through the Way of Transcending Western Ones

Jiang Chang

Abstract： Modern Western values not only influence the world development deeply, but also lead to the increasing integration and assimilation of human values directly. The paper has made an analysis on the formation, benefits and problems of Western values. In the process of overcoming the drawbacks related

---

* 江畅，湖北大学哲学学院教授，高等人文研究院院长。

to Western values, it is very urgent and necessary to seek for Non-Western values which means Asian values will play an important role in building advanced values beyond Western values.

Keywords：Western Values；Non-Western Values；Asian Values

现代西方价值观（以下简称"西方价值观"）伴随着强大的现代西方文明逐渐流播到全世界，深刻影响着世界发展的进程，遂使整个人类价值观日益一体化和趋同化。然而，西方价值观存在着一些不可克服的根本缺陷和弊端，西方价值观假如世界化就会加速人类的畸形发展。为此，整个人类特别是具有丰富历史资源和诸多独特优势的古老亚洲，应该努力构建超越西方价值观的更先进的价值观，从根本上改变今天西方价值观日渐全球化的世界格局。

一　西方价值观的形成、优势和问题

西方价值观的形成可追溯到西方商业革命时期意大利地中海沿岸市场经济的兴起。从那时到 20 世纪 50 年代达到成熟形态，历时约 600 年。这是一个漫长的"血与火"的艰难历程，中间经历了文艺复兴、宗教改革、启蒙运动、政治革命、产业革命、经济学革命、哲学革命、科学技术革命，乃至世界大战、世界性经济危机等一系列革命运动和历史事件。西方价值观就是在这一系列伟大革命运动和重大历史事件中主要由思想家和政治家构建起来的，它是人类历史上第一个人类自觉构建的价值观体系。

在整个西方价值观构建的过程中，西方社会形成了关于社会发展的各种不同流派和思想体系，其中最有影响的是自由主义、共和主义和社会主义。在这三派主要观点争论交锋的过程中，自由主义最终成为西方社会主流价值观和价值体系。自由主义就是西方价值体系的理论形态和思想体系。自由主义内容极其丰富，概括说来，它是以个人幸福为终极价值目标，以利益、市场、科技、环保、责任、自由、平等、公正、民主、法治等为核心价值理念，以个体至上、天赋人权、私有财产神圣不可侵犯、主权在民、在法律下治理国家、三权分立等为基本价值原则的价值体系。"个人自由居于自由主义的核心位置"①，可以说，自由主义是以个人自由权利为根本价值取向的观念价值体系。依据这种理论构建起来的社会价值体系的基本要素是市场经济、现代科技、民主政治、法律统治。

西方价值观深刻改变了西方社会并通过西方社会深刻影响了整个人类社会的进程，使人类社会从贫穷落后的传统文明走向繁荣昌盛的现代文明。毫无疑问，这种模式有其旺盛的生命力和强大影响力，而根源则在于它的巨大优越性。"这种优越性主要表现在，它致力于把人从各种束缚中解放出来，努力扩大人的独立自性，刺激和鼓励人向内挖掘潜能向外征服世界，这不仅使人获得了自由，使我们的世界日益成为自由的世界、民主的世界，而且使人的能量最大限度地发挥了出来，使我们的世界日益成为富裕的世界、文明的世界。"②

我们应该承认西方价值观的基本合理性，也应该承认其巨大历史功绩。但是，我们更应该看到，西方价值观虽然看起来是个体主义、自由主义的，但其根本性质是资本主义的。或者更确切地说，虽然它的出发点和目的是个人解放、自由和幸福，但这种价值观在使人获得解放和自由的过程中却发生了异化，最终走向了以资本增殖为轴心，资本渗透它的整个结构和功能，资本控制一切。其结果，个人虽然从专制之下获得了解放，也获得了自由，但根据这种价值观构建的社会整个地被资本所控制，个人也因此而为新的奴役力量即资本所奴役，而没有真正获得解放、自由和幸福。由此看来，西方价值观实质上是一种资本主义价值观，是一种异化了的社会价值体系和发展模式。

二　寻求非西方价值观的现实紧迫性和历史必然性

20世纪以来，异化了的西方价值体系日益暴露出一些弊端，其中最

---

① 〔美〕马塞多：《自由主义美德》，马万利译，译林出版社，2010，第10页。
② 江畅：《幸福与和谐》，人民出版社，2005，第417页。

为突出的有贫富两极分化严重、周期性经济危机频发、恐怖主义盛行这三大问题。这些显性问题的深刻根源在于以市场经济为基础的现代化。这种现代化有三个最为突出且难以克服的痼疾：一是"原子化"问题。所谓"原子化"问题，就是近代以来自西方扩散至全球的现代化以孤立的个体为社会的实体，一切以个人的权利、个人的利益为轴心，不考虑共同体或社群，更不考虑全人类。二是资本化问题。市场经济原本是一种经济形态，其机制和原则只适用于经济领域。然而，在现代化的过程中，经济领域的市场化逐渐渗透到了整个社会生活。不受制约的资本逻辑和力量足以使整个社会和人的心灵彻底物化和奴化。三是极权化问题。现代西方社会成功地实现了对大众心理意识的操纵和控制，人们内心批判向度的丧失，促成各个领域的一体化。这三个问题并不是彼此孤立的，而是相互缠绕、相互支撑的。

所有这些难以克服的问题及其严重后果表明，西方价值观虽然可以带来人类的繁荣，但这是以人类不可再生资源迅速消耗、人类生存环境日益恶化、人类身体生物学结构加速变异为沉重代价的。西方价值体系的巨大物化力量，正在摧毁一切与之抗衡的异己力量，消除扩散途中的障碍和阻力，使这种模式迅速世界化、全球化。西方价值体系是一种加速人类毁灭的社会发展模式，伴随着西方价值体系世界化进程的加快，其负面作用还会进一步增大。在西方价值观的弊端及其后果日益显现的今天，非西方国家再也不能简单地照搬西方价值观，更不能搞所谓全盘西化，而是要采取强有力措施抵制西方价值观的扩张和渗透。什么样的措施是强有力的？当然不是把国门关起来，在信息化时代，一个国家的国门也不可能完全关闭。真正强有力的措施，是在学习借鉴西方价值观的基础上超越这种价值观，构建比西方价值观更适应人类可持续发展的、使人类真正幸福安宁地生活的更先进的价值观。构建超越西方价值观的更先进价值观，是从根本上克服西方价值观给世界已经带来的和可能带来的问题和灾难的唯一出路。

20 世纪以来，非西方国家不少思想家和政治家一直在探寻不同于西方的价值观，但到目前为止，尚未取得真正的成功。的确，他们的失败在一定程度上更强化了西方价值观的优越感和竞争力。但是，过去不成功并不意味着将来不成功，更不意味着永远不成功。虽然西方价值观在目前情况下拥有强大的竞争力和影响力，甚至由于它强有力地刺激和满足人性中某些本能或原始需要而具有特殊的诱惑力，但它的根本性问题及其所导致的现实后果应该足以使非西方人乃至整个人类警醒。西方社会由于马尔库塞所说的"极权主义"的影响已经基本上丧失了自我批判和自我变革的能力和力量。① 在这种情况下，如果非西方国家不抵制西方价值和文化的扩张和影响，任由整个世界"西化"，整个人类也将会丧失自我批判和自我变革的能力和力量，成为"极权主义"的人类。果真如此，人类不久（也许 50 年或 100 年以后）就会面临灭顶之灾。全人类西方价值体系化就是极权主义化。在全人类这种极权主义化日益深重的情况下，非西方国家要清醒地意识到，构建超越西方价值观的更先进价值观不只是非西方国家可持续发展的需要，而且对于人类的未来发展也是一项十分紧迫的任务。

构建超越西方价值观的先进价值观不仅具有现实的紧迫性，而且具有历史的必然性。世界的一体化只能是分权式的、民主式的，是多元主体的。作为世界主体的国家即使在各个方面都与世界接轨，也仍然能够拥有自己的价值体系、独特生活方式和民族特色；仍然能够拥有独立性、自主性和完整性。人们把作为世界主体的国家比作一体世界中的"极"，这是十分恰当的。多元主体的世界就是一种多极的世界。只有世界的多极化，才会有世界的多样化，而世界越是多样化，世界就越会结合成为一个整体。各民族找到自己的发展之路，可以实现本民族乃至人类更好的发展，也可以为西方价值体系突破自身不可克服问题的解决提供借鉴，从而实现整个人类价值体系、发展模式和生存方式的多元化、多样化。如此，整个世界就会更绚丽多彩，更充满生机和活力。

当然，构建超越西方价值观的先进价值观并非只意味着各国构建本

---

① 参见〔美〕马尔库塞《单向度的人：发达工业社会意识形态研究》，刘继译，上海译文出版社，2008，第 16 页。

国的独具特色的价值观；超越西方价值观的先进价值观也可以是区域性，如亚洲价值观、非洲价值观、拉丁美洲价值观等；也可以是整个非西方国家共同的价值观。西方价值观本身就并非只是西方某个国家的价值观，而是西方各国共同的价值观，而且同中有异。问题的关键在于西方价值观本身存在着致命的缺陷，非西方国家不可再采用这种价值观，而必须构建起更先进的同时也更适合本国本地区的价值观。

三 亚洲肩负着构建超越西方价值观的 先进价值观的特殊使命

构建超越西方价值观的先进价值观不太可能依靠西方。在 20 世纪甚至更早以前，西方许多学者已经深刻意识到了西方价值观的问题，但他们生活在西方世界，缺乏非西方的文化背景和社会实践，因而很难给人类提供超越西方价值观的先进价值观。这种价值观需要非西方国家的思想家和政治家根据本国或本地区的历史文化和社会实践来构建，而就地区而言，可能性最大的是亚洲。在非西方世界中，亚洲具有诸多构建先进人类价值观的独特优势。亚洲除了是人口最多地区，其明显优势至少体现以下四个方面。

首先，亚洲有悠久的历史、文化传统和丰富的历史文化资源。根据亨廷顿的看法，在这 5 个仍然存在的古代文明中，除西方文明之外，其余 4 个文明都属于亚洲。它们是中国文明、日本文明、印度文明和伊斯兰文明。而在 8 个现存的主要文明中，有 4 个属于亚洲。① 亚洲的这 4 个文明不仅历史悠久，有自己独特的价值观和文化，更重要的是，除日本文明之外，其他文明没有完全被西方文明吞噬，对西方文明依然保持着强大的张力，可以说是目前世界上尚存的抵御西方价值观的力量。

其次，亚洲人都是土生土长的本地居民，他们祖祖辈辈生活在这里，

---

① 参见〔美〕塞缪尔·亨廷顿《文明的冲突与世界秩序的重建》，周琪等译，新华出版社，2002，第 29 页。

这里是他们的家园，因而亚洲人有强烈的民族认同感和独特的民族性格，很难全盘西化。即便是日本，虽然经过了明治维新时期的"全盘西化"和第二次世界大战后的"西进运动"，但日本的本土文化以及中国的儒家文化仍然对今天的日本社会和人民发生着深刻而广泛的影响，并且形成了与西方思想相融合的具有日本特色的儒学。

再次，近代以来，亚洲思想家和政治家对构建具有本民族特色的发展模式做出了艰难的探索，积累了丰富的思想理论和实践经验。自近代"西学东渐"和列强入侵以来，亚洲国家的仁人志士就开始了一代又一代的对适合本国和发展道路的艰难探索。这些政治家和思想家不仅留下了宝贵的思想，也留下了难得的经验教训。这一切为构建超越西方模式的更适合亚洲的先进模式奠定了良好的基础。

最后，亚洲意识正在觉醒，亚洲迅速崛起，亚洲命运共同体正在形成之中。有政治家预言，假如说 19 世纪属于大英帝国，20 世纪属于美国，那么 21 世纪就属于亚洲。照目前的趋势看，中国很快将成为世界第一大经济体。再加上日本延续的实力和印度的迅速崛起，这些国家使得亚洲成为不可小视的力量，但同时也使实力的天平向亚洲大陆的北部和东部倾斜。① 今天的亚洲已经拥有世界 1/3 的经济总量，是当今世界最具发展活力和潜力的地区之一，在世界战略全局中的地位进一步上升。习近平指出："亚洲国家逐步超越意识形态和社会制度差异，从相互封闭到开放包容，从猜忌隔阂到日益增多的互信认同，越来越成为你中有我、我中有你的命运共同体。"②

以上所述表明，亚洲不仅已经形成了对西方文明的挑战，而且具备了超越西方、构建自己的价值观和发展模式的可能性和必要性。亚洲作为具有丰富历史文化底蕴同时又充满生机活力的地区，不仅肩负解决本地区的价值体系构建的责任，也肩负着为人类构建超越西方的更先进价

---

① 《外媒：21 世纪属于亚洲》，2011 年 11 月 19 日，新华网：http：//news. xinhuanet. com/world/2011 – 11/19/c_122305133. htm

② 习近平：《迈向命运共同体 开创亚洲新未来——在博鳌亚洲论坛 2015 年年会上的主旨演讲》，《人民日报》（海外版）2015 年 3 月 30 日，第 2 版。

值体系和发展模式的重大责任。亚洲各国要履行自己的历史使命，需要进一步增强亚洲意识和责任意识；进一步解放思想，营造思想自由的社会环境；进一步学习、借鉴西方价值观和文化，并在此基础上致力于超越它，构建比西方价值观更先进的亚洲价值观。

A Study on the Education of Core Value & A Practice of Ultimate Virtue

Kim Young Suk[*]

Abstract: Originally, the aim of learning is '格物致知', that is, brightening the principal of things. The aim of religion is pursuing the unchanging valid truth and realizing it. I think philosophy and theology also start in revealing the origin（始原）and basis of human beings and in finding the wisdom of heaven to answer to "what is a righteous life?" There were a lot of educations at school, nobody found the truth and happiness. According to Proverbs 1: 7 in the *Bible*, "The fear of the LORD is the beginning of knowledge", John 8: 32 says "knowledge will set you free". In the Chapter 20 of《中庸》writes '知天命', '知人', '事亲', '修身', '君子'. It means as humanity is the children of God, when they know God, they can see the truth. So far, all people have been locked due to a fixed mind set from dark learning and education. People wanted to be from the spiritual prison of their consciousness, but they could not be free by their false consciousness, tightly bound desire, and finally are weakly dying. Thanks to people's consciousness, their relationship is neither comfortable nor happy. I have taught students for 29 years at schools. I never saw public education systems that enable students to be satisfied or happy. This is because schools did not teach the

---

[*]　Kim Young Suk, the international director of IANC.

ethics for Common Good, the view of moral for co-existence and co-prosperity, the education for the respect of life by priority. Schools emphasize in entering good college or having good jobs and incite extreme individualistic selfishness. That is, schools raised students Ego. So the students ignore and bother weak students. And they do not love each other, regard others as their rivals. Naturally, their relationship becomes desolate and heartless, humanity's happiness get small gradually. In other words, the school did not educate true philosophy and core value that enable students to realize the infinite happiness inside of them and to emancipate human beings from their consciousness（ego）. That is the present state of the schools' education.

Now, the schools should get out of competitive educations that cultivates selfishness. The school should educate fostering the Common Good of mankind. Also it is urgent that education to develop Righteous men, saints, to open a new peaceful era on the global village. Now is the time when the schools educate to enable students to be reborn as neohumans, saints, by teaching the students to enlighten the truth and practice ultimate virtue. The writer in this paper will speak of the importance of core value as an alternative for how all humanity become peaceful and truly happy.

And this paper has a meaning by suggesting a methodology to practice 'Common Good' and 'Ultimate Virtue'.

Keywords：Respect of Life；Neohumans Culture；Public Benefit；Public Philosophy；Common Good of Humanity；Co-existence & Co-prosperity；Ultimate Virtue；Common Good

核心价值观教育与终极美德实践研究

金英硕

摘　要：最初，学习的目的是"格物致知"，即揭示事物的本质。

而宗教的目的则是追求不变的有效真理并使其成为现实。我认为哲学和神学也开始揭示人类的起源（始原）与基础，并寻求上天的智慧来解答"何为公义？"在众多教育学派中，没有人找到真相和幸福。据《圣经》箴言1：7中写道，"敬畏耶和华乃是知识之始"，《约翰福音》8：32说道，"知识将让你自由"。而在《中庸》第20章中也写道："知天命"，"知人"，"事亲"，"修身"，"君子"。这意味着人类作为上帝的孩子，当他们知道上帝的时候，他们才能看到真相。迄今为止，无知的学习与教育固定了所有人的思维模式。人们想挣脱意识的精神牢笼，但却被自身错误的意识所束缚，被欲望牢牢捆绑住，最终缓缓消亡。意识使人们的关系既不舒适也不高兴。我在学校执教29年，从未见过公共教育体系能使学生满意或高兴。这是因为学校并没有优先教授学生共同利益的伦理观，共生共荣的道德观，也没有教会学生尊重生命。学校强调的是学生被不错的大学录取，或是拥有好工作，从而鼓励极端个人利己主义。也就是说，学校提倡学生以自我为中心。因此，学生会漠视或麻烦弱势学生。学生之间不互相爱护彼此，而是把别人都当成自己的对手。自然而然地，学生关系变得冷淡和无情，渐渐地人类的幸福越来越小。换句话说，学校并没有传授真正的教育理念和核心价值使学生认识到自身内在的无限快乐，也没有将学生们从他们的意识（自我）中解放出来。这就是学校教育的现状。

现在，学校应该避免会培养自私主义的竞争性的教育。学校应当以促进人类的共同利益为教育目标。此外迫切需要教育培养正直的人和圣人，在地球村上开启一个新的和平年代。现在正是学校揭示真相、实践至善，教导学生使其重生为新人类和圣人的时候。在本文中，笔者将提到作为全人类和平、真正幸福的选择的核心价值的重要性。

本文建议用方法论来实践"共同利益"和"至善"，具有一定的意义。

关键词：尊重生命 新人类文化 公共福利 大众哲学 人类的共同利益 共生共荣 至善 共同利益

I Introduction

Today a lot problems on the earth drive all humanity to destruction. They are food problems due to being polluted by heavy metals, air pollutions, low pay, industrial accidents, political persecution and tortures, nuclear weapons, and the violation of human rights and so on. These are anti life, the destruction of life, a trend of regarding human life lightly, and the loss of human dignity. All those problems result from the following two factors. One is the maximization phenomenon of distinguishing discriminating knowledge by a dichotomous way of thinking. The other is anti ethical monopoly and occupation from the expansion of desire and possessiveness. These phenomenon spread to the world and influence on one's view of life and view of the world. Nowadays if human beings are not reborn as neohumans, a new kind of mankind, through the spiritual culture and core value of Asia, they will not adapt to the new change principle of the universe. They may face a serious crisis, may cause the extinction of human kinds. Now we live in the revamping era when the destruction of human beings will not only be humanity' subversion, but also be the crisis of the life or death of everything living on the earth. It will make a big impact on the evolution and change of the universe. We should realize if all humanity will not get out of their wrong values and philosophies and will not be reborn as neohumans, who will be the leaders of a new era and move in saving one's life, Singularity is near to all humanity and the universe, which is totally different from Ray Kurzweil' s "Singularity is Near".

Then what is the ultimate aim of the existent learning and religious philosophy? That is the realizing and completion of the truth. However humanity's truth was the expedience of partial enlightenment, so nobody recovered their original nature. In fact the basic aim of all learning is reinstating the original nature of humans and becoming the man of heaven. That is recovering the nature of God and the man of God. Therefore, if there is no education for recovering the nature of human beings and for fostering a well-rounded person, the education is useless.

As I do not know exactly about foreign schools, I will narrate Korean public schools' problems.

1. The students who learn with repeating memorization forget after exams,

2. Schools uniformly teach very difficult knowledge to students who are not interested or do not have to learn, so the education is not helpful to a lot of students in the future. A lot of students just spend time at schools as inferior students.

3. Schools teach incomplete philosophies and values of life that lack morals

4. Schools infuse students with wrong thoughts and philosophies as truth and make them believe blindly.

5. As schools teach separated subjects such as biology, physics, chemistry, students cannot understand things from the whole.

Though their studying at school may be helpful for entering good universities and having good jobs, the education is goading competition and for standing a line. Solving math problems, repeating memorization, and teaching by rote, students lost interest on their studying. It is very difficult developing students' talents and individuality. Therefore, although students study a lot, the education is not helpful for developing human nature and the course of their life.

Now, schools should get out of the ideals and system of wrong education system. Also they need to educate the original character of humanity, ethics, creativity that one can stand by oneself, and spiritual development to seek happiness and the truth. Where can one put their true value? How can one live righteously? Who is humanity? How can man and heaven become one? How can one live out mutually? How can societies become one? Now is the time when schools should have the value and aim that teaches integrated study and the win win truth to make all mankind become one and the world become one.

The reason that the world is dark and ignorant is because there was no philosophers or educators who have bright wisdom. So humanity still wander. Here, the importance of the education of new core value comes to the fore. As mentioned above, schools became the places where students grow egos, produced maladjusted students, and caused violence. Originally humanity was God, so the blood of God that lived happily forever without any panics about diseases and death is flowing in their vessel now. It is natural that students cannot be satisfied with present school system. Now is the time when schools educate the wisdom and philosophy that enable them to be reborn as the complete children of God. Then the earth can be changed into heaven. I think schools need to teach reinstating their original nature, whole rounded education facing the new era.

II The Importance of the Education of Core Value

So far, the civilizations and science have destructed life and killed each other and have displayed their power. I think as there are no cultures to save life and the win win philosophy to enable all humanity to become one, the global village faces crisis. Now is the time when we need to study to establish core values and valuable philosophies through the classics, the sound of heaven, and the order of heaven （天命）. What is establishing the view of core value for new life? Introspecting human history backward, we can see human beings have lived with very ignorant and valueless aims and philosophies. In spite all humanity is their brothers, they have committed to kill each other and waging wars. Now we should throw away the life of hurting each other and hating, and the conflicts of thoughts and illusion and we have to change our aims into win win life. To open a new era, we should find a new core value. I think it is the most important to have a philosophy of saving life, immortal life, and eternal happiness. To realize these core value, the study and education of the root and the original hometown of mankind （人即天，人即神） have to be preceded. Also, by practicing public philosophy and common goodness that are public benefit and finding win win wisdom, becoming saints, neohumans, is the most valuable. Then, what is the core value of Asians? Let me examine one by one.

1. Humans are heaven （God） （人即天，人即神 in 三一神告）

Human beings are originally one brother sharing the blood of heaven and one ancestor from the view of the overall world. They are one body that is connected with a line and net and they have the same genetic trait like holistic organic bodies and the heart of heaven. So human beings are God that is in the blood of God （'天命' or '天神'） genetically. Thousand years ago, humanity was deprived of their original nature of heaven （the character （天性） of living in heaven （神国） due to the accident of the forbidden fruit （being caught by the mind of 耽嗔痴 in Buddhism）, they have lived in unhappiness and pain and have died. A Korean ancient scripture, '天符经 （Cheon Bu Gyeong）' records "本心本太阳昂明", "人中天地一". Additionally, part '神训' of '三一神告' says "降在尔脑", "自性求子". Those words are the words of heaven revealing the basis of humans. They mean that humanity was originally born with a nature like one sun, the energy of heaven and earth becomes one and stays in mankind. Also the two words in part '神训' of '三一神告' involve a significant meaning, 'find out the seed of heaven because the nature （天性，神明） of heaven （God） came into human beings.' Like that, Korean ancient scriptures have a high level philosophy that is a core value of Asian and enables all the people of the world to become one and one brother to make the world peaceful.

2. Having God in one's heart （侍天主） and respecting God and loving humanity （敬天爱人）

There are a lot of philosophy and prophetic books like mentioned above in Korea. Therefore, by studying Korean ancient history and spiritual culture, we can see the human future will be bright. There was the Poongryu Tao, Fairy Tao, which sought to recover the original nature of human and reinstating their original figure（元始返本）and（克己复礼）. People tried to find out the way to change one's body and recover free bodies flying freely in the sky. That Korean religious movement that returns to their original hometown appeared as Donghak. The philosophy that turned up in the process is having God as one's owner（侍天主）and serving and regarding human beings as God（敬天爱人，事人如天），that movement of the spiritual reformation lasted for 150 years, which has been connected to the advent of neohumans, saints. I am anticipating that the spiritual culture would be the ideology of education for not only Korean students but also the students of the world.

3. The love of brother and the spirit of the brotherhood of mankind
The spirit of the love of brothers and the universal brotherhood.

First, the way of all humanity becoming one is to realize that we are not animals but the children of God. As we spiritually exist, we should live with the pride that we are God. In addition, all humanity is the branches of God because they have the blood of God. In other words, as all humanity has the genetic trait and nature of God, by demonstrating brotherly love, we should seek the way of living happily in a harmonious and peaceful world. If we do not establish a new value and do not foster neohumans, we will not be able to solve food problems, population problems, and environment problems, and the preservation of ecosystem will be impossible. If human beings learn the new value and new spiritual culture and become neohumans, all problems will be solved. I think the clues of all the basic problems of birth, old age, diseases, and death can be found by practicing the value and philosophy.

The ancients and scriptures record that mankind was originally freely existed and did not experience birth, old age, diseases, and death. Why did they lose their basic nature and were changed? That's because human beings lost their bright conscience like the sun（明德本心）. They forgot that all humanity was brothers being controlled by evil spirit that is consciousness (ego) and raise sins involuntary acting like animals and killing each other. Now is the time when we should be beyond the thought of darkness and ignorance in us and seek the nature of brilliant heaven's wisdom. Also we should study on how to fight against the ignorant thoughts and desires arising every second in us and defeat them (克己修身修心, ‘大道正法’) not to fight or compete against neighbors or others. Those who do not cultivate even their mind (修身) cannot do anything. We should open a new era with the method of becoming saints.

The only way of overcoming the crisis of this era is in finding the scriptures and the wisdom of prophets and opening a new way for all humanity. If one thinks of all things under one heart and conscience (一心 and 良心), the heart of God, all humanity is one brother and one body. And regarding everyone as my body, regarding everyone as God (爱邻如己) and acts, they will surely become saints (fairies or neohumans). Living with this heart is " the movement of saving life" .

In conclusion, the core values of Asians is the thought of public benefit. The philosophy of fostering saints and the spiritual culture for saving life are based on the recovery of human being, the thought of respecting life, and the thought that mankind are heaven.

Here are the Five Merciful Philosophy and the Law of Liberty that enables all humanity to be reborn, one heart & one body philosophy that will be a new Asians' mainstream culture and philosophy with core values.

Because they do not have the meaning of not only individual good, but also it contains ‘ Common Good (共同善) ’? ‘ Public Good (公共善) ’ that are connected to societies, countries, and the lives of the whole global village. Also they are the public philosophies with the core values of a cosmetic dimension. This enables people to get out of all disputes, conflicts and birth, old age, sickness, and death.

Ⅲ The Practical Methodology of 'Ultimate Virtue'

What is 'Ultimate Virtue（至善）', 'The Highest Good（最高善）'?

The reason that 'Ultimate Virtue（至善）' in three doctrines of 大学 among 4 scriptures（四书）of Confucius receives attention nowadays is evident that so far the study on Common Good to produce humanitarianism（弘益人间）has been rare. As each person has a philosophy, each country or society has two 'Common Good（共同善）' 'and 'Public Good（公共善）'.

1. What is 'Common Good（共同善）' and 'Public Good（公共善）'?
'Common Good（共同善）' means Public good（公共福祉）that is common interest the whole society. 'Public Good（公共善）' is good for not only each individual but also society, country, and all humanity. This mean a whole profit is established when a lot of people's interest is well harmonized unlike individual interests. Here, the difference between them is that individual becomes main in 'Common Good（共同善）', individual cannot become main in 'Public Good（公共善）'. Finding the methodology of 'coexistence and co-prosperity' living happily together and practicing the way, when the above two conditions are satisfied, 'the Big One Peaceful World will be established. Like that, the seeking of Common Good is a core principle that enables the modern society with various members and complex social system to move healthily. However, as humans are the co-existent ones（共存的存在）that get along with others, if they put private interest before Public Good（公益）, the community will be in a state of confusion and the society will collapse. Furthermore, if Common Good gives priority too, groupism and power supremacist may violate personal dignity, we should exercise caution. Therefore, the pursuit of value of Common Good should put aim in not only the dignity of personal value but also the human being lives of the whole members. Viewing from the theory of Tomas, the aim of community is to live

a life of a ultimate virtue. The great ethics and a ultimate virtue focus on making humanity's behavior good and community seeks the completion of its members' personality.

In this sense, when Individual Good is considered from Common Good, Common Good from Individual Good, mutual accordance is established.

However, if Individual Good that is realized through Common Good do not aim righteously, it will be still under a incomplete condition. Therefore, the good of humanity can be seen only when Individual Good and Common God that maintain a good relationship with ultimate virtue are harmonized. So 'Ultimate Virtue' means 'Common Good' and 'Individual Good' go well together. And it is 'The Highest Good（最高善）' to make all humanity's mind to become one. Let me introduce the methodology that enables human being to reach ultimate value.

2. The Practical Methodology o 'Ultimate Virtue'

So far, mankind did not know even their basic root and original hometown. Now as we know about what ultimate virtue is, what the original hometown and the root of humanity are, we need to study on a new philosophy and the law of the new norms and the new orders to recover their original state. The writer of this paper will present the practical methodology of ultimate virtue.

1）The thought of the three '三敬' and '五恕哲学'

'The thought of the Three Respecting（三敬）' is respecting heaven（敬天）, respecting humanity（敬人）, respecting all things（敬物）, which is based on the thought of Donghak. I would like to emphasize on the movement of saving life and education to reborn as neohumans by recovering one big spirit（大同一心）that loves the life of all things in the universe and regards them as my body. Let me explain about the term of this new philosophical movement. The mental attitude and the philosophy to reach 'Common Good' and 'Ultimate Virtue' are '五恕哲学'. '忠' is the expression of 'conscience', the nature of human beings. '恕' expressing '仁义' of Confucianism means a merciful heart '慈悲心' and '悉有佛性' of Buddhism.

Also '恕' means 'forgive', 'sympathize by understanding', and 'think one as my heart and my body'. Then what is '五恕哲学' （5 forgiveness philosophy）? It is a logic that only if one fosters the heart to love 'heaven', 'earth', 'humanity', 'all things with figures', and 'air and water without figures' as my body, they can become 'new men', 'neohumans', 'saints'.

In other words, '五恕' is '敬天' （respecting heaven）, '敬地' （respecting earth）, '敬人' （respecting humans）, '敬物' （respecting all things）, and '敬命' （respecting life）. Furthermore, it means the saving philosophy that regards the world, the heart of the universe, and unseen lives as my body and communicate with them.

2）'爱邻如己', '敬人如天'

All scriptures of the west as well as Asia commonly record that the law of '爱邻如己' will be practiced. 'Love your neighbors as my body', "Regard everybody as you serve heaven." I think that there is no higher rule than this rule. This law, 'Serve everybody as God and love them' is the law to recover the nature of humans and go into heaven. It is not a worldly law. The next step is 'Regard everyone as my body' 'The law to overcome one's body and mind' is the law of mind that enables mankind to be reborn as neohumans.

3）The practice of the Law of Liberty and a conscientious life

First, to practice the law of heaven, you should live a righteous life without any regret on my conscience. Being based on a conscientious behavior and heart, the practicing of the Law of Liberty enabling people to stay in the utmost joy land is possible.

What is the Law of Liberty?

The Law of Liberty is beyond selfish discernment, a law not to commit sins, a law to enable people to get out of birth, old age, diseases, and death, a law of heart not fighting each other, a one to enable you, I, and the world to become one, a law of heart to make all living things, heaven, and the heart of the cosmos to become one.

4)'Altruistic behavior（利他行）'and the life in the contrast of what one wants to live

Most modern people take precedence over their own interests first, they lack in considering others, respecting others, and serving them as their seniors. So the society is like a desolate desert. We should wake up and get out of the stereotype and desire and find out a way to get along well with neighbors. To do that, you should not think of your only personal interests and prosperity but to help poor hungry neighbors and to practice the love of mankind are the matrix for the life in contrast of what they want to live. For this love be realized, one should give something to others when they do not want to give something to others. When one does not want to help others, they should help others overcoming their mind. Then the acquired ego loses its power and one's conscience starts to grow. If one practices the life in contrast of what way they want to live, their anguish, agony, and selfish disappear, they will come to have a power to get out of their spiritual prison. Those who know this truth practice this love by donation, offering free meals, and charitable work. The practicing of altruistic behaviors and the life in contrast of what one wants to live are ways to remove the root of desire. Then the ways will open a era of immortality, people will be reborn as fairies（重生更生）.

Additionally, practicing ultimate virtue and the way of practicing need people's efforts and sacrifices. But it is a methodology that enables people's mind and bodies to become healthy, to acquire happiness, and to reach nirvana. In a word, if one practices the One Body Philosophy and the methodology of ultimate virtue in their real life, they will be completed as neohumans that become a light of the world. They will not only save themselves but also all things that do not have the wisdom of heaven and are dying. Therefore, they realize the heaven of heart in their bodies through ultimate virtue and enjoy an eternal happiness and joy. I came to know that one can stay in a state of true happiness and ultimate virtue when one recovers the nature in them. So ignominy and the seven passions do not arise in them and they are in a selfless condition（'无我境地'，'物我无亡喜者'）. I think the Necessity of Development Rounded Righteous men（全人，义人）, Neohumans who are in ultimate virtue and join in the movement of saving the earth is urgent.

IV Conclusion

Today is neither an age of materialism nor a era of scientific technology. Though people enjoy the affluence of material, the poverty of their heart becomes worse than old times. This is the era of the heart and spirit. Now is the time when we go toward eternal life hand in hand on the basis of 'the wisdom of bright and ultimate virtue' beyond the expediential, partial, and ignorant knowledge. Also all humanity should pay attention to the new culture of neohumans and prepare for beyond the global village, the era of the universe. For this new era, homes, schools, and societies should study on what they should teach, on what they should put their core values, and how they plan their life. We need to study on the definition of true life and righteous ultimate virtue and teach students. Further it is the time when we rethink whether humanity's ultimate virtue and happiness will be able to be accomplished by the materialistic civilization.

At this point of time when the necessity of the new philosophy and the new law is emphasized, it is meaningful to mention about the history of the laws. The laws were recorded well in the old scriptures and each religious scriptures. Among them, there are laws, norms, and ethics on the sociable orders such as the Ten Commandments in the Bible and the 10 good law and 280 rules in Buddhism, the Three Gang 5 Loon（三纲五伦）and etc, but the society has become desolate and its disputes and conflicts have got serious. The existent religions, philosophies, and theology do not function their basic aims and their roles, their teachings are partial. This means there is no righteous great Tao. The study on new order and law of a new era is urgent in this era. Choi Si Hyong of Donghak suggested 10 rules (十毋天) to prohibit something against heaven. Additionally Namsago, a Korean prophet of around 500 years ago, suggested 23 rules. Furthermore, through 4 angels, Choi Jewoo, Gang Jeung San, Park Tae Sun, and the Victor Cho Hee Sung, who appeared according to Yin-Yang and the Five Elements of theory in Korean religious movements, the last complete law that realize the great righteous law to produce saints, neohumans, was proclaimed in the early 1980. That is the Law of Liberty, which is the law of mind that enable all religions and Dharma to be unified (万教万法归一) into one. Also, it is called a new philosophy of the "One Heart One Body Philosophy (一心一体)' in the International Academy of Neohumans' Culture.

The development of medical and scientific technology caused activation of the social welfare facilities, the number of healthy old people grows due to them. That is, now is the time of an aging society and longevity. Furthermore, if Asians' core value and the culture of spiritual opening are developed, the last paradigm of the Hanryu will correspond to the ultimate aim and the final issue of world religious movement. If all human beings join the movement of saving lives, practice and learn public good and ultimate virtue, the wind of neohumans' culture toward the era of immortality and the dream society will arise beyond agelessness. The cultivating methodology for practicing core value and ultimate virtue will be the law of the new era and be the basis of the new society and the education philosophy. Muje in Hancountry and Shih Huangti unified China, enjoyed their prosperity and tried to find elixir in Samsin mountain, the hidden manna of heaven. However, as they failed in cultivating their mind, they lost all things and died. Recently a lot of books on the new era have been produced. For example, "The Universe Within" by Neil Turok, "The Unseen World" by Lee Gang Young, a Korean particle physicist, "Singularity is near" by Ray Kurzweil, "Dream Society" by Rolf Jensen, "Ageless Body Timeless Mind" by Deepak Chopra, "New Science Changes the World" by Bang Geon Woong, and "The Emerging Ming" by Karen Nesbitt, Ph. D. Shanor.

The 38th parallel of Korea, Military Demarcation Line, means not only Korean division but also all humanity's mental state. This phenomenon begins from the ignorant philosophy that although all humanity is a tree sharing one blood, they think they are different from each other. Now is the time when intellectuals take the lead in practicing a big love respecting heaven and loving mankind and communicating in each culture. If all human beings start to become saints, neohumans, the inter-Korean border collapse and the world will become one world, and it will be changed into the paradise.

Encouraging Values to Ensure A Future: Asian Values for the Future of the World

Abstract: The paper, with the background of enlightenment, points out the weakpoint of western values which take profit-making as the sole goal of society and make corrupt practice rise to the world stage. The paper holds that we should re-think Asian values from the perspective of dialogue and mutual sharing, because the thoughts from our ancients can help us solve contemporary social problems, therefore different ethnics and culture should learn from and dialogue with each other in the time of globalization and creat a new Asian values.

Keywords: Enlightenment; Western Values; Asian Values

倡导确保安全未来的价值观：指向世界未来的亚洲价值观

托马斯·梅纳帕拉皮尔

摘　要：以启蒙为背景，本文指明了西方价值观所具有的缺陷，认

---

* Thomas Menamparampil, Professor of Philosophy, nominated for Nobel Peace Prize in 2011.

为西方价值观倡导的盈利一旦成为社会的唯一目标，将给社会带来危险，并使腐败成为世界性的问题。本文认为，从对话和共享的角度反思亚洲价值，亚洲祖先们留下的思想智慧能有效解决当代社会的诸多问题，主张在全球化时代各民族、各文化的人们必须相互学习、相互对话，在团结的基础上创造一种新的亚洲价值观。

关键词： 启蒙　西方价值观　亚洲价值观

1. Apology about One's Culture Vs. Resistance to Anything Unfamiliar

Pressed hard by the raw realities of a globalizing world, people in Asia, especially those who belong to humbler and weaker communities, are beginning ask questions. Some become **apologetic about their cultures** and hesitant about the cultural assumptions of their own community, particularly when they do not seem to help in coping with the problems in a fast changing world. To them their own traditional values appear outdated. They stand for outright rejection of the old in an eager desire to profit by what is new.

Others, on the contrary, are extremely proud of their cultural/civilizational identity and inherited traditions. They are determined to offer fierce **resistance to anything unfamiliar** and alien. Some among them do not hesitate to go to exaggerations and enjoy making a display of their attachment to their traditions, even to what has become irrelevant, obsolete and unhelpful.

While the former forget the importance of historical and cultural continuity, the latter show no confidence in the dynamic element at the heart of their own culture that knows how to adapt to changing situations without compromising the core values of their collective identity and inner genius.

2. The Role of Enlightened Persons

These are contexts which invite **enlightened persons** to study changing trends and new ideas with an open mind and self-confidence in order to draw profit from whatever is good. They should at the same time deepen their understanding of their own heritage and cultural **values** in order to **re-interpret** them to the other members of their community and make them respond to contemporary needs.

It is when diverse streams of thought converge, they fertilize each other, and a 'new world of ideas' comes into existence, holding out hope for the coming generations. **Convergence of thought** and the complementary nature of human aspirations invite us to affirm our belongingness together.

3. Reflection on Asian Values is in View of Dialogue and Mutual Sharing

A reflection on '**Asian Values**' is not meant to be a chauvinistic self-assertion of emerging nations, nor a claim to superiority. It is merely a **humble search** for our core identity and an expression of our intense desire to re-interpret our civilizational assets to respond to the needs of our times, and share the resulting insights among ourselves and others who are interested. Some of these insights may prove to be a lamp on humanity's path to the future.

Similarly, the affirmation of 'Asian Values' is not intended to be a defence of authoritarianism or various forms of cultural or national fundamentalism. Nor is it an underestimation of modern concepts like human rights, the rule of law, accountability, democracy, participation, political-economic-gender equality, dignity of the individual. What these modern concepts stand for were articulated in diverse formulations in diverse cultures in different periods of history. After all, all human values have their roots in **identical human nature**.

What we would like to emphasize is that, today, their various incarnations must be brought to **dialogue with each other** with mutual respect so that our common destinies can be shaped purposefully. This International Conference is oriented to that end.

4. The Danger that Values Decline and Fall in a Market-driven Society

Of course, in a market-driven society the values that are esteemed most are efficiency, productivity, speed, marketability, management and such others. The traditional Indian emphasis on self-search and the Chinese on self-cultivation is not a denial of the importance of practical values in a world where Economy has assumed immense importance. Asian values do not stand on the way to the rationalization of the Economy, but they insist that the Economy be also human and humane.

Christopher Dawson said decades ago that a society is seriously impoverished, if it is "**emptied of all** the values that are not explicable in economic terms" (Dawson, 2002: 26). It is good for us to be aware what disasters await human society, when a **value-free** market is allowed to dominate human lives.

When people are evaluated only in market terms, i. e. , when human beings are classified merely as "**labour**" or evaluated solely in reference to the "**market**", their status sinks. In other words, when their worth is calculated only in terms of their use to the economy, they become less than human beings and bearers of dignity. And yet, the tragedy today is that entire nations are opting for this form of self-abasement by making **economic growth their sole goal**.

5. Dangers When Profit-making Becomes the Sole Goal of a Society

When mighty enterprises like Big Corporations or Government Departments make profit-making as their sole ethical norm, they become less and less accountable to anybody. Today's top managers have the power to set their own remuneration, with no upper limit (Piketty, 2014: 24). They can amass enormous sums by bringing business and political power to join hands together towards that end. They manipulate mass media, impose uniform ways of thinking and acting on society, monopolize knowledge, subject people to **consumeristic habits**, imprison them in artificial environments and even isolate them from natural settings. They flaunt their wealth humiliating the poor whom they see as getting poorer and poorer. Those who fall victims to their mesmerizing and **psychologically numbing** influence, lose their concern for society, commitment to compassion and solidarity; they lose sight of ecological responsibilities and grow in their greed for wealth (Hathaway, 2009, *xvii*), often acquired unethically.

Adam Smith had argued that the economic dynamism stimulated in society by the self-interest of individuals can benefit the entire society, even when not intended. However, Nobel Laureate Liu Xiabao points out that to make the self-interest of the majority purposeful, we need a minority of **moral giants** who can make ' **selfless sacrifice** ' . "The appearance of single martyr can fundamentally turn the spirit of a nation and strengthen its moral fibre. Gandhi was such a figure", said Liu (Guha, 2014: 39) .

6. Corrupt Practices Have Risen to the World Stage

The tragedy in our times is that corrupt practices have risen to the world stage.

No one can plead to be totally innocent. That is why all must join hands together in order to wipe out this plague from society. Corruption is not only about the **wrong use of money**, but also about the **wrong use of power**. It is not only about taking bribe in government offices, but also about various forms of manipulation and blackmailing, political arm-twisting, pushing a particular party's or ethnic group's interests through underhand ways, unfairness of dominant classes and castes to weaker sections, the imperceptible manner of bulldozing or marginalizing legitimate claims, silencing the voices of the weaker communities, physical elimination of political opponents or commercial competitors, interfering with election processes, using 'strong men' for vacating land or realizing bills, fixing matches, selling drugs. Corruption also has reference to hidden transactions, unpaid salaries, underpaid employees, unfair pressure.

The **globalized world has become a hiding place** for corrupt business. The global market provides distances, creates anonymity, gives opportunities for dishonest deals, enables one to take advantage of the weak, evade laws, and make an unfair proportion of profit. Let us make a distinction: 1. if greater profits are made through harder work, greater efficiency, more effective customer service or through path-breaking innovation, it is certainly legitimate. 2. But if it is made by underpaying the worker, evading taxes, ignoring safety laws, producing counterfeits, ruining the environment, abusing customer confidence, falsifying accounts or labour figures, double book-keeping, deceptive advertisements, industrial espionage, it is undoubtedly criminal.

Investigative journalism has often highlighted specific cases of dishonesty and unfairness. But media men also can bend to mammon, and sell their services for money: cooking up stories to defame or defend a party leader, **distorting facts** to press an argument, presenting allegations as proven truth for minor favours. Plagiarizing, pirating cassettes, and violating intellectual property rights are very common in our days. Engineers in government service get opportunities to embezzle huge amounts. Doctors are accused of patronizing particular pharmaceutical companies or diagnostic centres, and even dealing in human organs. When citizens are not alert, the mechanisms of accountability and sanction are not activated, and structures of enforcement lie idle. Society remains silent. You and I give a tacit approval.

7. Do Our Asian Ancestors Have a Message in Such Contexts?

We may take a message from Buddha's teachings. The economy had grown brisk in his days: credit, debt, interest and market—everything was in full function. There were rich people going bankrupt and poor people gathering a fortune, honestly and in other ways. A warning against corruption was timely. A passage from early Buddhist poetry says, "**Let no one deceive** anyone else, nor despise anyone anywhere. May no one wish harm to another in anger or ill-will" (Samyutta Nikaya, 146 – 148).

Similarly, a Taoist teaching says, "When rulers live in splendour and **speculators prosper**, while farmers lose their land and the granaries are emptied; when governments spend money on ostentation and on weapons; when the upper class is extravagant and irresponsible, indulging themselves and possessing more than they can use, while the poor have nowhere to turn. All this is robbery and chaos. It is not in keeping with the *Tao*" (*Tao Te Ching 53*). Are we in such an age? At another place the *Tao Te Ching* says, "The **sage does not accumulate**. The more he does for the people, the more he saves. The more he gives to people, the more he has" (*Tao Te Ching 81*).

In Confucian tradition, a gentleman is concerned with what is right; the inferior man with profit, with material welfare. Mencius too looked down on the profit motive. Science, technology, and efficient economy have given us good things, but they must be regulated by the norms of wisdom contained in our cultural traditions. Truly, "A gentleman takes as much trouble to discover what is right as lesser men take to discover what will pay" (*Tao Te Ching 81*) .

In the West, the first generations of capitalists were models of self-regulation. Their aim was to earn, build up capital, invest, and not to overspend. In fact, Weber and Keynes refer to high accumulation and low consumption (Sachs, 2011: 150) . Today's capitalists on the contrary tend to profligacy, eager to display: they believe in lavish parties, weddings, anniversaries, election victories. Concentration on fortune-hunting has thrown up a class of super-rich and dumped the weak in dire poverty (Sachs, 2011: 152) .

8. Imbalance in Economy

Economy organized on a vast scale, whether controlled by the Government or by Corporations, tend not to respect persons, human concerns, families, communities, values, natural environment. **Gigantism always has its victims**. No wonder Henri Bergson thought that man was designed for very small societies. We are not, of course, opposed to the bigness of things, but are anxious that its weaknesses should be recognized. Correctives should to be sought. There is evidently some imbalance when "Companies are competing against countries—not just other companies" (Charan, 2013: 7) .

The manner in which some companies do that looks more like an expression of the **aggressive and destructive streak in human nature** than of its constructive instincts. They ignore the inner worth of human beings, underestimate persons, communities, cultures, nature's gifts to humanity, ethical and aesthetic traditions. After having invaded and damaged millions of human lives and ruined the environment, when things go wrong, the only solution that profit-makers can propose are drugs, tranquilizers, sedatives, stimulants, and antidepressants (Fleischcker, 16); not silence, reflection, self-criticism or self-improvement, the way Asian sages have suggested.

9. When Giants Fail, Poor People are Asked to Help

Meantime consumer goods are in abundance, and most people are happy. They do not know what they are missing, how they are **losing values** that have taken shape over centuries and what their fate ultimately will be. Gradually **speculators take over** the economy. And then, of course, there comes the **collapse**. If a collapse had not taken place, one would not believe that it was possible. But it has taken place. The reasons for the recent economic meltdown are not hard to find.

And when, during periods of recession, corporations and banks collapse and are gasping for breath, it is the tax-payer's (the average man's) money that is being used to bail them out. It is as though the poor are rushing to the **rescue of the rich**. This may sound paradoxical, but this is what is actually happening.

It is similar to the paradox about International aid that has not reduced inequality or brought the needed assistance to the poor. International aid so often turned out to be the poor in rich countries coming to the aid of the rich in poor countries, and then the poor in poor countries being compelled to pay back the debt to the rich in rich countries. Thus, even plans formulated with **good intentions go wrong** in unforeseen ways.

10. Postcolonial Anxieties

There was a time when the main Asian anxiety was about winning freedom. Once freedom was won, other problems began to manifest themselves. Newly independent nations had to deal with **outdated economic systems** and fiscal policies, shortage of capital, land reforms, and codification of law. Many of them had to build up for the first time political institutions like parliaments, electoral commissions and parties; national consciousness in the face of strong ethnic, linguistic and regional loyalties. They had to make primary education and health care accessible; maintain roads and railways; equip army, bureaucracy; handle chronic hunger, illiteracy, unemployment, red tape, corruption and religious fanaticism. The task was not easy for newly born nations or leaders inexperienced in administration. It is no use finding fault with the leaders of that era. They were trying to achieve what more advanced countries had done over centuries.

There were other worries as well. The right sort of political climate had to be created that would favour democratic participation and healthy collaboration. The concept of nation-state developed at the Treaty of Westphalia in 1648, with more or less homogenized citizenry, did not suit many of the multi-ethnic, multi-cultural, multi-religious nations of Asia. **Ethnic minorities** thought their interests could be neglected by the dominant majority. It is no surprise that discontented ethnic groups went in for secessionist wars wanting to set up independent nations. Diverse communities began fighting among themselves, going at times to the point of violence. Neighbouring countries claimed portions of each others' territories which they felt belonged to them in some earlier period history. And again, during the Cold War period, most nations were dragged into ideological polarizations, and ideology-led groups clashed within nations.

After the 80's, injustice was no more perceived along class-lines alone; it was more understood in terms of the neglect of weaker groups: women, lower castes, regional minorities, ethnic or linguistic minorities, migrants, poor indebted nations, victims of globalization and of new forms of poverty, of human rights violation, **damaged environment**, **wounded cultures**, cultural rootlessness, and communal violence. Many uncertainties also remained as how to deal with social problems like alcoholism, drug abuse, out of wedlock pregnancies, and sexually transmitted diseases, Speaking of values, new questions came up like cell research, euthanasia, death penalty. Traditional value-systems failed to adapt to new problems and to respond to the new needs.

11. Unfortunately Violence has Become the General Way of Protest

When values fail to exert a moral authority in society, **force comes to play a greater role** in obtaining social compliance, whether imposed by the Administration or inflicted on each other by fellow-citizens. Force used in excess takes the form of violence. Violence, once unsheathed, cuts in all directions. For example, if it was used for the struggle for freedom, it remains on for a long time in various shapes to harass societies even after independence.

Similarly, there is the danger that communities that feel marginalized along class, caste, ethnic, cultural, regional or religious lines, grow convinced that their voice would have persuasive power only if it is accompanied by a show of strength, not excluding violence. With this sort of conviction, a fear of **imposed unreasonableness** can catch up with society at various levels and influence various sections.

A response to it is likely to be equally unreasonable. After all, all radical Asian ideologies in recent history were a response to intense pressure under which a people/nation laboured. The more radical the pressure, the more radical the response. **One exaggeration invites another**. In such an atmosphere, even traditionally peaceful societies lose confidence in the peaceful styles taught by Asian sages. If a sense of balance and moderation is ignored and values forgotten, and if strong self-assertion becomes the norm across all emerging nations, tensions are bound to arise, with many uncertainties for Asia's future.

There is also an eagerness in all emerging nations to catch up with the developed world. Impatience for quick achievement runs the risk of surrendering to persons who over-claim power, which in turn can lead to power-struggle and initiate a cycle of violence. Similarly, in the economic field, **growing anger** against mounting inequality can threaten the future of our societies.

Meantime natural resources are being over-tapped, environment is in peril, and stiff competition rises to merciless heights.

12. Reflection on Values Has Become Absolutely Necessary Lest We Perish

Sayyid Qutb says in *Milestones* "Humanity is standing today at the brink of an abyss...because humanity is **bankrupt in the realm of 'values'**, those values which foster true human progress and development" (Mishra, 2012: 270). Already in 1916 Yan Fu had called for a return to Asian values in the face of gross injustices he witnessed, "How different are the principles of Confucius and Mencius, as broad and deep as Heaven and Earth, designed to benefit all men everywhere" (Herlee G. Creel, *Chinese Thought: From Confucius to Mao Tse Tung*, Chicago, 1971, p. 237). Sun Yat-sen wrote in 1924, the oriental civilization is one of Right not Might (Mishra, 2012: 214).

These are lessons that Asians themselves are forgetting. Ultimately we may have to learn some of our own teachings from others. In 1896, Liang Qichao pointed out, Mencius had taught that the rulers must be close to the people; now, he said, it is from the democratic West that we have to learn this lesson today so that we may be truly ourselves (Mishra, 2012: 144). One thing is certain: we all have to learn from each other.

13. A Few Key Concepts from Confucius

Ethical traditions develop in society in response to human needs for guidance in life together. The **Ethic of Responsibility** says that our fates are linked and that we all must be concerned for each other. Communities and cultures everywhere in the world have encouraged their people to develop sensitivity for each other, 'To know the anguish of others is to feel that anguish as our own'.

Confucian propriety (*li*) and righteousness (*yi*) can contribute to harmony and relationship. Confucian humanness (*ren*) corresponds to the Golden rule of love. Thus the Confucian message of social harmony and Taoist teaching of harmony with nature complete each other. It is an invitation to become fully human: calm, confident, trustworthy, open; with no fear, no guilt feeling.

Dhammapada teaches one "To avoid all evil, cultivate good, and purify one's mind".

14. Ancient Values Will Have to be Reinterpreted for Our Times and Given a Dynamic and Relevant Meaning
—The Example of Mahatma Gandhi

Society keeps changing. New situations call for new responses. In one period of Jewish history they realized that they should express their relationship with the divine not merely by offering sacrifices of rams, goats, and oils, but acting justly, mercifully and remaining humble (*Micah* 6: 7 – 8). There was a **radical change of perception**, new importance being given to justice, which grows even stronger in the other Israelite prophets.

Mahatma Gandhi reinterpreted the ancient concept of *Ahimsa* (non-violence) to suit a new need when he courageously brought it to the political field. He gave the word **new connotations** never perceived before. Non-violence was, for him, not mere passivity or weakness, or a sign of helplessness. On the contrary, it had a transformative quality, with immense power to change a situation, for example, by confronting an unjust law with active civil disobedience. By **reinterpreting the concept** of *Ahimsa* in this way, Gandhi universalized the message, making it meaningful to everyone in a similar situation anywhere in the world. Martin Luther King, Mandela, others felt inspired by Gandhi while pressing for their rights.

In a similar way, Gandhi gave to the Indian concept of **renunciation** a dynamic content, linking it with intense political and socially beneficial activity and making it sturdy, and giving it a spiritual purpose. It was not arbitrary instrumentalization of an idea, but in keeping with the Indian inclination of making concepts and norms context-sensitive.

And again, Gandhi introduced the concept of "**strong persuasion**" by appealing to the conscience of the opponent in respectful protest, in a non-violent and courteous manner of expressing non-acceptance. Similarly, his understanding of God as Truth made him inclusive, tolerant, and open. He was open to new ideas from anywhere in the world. However, he insisted on the 'language of continuity' between his society's past and future (Guha, 2014: 123).

The great Indian poet Kalidasa too welcomed the flow of thought from anywhere, but suggested that they be submitted to the wisdom of the good and the learned (Chandra, 2003: 56).

15. Self-Search, Self-discipline and Self-Enhancement Are for Social Good

The Muslim jurist-mystic Ayn al-Qudat al-Hamadhani (d. 1131) defined ethics as the "opinion of the heart". Mahatma Gandhi had a similar expression, the "inner voice". Cultivating this inner voice is calculated to remove the influence of all negativities like avarice, anger, resentment, self-seeking, in order to be able to create a serene atmosphere with the rest of the world. It generates a new set of attitudes and spiritual **values** like self-control, benevolence, patience, peace, non-injury, truth, endurance and tranquillity.

Nearly all Asian traditions give importance to the **development of the inner self through inner striving and discipline for creating an ethical climate in society**.

Interestingly, Paul Ricoeur's understanding of ethics is something similar: he sees ethics springing from our desires, needs and strivings towards **self-actualization** (Schweiker, 2008: 548). All these efforts are then calculated to self-actualization. But this attention to the personal self is for social benefit. Patanajali says a person who has become master of his/her self, hears "the cries of all creatures", offers friendship, compassion, joy, impartiality, and sensitivity to others.

Historically, values evolved in different cultures in different ways to suit the needs of individual societies. The difference often is in the emphasis. Personal effort can never be neglected. "Be yourself your own lamp and your own refuge," says Mahaparinibbana Suttanta (Chandra, 2003: 170). For, you can set yourself right with sincere effort. Even accumulated **Karma** can be transformed and set right by a moment's action of the mind. According to the Upanishads, *Moksha*, **unfettered condition**, comes from withdrawal and reflection on the deeper nature of things. "Sitting in forgetfulness" is considered most helpful for attaining the highest perfection and purity of oneself, *Nirvana* (Chandra, 2003: 153).

The Indian practice of cultivating **Mindfulness** can help one to reinterpret values in each context; for example, to decide how to combine justice with mercy, and wisdom with compassion. Asian sages always urged a holistic approach to ethical problems basing on the wisdom of doctrinal texts, philosophical principles, and also lived experiences. Hardened conceptual tools may not always help. In Buddhism, there are the Four **noble truths** to guide one in living a balanced and moderate life. Secular scholars would like to seek assistance from practical reason and the findings of human sciences as well.

Gurucharan Das makes an interesting remark that as the code word for

America would be 'liberty' and for France 'equality', the code word for India is *Dharma* (Das, 2012: 275). But this concept of *Dharma* will need to be reinterpreted in contexts, and applied to diverse problems: e. g. of corruption in offices, adulteration of goods in commerce, student indiscipline in universities, abuse of women in homes, exploitation of the weak in slums, provocation of an opponent in the political scenario. This is what makes Das emphasize the need for education in citizenship and 'public *Dharma*' (Das, 2012: 148), which would mean the ethic of uprightness in the public sphere.

16. Collective Self-Awareness, Healing of Collective Memories

As there are things to be set right in the inner consciousness of an individual person, there are **wounds to be healed in the collective self-consciousness** of a community, an ethnic group, a language group, a religious group, a society, a nation, a civilization. It is in this mighty undertaking that we keep failing at the global level and in individual contexts right round the world. Generally we study the immediate causes of tensions and conflicts and suggest remedies. Our social analyses have remained at the superficial level and often ideologically conditioned. We should not be satisfied with the obvious, but should dig further down and search into the collective psyche of communities.

Could there be a profound sense of hurt kept alive by the memories of humiliations one's community has suffered (e. g. during the colonial or post-colonial period) or of by the guilt feelings for injuries one's community/nation has inflicted on others? **Psychic wounds remain**, whether they be personal or collective, until they are healed. Anger and resentment of a community/nation/civilization remain submerged, and even if ineffective today, tomorrow they find self-expression in hate-speech or outright violence. We need to attend to the ongoing sense of victimhood, and bring healing to the ire that remains buried deep within the consciousness of communities, nations.

Until we succeed to handle **collective grievances** with the delicate skill of a physician, and help each other and get over our postcolonial complexes, we do not become truly free; we have not yet become independent.

Similarly, lingering wounds may be in the collective unconscious of an ethnic minority, a language group, a religious community, or a nation, prompting a belated response in one manner or the other. These wounds need to be healed. The task I am proposing certainly is not easy. But that is the mission of responsible intellectuals in the world today. In this endeavour they need to have a non-sectarian, non-partisan attitude, guided solely by the values one cherishes for the common good. It is a world-transforming undertaking.

17. Wounds Inflicted by One's Own Success is Hardest to Heal

While hurts inflicted by an opponent is hard of healing, those inflicted by oneself is harder. The complacency and over-confidence that come upon oneself from unqualified success is the hardest to heal. Christopher Dawson argues that many successful civilizations/nations fell victims to these very weaknesses precisely in periods of their eminent success, weaknesses to which they grew blind. When they began **marginalizing the values** by whose strength they had grown and attained success, they were placing themselves on the way to decline.

For example, he says, the Hellenic civilization collapsed on its own with the "disappearance of those vital characteristic types in which the spirit of the culture had embodied itself". Once they cut off their roots with their past, true **Greek values** and institutions disappeared, and their society became an impersonal exploitative hierarchy. There was clearly "the degradation of the Greek type". Thus, "Hellenism withered from within" (Dawson, 2002:

62 – 63）.

Dawson makes similar comments on the decline of Roman society with the weakening or **Roman values**. "Rome became more and more a predatory state that lived by war and plunder, and exhausted her own strength with that of her victims" (Dawson, 2002: 67). Cities became parasitic.

George Friedman feels, in the same way, that ambition for money and power "devastated the **republican values** that were the greatest pride of Roman citizenship" (Friedman, 2012: 31). Recent history of nations confirms the same lesson. Friedman believes that even "German, Japanese, French and British power declined" only through their successes that led them to irresponsibility and wars (Friedman, 2012: 17).

Today the confrontation between nations is less in the battlefield than in the market. But *Dharma* can be taken to the area of commerce as well. Gurucharan Das says that it is the business man with high sense of *Dharma* that will gradually win trust and retain the market (Das, 2012: 160). Similarly, if *Dharma* is taken to field of politics, Asian nations may be able to put tensions behind as a warring Europe did by abolishing war and forming the European Union. The experience of ASEAN which brought nations in tension together shows that this is possible.

18. Cultivating Social Sensibility

As bodily self-awareness has a healing power, so too, when one cultivates **collective self-consciousness and social sensibility**, it paves the way to social healing within that society. Responsible members of the community therefore should reflect on the vexed questions that harass the community, e. g. caste-system, growing economic inequality, gender prejudice, ecological degeneration, memories of collective humiliation, communal tensions.

Similarly, in a politically competitive world, there can be lingering fear in countries and communities that have gone through negative experiences, if they see a show of strength in neighbouring peoples and excessive eagerness to outsmart others, before which they feel inadequate. On the contrary, they are edified when they see self-restraint and mutual assistance. And they rejoice at the success of an achieving neighbour.

19. Symbolic Gestures and Prophetic Actions that Heal

Whenever we violate these and other helpful norms of human processes, and whenever we choose to move against the **flow of the cosmic order** and ignore *Dharma*, we hurt ourselves more than others. Time may pass, but the consequences remain.

We need **prophetic personalities** to bring healing to societies. Gandhi had the singular ability to pass on powerful messages through symbolic actions. His intense activity of spinning cloth, frequent stay among the lower-caste communities and other activities, were pointers to an imbalance in the social structure.

Many of his **prophetic gestures**, including his manner of relating with people, and the very way of dressing, had a challenging message for the collective psyche of millions. They provoked thought, acted as a corrective and served as an encouragement as required in each context. It was his determined effort to keep to the **Middle Path of balance** and always show respect to the opponent.

20. Asian Togetherness, Asian Values

The **longing for Asian togetherness** is nothing new. There has been mutual borrowing down the centuries. During freedom struggle, Asian leaders kept touch with each other. In spite of the differences in ideologies, they respected each other. In today's context let me refer briefly only to a few of our leaders who dreamt about this togetherness in Asia and collaboration in the world.

Rabindranath Tagore was one of those who were concerned for Asia's future from his earliest years. He kept closely following the stirrings for freedom in China. For him, Asian togetherness was only a part of global togetherness. It was always his effort to harmonize the ideals of the East and West (Guha, 2014: 122). He firmly believed that one's own country can never be considered greater than the **ideals of humanity**. He discouraged any fascist attitudes (Mishra, 2012: 226).

He was very emphatic when he said, "When organized national selfishness, racial antipathy and commercial self-seeking begin to display their ugly deformities in all their nakedness, then comes the time for man to know that his salvation is not in political organization and extended trade relations, not in mechanical rearrangement of social systems, but in a **deeper transformation of life**, in the liberation of consciousness in **love**, in the realization of God in man" (Michael Collins, *Empire*, *Nationalism and the Postcolonial World: Rabindranath Tagore's Writings on History, Politics and Society*, New York, 2011, p. 67).

Tagore cautioned his countrymen against any form of militant nationalism, which would, he said, only yield its 'harvest of antipathy'. What he ardently sought was a regeneration of Asian spiritual civilization. He was perfectly convinced, "Great civilizations have flourished in the past in the East as well as in the West because they produced **food for the spirit** of man for all time" (Rabindranath Tagore, *Crisis in Civilization*, Delhi, 2002, p. 260).

Referring to Asia's haste to catch up with others in an un-reflected manner he said, "Take count not only of the scientific perfection of the chariot but of the depth of the ditches lying across its path" (Mohit Kumar Ray (ed), *The English Writings of Rabindranath Tagore*, Vol. 7, Delhi, 2007, p. 970). He spoke with passion when he said, "Nations who sedulously cultivate **moral blindness** and the cult of patriotism will end their existence in a sudden and violent death. " History has repeatedly proved this true.

Nehru too was extremely eager to bring Asian societies together (Mishra, 2012: 249), which found expression in Pan-Asian Conferences, the Bandung Conference, the formulation of the *Panch Shila* and other initiatives. He found friends in Sukarno and many others who held similar views. Ho Chi Minh was another leader who often spoke of the "**Great Asian Family**" and kept in touch with Nehru (Guha, 2012: 77) .

Though Lee Kuan Yew admired the result-oriented approach of the West and its scientific and industrial success, from the 80's he began to speak more and more of **Confucian values** (Guha, 2014: 258) and ' AsianValues ' . After Deng Xiaoping began observing the experiences of Singapore with interest, Lee considered it a mission to propagate a happy harmony of Asian and the Western values.

21. We All Have to Learn from Each Other

In this globalized world, we all have to learn from each other. " The great civilizations of the past have often been focused on their own cultures. In the future, they will increasingly study the greatness of other civilizations " (Martin, 2006: 388) . Even the most developed nations are beginning to recognize their own incompleteness without others. There is general recognition of human interdependence, a conviction that we belong together, that our needs are identical, and that we need each other. Despite growing distances between self-centred communities, there is visible convergence of thought, fusion of longings, and a desire for togetherness.

For example, there is a sudden revival of interest among environmentalists to study the **traditions of tribal communities** in remote areas when exploring ways to control pollution, ecological destruction, species' extinction, over-tapping of non-renewable energy; ecological balance, appropriate use of land, harmony between humans and other species. They have sought inspiration from personalities like Tagore or Gandhi who manifested great esteem for life in the villages, the simplicity of the people and the beauty of uncontaminated nature.

While we do not claim that such models have the final word in these matters, they seem to propose a corrective to industrial recklessness, an impersonal economy, and over-confidence individual civilizations. Wisdom consists in drawing profit from each others' experiences.

22. Communities, Cultures, Ideologies and Religions Must Dialogue

Gradually people are awakening to the fact that Economy is dependent not only on capital and labour, but also on **values** like traditions of trust, skills developed in cultures, and habits of the mind, which we call the **social capital** of a society. They are sustained by ethical convictions deeply embedded in cultures. These values can be brought meaningfully to day-to-day social processes only if cultures, communities ideologies, and religions, dialogue. Life together becomes possible only by searching for consensus among these various traditions.

As we have already seen, ancient values have to be made relevant by bringing them to concrete situations and face to face with issues that society considers important today, e. g. democracy, economics, technology, natural sciences; ecology, feminism, and postmodern perceptions. They have to be put in relationship to responsibilities in the areas of accounting, management, finance, marketing, communication technology, treatment of workers, and others. Only in this way will the global civilization emerge as truly human and meaningful.

23. 'Terrorism' can be Confronted Best by Values

Let us take another example. The best way to confront the so-called 'terrorist' force is not the use of greater force. Human ingenuity must suggest other solutions as well. We have referred to some of them in earlier sections. Gandhi believed that **mind-power is stronger** than muscle-power and gun-power in the long run.

When we fail to agree on moral values among ourselves, various types of inter-community tensions and social fragmentation are bound to occur. Common codes of conduct must be evolved. Increasing cyber crimes, for example, call for a global ethical code. In 1993 Hans Kung suggested a **Global Ethic** in the Parliament of World Religions in an effort to broaden areas of agreement (Schweiker, 2008: 488).

The values of various cultures are complementary, and not one exclusive of the other. Diverse needs compelled communities to emphasize diverse values as required in specific circumstances. However, the **Golden Rule** of 'doing unto others as one would like others to do to you' seems to have the widest acceptance. In the same way the **sense of responsibility and benevolence** for the poorest and the most neglected may be considered universal. Some societies emphasize justice, others compassion; Africa may give importance to 'communal ties and social cohesiveness', the western society to individual rights, Asians to family values.

24. Religious Believers and Ardent Secularists Must Dialogue

Those with secular convictions accuse religious believers for being partisan, forgetting that they too often show themselves partisan when they apply 'rationality' only to some areas and not to others. That is why religious and secular voices must engage one another, national and civilizational leaders must talk.

Values that are more widely acceptable must emerge from their conversation. That is the only way to solve problems like social tensions, civil wars, cultural oppression, political autocracy, economic stagnation, forced migration, and increase in the volume of refugees.

25. Humanity Has Become Interconnected and Interdependent

It is not that no progress has been made in **matters of common interest**. Kishore Mahbubani lists a number of areas where common understanding has been deepening at the global level: there is growing acceptance that rulers are accountable to the people (Mahbubani, 2013: 40); that a win-win approach is better than cutthroat competition; that the work ethic of discipline, competence, teamwork is required to make a breakthrough in economy; that the health of the masses is the best asset of the nation; that healthy food and clean water are a must to ensure high production; that the future of a society depends on fair access to education for all people.

It is usually believed that ideals converge while practical interests divide peoples. Mahbubani argues that in the present day the opposite is true. In our times, it is evident that **economic interests are bringing peoples and nations together**. In this area all speak the same language (e. g. , the language of science and technology). The strategic interests of the developed and underdeveloped world have become interdependent. Global trade keeps growing in volume. There is visible upward mobility everywhere; many more millions have risen to the levels of the Middle Class. Global interests in the areas of ideas, ideals, information, compassion, assistance keep widening. International travel is expected to touch 1. 6 billion by 2020. So, Mahbubani argues that in today's situation material interests of people converge; but it is their **minds that have not found the way** to move forward together (Mahbubani, 2013: 81 – 82).

"Postwar Asian experience demonstrated that later modernizers were actually advantaged relative to more established industrial powers, just as earlier liberal trade theories had predicted" (Fukuyama, 1992: 101) .

A **new human consciousness** must emerge, one that encourages togetherness (Mahbubani, 2013: 74) . But if each nation seeks only its own interests, the common good comes to be clean forgotten. What actually happens is that national leaders are caught in strategies of **populism** and are eager to advance their own personal interests, or those of the dominant group, or the nation's own short term interests. There are few statesmen who are able to transcend these limitations.

But we know that the future belongs to those who ensure a fair deal across different income classes, ethnic groups, and regions, and put their collective interests in relationship to the global good. Historian Fernandz-Armesto had predicted decades ago, "**Increasing inter-connectedness** seems to lead to increasing interdependence, which in turn demand new, ever wider, ultimately worldwide 'frameworks' for action, transcending old nations, blocs and civilizations" (Fernandez-Armesto, 2001: 560) .

26. The Role of Intellectuals

You have become a disciple in order to benefit the world (*Silabhadra, the Buddhist professor of Nalanda University, to Hiuen Tsang from China*) .

Intellectuals must develop a sense of responsibility. " The ideas of economists and political philosophers, both when they are right and when they are wrong, are more powerful than is commonly understood. Indeed the world is ruled by little else", said John Maynard Keynes. Practical men (actual rulers) are often **slaves to outdated ideas,** he argued (Stiglitz, 2012: 151) . Hence even the most anti-intellectual society today has need of people who have ideas towards togetherness if they wish to make headway.

The recent book of Thomas Piketty, *Capital in the Twenty-first Century,* refers to the "rising human capital hypothesis," which argues that '**human capital**' is far more important than financial capital and real estate, capable managers more than rich stockholders, specialized skills more than the unearned advantages of nepotism (Pikettty, 2014: 21 - 22).

However, 'human capital' is not only knowledge and skills, but also **values** like motivation, sense of purpose, sense of belonging, mutual trust, energies for resilience, and absolute determination. While knowledge and skills will decide the direction of the economy, **values** alone will ensure cohesion to a community and a future to a society. Here is where **intellectuals with vision** can help. They are more powerful than actual power-wielders (Mahbubani, 2013: 64).

Confucius taught, "Persons of humanity are like this: wanting to develop themselves, they also develop others; wanting to achieve things themselves, they also allow others to achieve what they want (*Analects 6. 28. 2 - 3*). And again, "But if even a simple peasant comes in all sincerity and asks me a question, I am ready to thrash the matter out, with all its pros and cons, to the very end" (*Analects IX, 7*).

The Rigveda had said, "One ignorant of the land asks of the one who knows it; he travels forward, instructed by the knowing-one. This, indeed is the blessing of instruction, one finds the path that leads straight forward" (*Rigveda X, 32. 7*).

In times of troubles, we need new motivators to urge society on. It is for us to develop motivation for carrying a **hope-filled message to Asia** and to the **world**. " Let your aims be common, and your hearts be of one accord, and all of you of one mind, so you may live well together" (*Rig Veda 10. 191. 2 - 4*). "Let us have concord with our own people, and concord with people who are strangers to us.... May we unite in our minds, unite in our purposes, and not fight against the divine spirit within us" (*Atharva Veda 7. 52. 1 - 2*). "Consider the family of humankind one" (Jainism, Jinasena, Adipurana).

References

Chandra, Ramesh & Mittra, Sangh, *Buddha: A Revolutionary and Reformer*, Commonwealth Pub. New Delhi, 2003.

Charan, Ram, *Global Tilt*, Random House Books, London, 2013.

Das, Gurucharan, *India Grows at Night*, Allen Lane (Penguin), London, 2012.

Dawson, Christopher, *Dynamics of World History*, ISI Books, Wilmington (Delaware), 2002.

Ferguson, Niall, *Civilization*, Allen Lane (Penguin), London, 2011.

Fernandez-Armesto, *Civilizations*, Pan Books, London, 2001.

Friedman, George, *The Next Decade*, Anchor Books (Random House), New York, 2012.

Fukuyama, Francis, *The End of History and the Last Man*, Penguin Books, London, 1992.

Guha, Ed. *Ramachandra Makers of Modern Asia*, Belknap Press Harvard, Cambridge, 2014.

Hathaway, Mark & Boff, Leonardo, *The Tao of Liberation*, Orbis Books, New York, 2009.

Hobsbawm, *Fractured Times*, Eric Little, Brown New Delhi (Noida), 2013.

Mahbubani, Kishore, *The Great Convergence*, PublicAffairs, New York, 2013.

Martin, James, *The Meaning of the 21st Century*, Eden Project Books, London, 2006.

Mishra, Pankaj, *From the Ruins of Empire*, Allen Lane (Penguin), London, 2012.

Picketty, Thomas, *Capital in the 21st Century*, The Belknap Press, Harvard, 2014.

Sachs, Jeffrey, *The Price of Civilization*, The Bodley Head, London, 2011.

Schweiker, William, Ed. , *Religious Ethics*, Blackwell Publishing, Oxford, 2008.

Sharma, Ruchir, *Breakout Nations*, Allen Lane (Penguin), London, 2012.

Stiglitz, Joseph, *The Price of Inequality*, Allen Lane (Penguin), London, 2012.

Religious Pluralism as A Proper Ideology for Harmony and Peace

Warayuth Sriwarakuel

(Assumption University of Thailand)

Abstract: Harmony is something desirable. It is needed both in nature and in society. Man is an important factor to promote or destroy harmony. Human beings are different from animals in that they have two levels of reason and faith. Whereas it is obviously probable that animals can learn how to use induction, humans can use not only induction but also deduction and metaphysical reasoning. Similarly, whereas animals can have only animal faith, namely, trust in their environment, humans can have not only animal faith but also human faith, namely, trust in their ideologies. In this paper I would like to argue that among religious ideologies, religious pluralism is the authentic dialogue for harmony and peace especially in the age of globalization.

Keywords: Religious pluralism; Harmony; Peace

和谐与和平视域中的宗教多元化

Warayuth Sriwarakuel

摘　要：和谐是值得拥有的。自然和社会都需要和谐。人类是促进或破坏和谐的一个重要因素。不同于动物,人类有理智与信仰。人类不同于动物的地方在于,他们有两个层次的理性与信仰。显然动物可以学习如何使用感应,而人类不仅可以感应,还会演绎以及形而上学的推理。同样地,动物只能有动物信仰,即信任他们的环境,而人类可以不仅有动物信仰,还有人类信仰,即信任他们的意识形态。我在本文中认为,在宗教意识形态之间,宗教多元论是全球化时代真正能带来和谐与和平的对话。

关键词:宗教多元论 和谐 和平

Why Harmony Matters

What is harmony? It implies a kind of relation between things. What kind of principle supports the harmonious relation? According to the philosopher Charles Hartshorne, it is the principle of likeness in difference. Thus harmony is similarity in diversity. Harmony is essential for both nature and culture. In nature there are both similarities and differences. It is obvious that there is harmony in nature. Harmony in nature can be observed through the balance between the opposites, namely, similarities and differences. If we need harmony, we need to make the balance between similarities and differences. If we put an emphasis on either side of the two opposites, then disharmony or imbalance will occur. Thus too much and too little must be avoided. The middle way is a proper path for harmony. Let see the opposite between similarity and difference. If we emphasize too much upon similarity, we will face with the problem of monotone. On the contrary, if we put an emphasis too much on difference, we will face with the problem of chaos. Let us see the problem between the two ideologies in political philosophy, namely, liberalism and multiculturalism. Liberalism holds the thesis that "Everybody is just like us" whereas multiculturalism holds the thesis that "Everybody is just different from us. " Both ideologies have loopholes because they hold extreme theses. While liberalism emphasizes too much upon similarity, multiculturalism emphasizes too much on difference. To take a middle way, we need to follow what I call "the Hartshornian Way". To see how liberalism and multiculturalism are wrong, we can do like Hartshorne does by adding "in all aspects" at the end of each thesis. Let see the liberal thesis first. We can see clearly that "Everybody is just like us in all aspects" is obviously wrong. Similarly, as for multiculturalism, "Everybody is just different from us in all aspects" is also obviously wrong. To be correct, we need to take the middle way, "Everybody is just like us in some aspect and different from us in another aspect. "

Why Religion Matters

There are many ways to define human beings. One definition which is relevant to this paper is: man is a basically religious being. Man has come to existence with a basic belief in the supernatural being. Justification or refutation is just a later stage. Religious tradition is one of the most powerful forces in life. Religion has been with human beings since the beginning of human existence. What would have happened if there had been no religion?

Neither Exclusivism nor Inclusivism

There are at least three main religious ideologies among different believers, namely, exclusivism, inclusivism, and pluralism. Exclusivism holds the thesis that our way is the only true way to reach salvation, and that all the other ways are wrong. Inclusivism holds the thesis that even though all other ways are true like ours, they are less true. Pluralism holds that there are many ways to reach salvation. Neither exclusivism nor inclusivism is proper for harmony because both fail to promote authentic dialogue.

What Religious Pluralism Means

Many people are reluctant to accept religious pluralism because they think that it is similar to religious relativism. In fact, the two schools are different. Religious relativism holds that anything goes. All ways are true according to the judgment and approval of their believers. Religious pluralism holds that their true ways do not depend upon the judgment and approval of the believers. We may divide pluralists into two main groups: Pluralists in ends and means, and pluralists in means but monists in an end. Scholars like John Hick and Buddhadasa are pluralists in means but monists in the end.

Why Religious Pluralism Matters

Religious pluralism is the only proper ideology for an authentic dialogue in the age of globalization. This ideology will eventually lead us to reach mutual understanding, peaceful co-existence, enrichment, and cooperation.

论坛专题

亚洲价值观和伦理秩序探微

刘可风[*]

摘　要：关于亚洲价值观的争论不是纯学术之争。亚洲价值观不是所有亚洲人和亚洲国家一致认同的价值观，而是起源于亚洲的并且可能对亚洲的未来发展有益的价值观。亚洲人的需要就是亚洲价值观存在的价值。但是我们必须明确，以国家为本的亚洲价值观是否已经完成了由传统身份制国家观向现代契约论国家观的转变；亚洲价值观中与威权主义的肯定的国家观相反相成的无政府主义的否定的价值观的强大作用力是否被我们认识；在儒家传统伦理所维护的"三纲"秩序被打破以后，我们能否建立起不同于"丛林法则"的"园林法则"伦理新秩序。认清和解决这些问题，亚洲价值观才能成为亚洲发展的未来价值目标，反之则可能成为亚洲发展的障碍。

关键词：亚洲价值观　国家观　伦理秩序　园林法则

Tentative Study on Asian Values and Ethical Order

Liu Kefeng

Abstract：The discussion about Asian values is not merely a purely

---

* 刘可风，中南财经政法大学副校长、教授。

academic debate. Asian values here is not the values that all the Asian people and countries approve, but should be the values that originate and benefit to Asia. Requires of Asian values made it worth to exist, however, we need to clearly aware that the advocating of "country first" Asian values whether changed by the modern contract theory from the traditional identity national view. Moreover, whether we notice that there are powerful reaction between certainly authoritarianism and negative anarchism. Furthermore, whether we do establish the "garden law" other than the "jungle law" after the traditional ethic order of Confucianism was broken away. Identify and solve these problems can help Asian countries achieves the future expects, otherwise they will become the factors that block the sustainable development.

Keywords: Asian Values; National View; Ethic Order; Garden Law

20 世纪 90 年代以来，围绕"亚洲价值观"，众说纷纭，莫衷一是，争议此起彼伏，经久不衰。总括起来，可以分为：有无之争，是非之争，优劣之争，存废之争，进退之争，源流之争，统分之争，成败之争，正负之争，虚实之争，因果之争，传统现代之争，动力阻力之争，主动被动之争，肯定否定之争，先验经验之争，等等。笔者认为，这些争论，是不会达到一致认同的有效结果的。因为"亚洲价值观"本身就是一个完全意义上的价值命题，争议各方都有自己先在的既定的价值立场和价值取向。它不是学术之争，在一定意义上，它类似于一种政治观、宗教观。不论它是不是人们"想象的"、"虚拟的"和"预设的"，或者是不是对已有事实的反映，作为一个概念，它的存在与否，取决于人们的需要和相信。信则有，不信则无。

众所周知，价值和价值观是有区别的。譬如：自由、民主、平等、和平、幸福，这都是人类共同的价值追求，但是，人们对这些基本价值的理解，所形成的自由观、民主观、平等观、和平观、幸福观，却是大相径庭的。这是处于不同国家、民族和时代的人，基于他们的社会状况、文化传统、阶级立场，乃至个人经历而必然产生的观念差异。因此，用洲际、国别来界定价值观，其实是缺乏根据的，也是很难被科学定义的。更不要说，把"西方"这一政治范畴和"亚洲"这一地域范畴放在同一逻辑层次上比对，加以非此即彼的解读和辩论，这在思维逻辑上是多少有些偏颇的。

但是，我们不是在讨论一个纯学术问题，而是在经济全球化加剧的背景下，在东西方强弱悬殊，西方发达国家咄咄逼人的态势下，在亚洲各国的经济社会发展遭遇困境和面临突破之机，讨论我们的命运和未来。我们可能需要重提"亚洲价值观"。我们的需要，就是"亚洲价值观"的价值。所谓"亚洲的"，与其说是"亚洲人共有的"，毋宁说是"发源于亚洲的并且对亚洲的未来有益的"。所以，我们不妨像经济学的人性假设一样，把亚洲价值观作为亚洲国家地区共同发展进步的假设前提。

为此，我们要对以往有关亚洲价值观的肯定的描述和评价做一定的分析，这种分析应该跳出单纯亚洲人的视角才可能是客观的。笔者以为，至少在三个方面，是被亚洲价值观的支持者有意无意地忽略了的。

第一，我们都承认，亚洲价值观首先是国家层面的价值观，即一种国家观。支持者们认为，正是在"国家第一"还是"个人第一"的问题上，构成了亚洲价值观与西方价值观的根本区别。这其实是存疑的。凡对西方稍有了解的人都知道，西方人在对国家的爱戴和尊崇、国家利益不可侵犯的神圣感和为国牺牲的使命感方面，丝毫不逊于亚洲人。比如著名的美国西点军校的校训，就是赫赫有名的"职责，荣誉，国家"。真正的区别在于对国家的理解：究竟是传统等级身份制国家观，还是现代契约论国家观。如果是后者，国家至上本质上就是人民至上，公民至上，纳税人至上；而如果是前者，个人是国家的附庸，国家是凌驾于个人之上的，国家至上就是维护森严的等级身份，维护作为国家化身的特殊个人。从亚洲的传统伦理渊源来看，显然亚洲价值观带有很深的前者的印记。现在需要反思的是，我们今天提倡的亚洲价值观，在坚持"国家第一"的价值导向时，是否自觉清算了旧的国家观而接受了新的国家观，而这正是中国乃至亚洲近现代知识分子所致力于解决的现代性问题。

如果这种国家价值观在亚洲各国没有完全实现新旧转变，则"国家第一"的价值取向就像是一把双刃剑，它可以使国家经济迅速起飞而给国民带来实际利益，也可以使这种一时繁荣的经济局面瞬间崩盘而给国民带来猝不及防的损失和灾难。

第二，我们都认同亚洲价值观与儒家伦理的血缘关系，所以无论是亚洲价值观的支持者还是反对者往往都把它与威权主义、贤能政治联系起来。这当然是有道理的。但是我们更要看到，但凡历史源流悠久的价值观，绝不是单一指向的，而恰恰是由两组对反的价值体系相反相成构成的。主流的强势的肯定的价值观念同时必然隐含着否定自身的因素，这种否定的价值观念几乎如影随形地与肯定的价值观念同时生长，都根深蒂固地埋藏于传统之中。比如中国几千年封建社会发展史，表面上看，靠的是维护以君权为核心的等级身份制而超稳定发展过来的，但是实质上，这种自上而下的严苛的家长制、专制主义，无时无刻不伴随着自下而上的分散主义、无政府主义，在社会生活中若隐若现地交替起作用。看似截然相反的东西实际上相互依存，缺一不可。有多大的威权，就有多强的离心力，它们互为存在的理由和前提。这也正是亚洲各国历史上反政府的民间情绪和行为倾向，以及运用暴力或非正常手段造成已遂和未遂的政权更迭，远多于西方国家的原因。看不到这一点，我们所提倡的亚洲价值观，就是片面的。

第三，当我们推崇一种价值观时，实际上是在讲两个层面的问题。首先是肯定某种可以在当时当地蕴含正面价值的伦理关系或伦理秩序，而后是选择维护这种秩序并实现其价值的道德规范。领导新加坡创造经济奇迹的李光耀先生曾多次强调：亚洲社会要想繁荣发达，最为重要的是要维护"五有"："第一，父子有爱；第二，君臣有义；第三，夫妇有别；第四，长幼有序；第五，朋友有信。"显然，这"五有"源自儒家"仁义礼智信"的"五常"说。可是，这里不是忽略就是回避了一个问题：自中国的汉代以来，儒家的"五常"一定是依附于"君为臣纲，父为子纲，夫为妻纲"的，即"三纲五常"。"三纲"是秩序，"五常"是规范，"五常"的作用和价值是为了维护"三纲"。"三纲"的秩序是不能颠倒和违反的，在"三纲"的秩序之下，忠诚和服从是"臣"、"子"、"妻"的美德和行为准则，对于作为纲的"君"、"父"、"夫"来说，他们对"臣"、"子"、"妻"并不需要忠诚和服从，而是享有远比西方价值观所提倡的更多的"自由"——为所欲为、不受任何制约的"自由"。有人说，对"三纲五常"，我们可以取其精华，去其糟粕，也就是颠覆"三纲"而保留"五常"。可是，皮之不存，毛将焉附？对于儒家思想来说，"三纲"失序，"五常"就没有了判定标准，进而失去了存在的意义。我们似可以这样判断，亚洲各国在价值观问题上出现分歧和迷惘，其原因并不是我们失去了传统道德规范，而是我们本想用传统道德来维护伦理秩序，为经济起飞保驾护航，但是事与愿违，在强大的经济推动力下，在经济发展如"过山车"般的跌宕起伏中，传统的伦理秩序基本瓦解了，而新的伦理秩序尚未建立起来。所以我们讨论亚洲价值观，如果只注重第二个层面的规范因素，而忽视第一个层面的秩序因素，就是舍本求末，本末倒置。当然，今天我们确实不能再回到"三纲"了，那么我们还要不要建立新的伦理秩序呢？这种新秩序有没有纲呢？如果有，应该以何为纲呢？

综上所述，今天，我们重提"亚洲价值观"，并不是要向全世界宣示一种与欧洲、非洲、美洲等诸大洲相抗衡的、迥异的，或者自诩比他们先进和优越的什么价值观，而是首先要尝试寻求重建顺乎自然、合乎人性、与亚洲各国现代经济社会发展契合的伦理新秩序。比如当代中国，重提"以人为本"，我们可以理解为"国家以人为纲"的伦理新秩序，它包含"政府以公民为纲，官员以人民群众为纲，国家中、家庭中每一个个人相互为纲"。在这种秩序下，我们再来考虑与之匹配的规范。

我们与西方价值观的区别，主要不在于是否建立这样的伦理秩序，而在于维护秩序的独具特色的方式。同样的伦理秩序，在不同的地方需要用不同的方式来维护。基于亚洲的文化传统，我们如果求助于从西方拿来的"丛林法则"，即由国家创造人与人之间自由平等竞争的环境，依靠"自由竞争，物竞天择，优胜劣汰，适者生存"来维护这种伦理秩序，实现其价值，结果可能会适得其反，演变成一种恶性竞争，自相残杀。因此，我们应该由国家营造一种人与人之间自由平等合作的环境，即采用"园林法则"，依靠"兼容并蓄，共同繁荣，求同存异，和而不同"来维护这种伦理秩序，这才有可能实现我们亚洲各国的未来价值目标。正如 2014 年 11 月在中国海口市召开的亚洲市长论坛（AMF）第四次全体会议上，伊斯坦布尔市长扎伊特·派索所说的："亚洲是一棵树，我们就是同一棵树上长出的不同的枝。"只有我们亚洲各国政府之间、人民之间、学者之间，摒弃前嫌，亲密合作，共同发展，我们的亚洲价值观才有价值，我们亚洲才有未来，人类才有未来。

Asian Spiritual Traditions: Birthing A Trans-Cultural Spirituality

Aloysius Britto [*]

Abstract: In this article, "Asian Spiritual Traditions: Birthing a Trans-cultural Spirituality", what will be explored is the vital importance of Eastern spiritual traditions, and its wisdom that the present world is in great need of. This article contextualizes this view in the present world context of the globalized industrial complex and the neo-capitalistic market economy. Our existential encounter with other religions is a matter of sharing our spiritual experiences and summoning us to a deeper and more mystical spiritual life. We should not immunize ourselves to the inner meaning of most profound truths of religion and their spiritualities. The life of Gandhi and his contribution to India will be highlighted. His struggle for India's freedom and sustainable life of the nation, built on self sustaining communities. Gandhi is one who showed us how to evolve from an ethnocentric to a global way of relating beyond ethnocentric boundaries. A universal spiritual mode of relating rooted in compassion and sustained by the awareness that reality is a reflection of the

[*] Aloysius Britto, Assam Don Bosco University. He has done his M. A. in Sociology from the Pune University in 1983, and has worked in Ishvani Kendra: Institute of Missiology and Communications from 1984 till date in missiological research for the Institute and as an editorial coordinator for its missiological digest, Ishvani Documentation and Mission Digest.

Divine.

Keywords：Asian Spiritual Traditions；Trans-cultural Spirituality；Neo-Capitalistic Market Economy；Interreligious Living Dialogue；Gandhi

亚洲精神传统：孕育一种跨文化精神

Aloysius Britto

　　摘　要：本文将探讨东方精神传统的重要意义及目前全球迫切需要的智慧。本文将这个观点渗透在当前全球化产业园区和新资本主义市场经济的世界背景中。我们与其他现存宗教的邂逅让我们能够分享精神体验，也促使我们拥有一种更深入、更神秘的精神生活。我们不应该逃避宗教及其精神的深刻真理的内在含义。本文将强调甘地的生活及其对印度所做的贡献。他为争取印度的自由和国家的可持续发展所做的努力都建立在自我维持的社区上。甘地向我们展示了如何从种族中心主义的方式进化到超越种族中心主义界限的全球化方式。这是一种普遍的精神模式，这种模式根植于怜悯心并把现实视为神圣的映照。

　　关键词：亚洲精神传统　跨文化精神　新资本主义市场经济　宗教间的生活对话　甘地

Introduction

In this article，what will be explored is the vital importance of Eastern spiritual traditions that even today，despite the ravages of modernization are custodians of a wisdom of which the western culture stands in the most urgent need. The uniqueness of the east is its living religious experience that sustained its people in the multi-cultural，multi-religious and multi-racial society down the millennia.

It birthed a trans-cultural spirituality which will benefit today's 'one planetary earth community'. Presently we need to be attentive to the voices from all over the planet to nurture a civilization of creative love and peace. Huston Smith intuited these insights from his lifelong study on *World Religions*: "For understanding at least in the realms of inherently noble as the great faiths of mankind, brings respect and respect prepares the way for a higher power love- the only power that can quench the flames of fear, suspicion and prejudice and provide the means by which the people of this small but precious Earth becomes one to one another" (Smith, 1991: 390). We today have to gain a new spiritual perspective and on this foundation, our spiritual and even our physical survival will depend. Our existential encounter with other religions is a matter of sharing our spiritual experiences and enrichment of our religious practices, revitalizing and summoning us to a deeper and more mystical spiritual life: Thomas Merton, Bede Griffith, Beatrice Bruteau and Diana Eck. Religions and their spirituality are much more than mere 'cultural phenomena' they are the vehicles of the most profound and precious truths to which we should not immunize ourselves to the inner meanings of which is governed by something, far deeper than mere mental categories, it opens up new avenues of existence and understanding, it leads us to that "light that is neither of the East nor the West" (Nasr, 1977: 61). The article contextualizes this view in our present world context of the globalized-industrial-complex and the neo-capitalistic market economy. The life of Gandhi and his contribution to India will be highlighted. His struggle for India's freedom and sustainable life of the nation, built on self sustaining communities.

I. The Human Search For Sacred Horizons

Sense for the Holy

The mentality of modern rationality and the scientific method has camouflaged the religious quest for being, it has closed us to the quest beyond ourselves, to an endlessly fascinating mystery of what makes us live, with faith, hope and love. Huston Smith says that "archaeologists have discovered no founding city of a civilisation that does not have a sacred centre" (Bryant, 1992: 11).

Anthony Giddens has sensed that this present globalizing world is "the runaway world", where we do not have a shared sense of direction of our history which appears out of control, and we do not know where we are heading. This "runaway world" needs a shared vision and spirituality-a sense of the holy (whole) without which it will perish by the weight of its own arrogance and "manufactured risk": global warming, overpopulation, pollution, unstable markets, and unforeseen consequences of genetic engineering. We still do not know the consequences of what we are habituated to do. What this world seeks for is not just knowledge but wisdom of humanity's ultimate destination that will liberate it from its deep anxiety and hopelessness (Giddens, 1999: 1 - 6). Hence, the role of religion in the globalised world is yet to be explored.

The utopian promise of a material paradise promised by the new economic social order has not brought any tangible result especially for the poor. On the other hand, the negative effects of globalisation have led to exploitation of labour, job insecurity, reduction in wages and consequently lower standards of living. The utopia of better life for the developed nations and promise to the poor have ended in the rich continuing to get richer and the poor becoming poorer. Worse still is the increasing influence of multinational companies and corporations on political decisions, especially of developing nations.

In the present times we need shamans, 'liminal personalities', communities and cultures that will enlighten and orient humanity to the larger vision of life that beckons us. We cannot exist as a people without a *trans-cultural maturity* which is far beyond just social adjustments, no longer limited by the culture in which one has grown, it is giving birth to a comprehensive self, who is a peacemaker going beyond violence, primitive perceptions of the other as a threat, and lives in the insight of this inner freedom of life (Gorman, 1985: 162) . "The only thing you have to offer another human being, ever, is your own state of being, as Meister Eckhart had said that there is no being except in the mode of being" (Dass, 1974: 6) This state of being is a *trans-cultural maturity* sustained by the new Shamans (liminal figures) of our age that's in transition to a planetary society.

Emergence of a New Consciousness: Need for Transcendence

Just as photosynthesis was a breakthrough moment in the relationship to the earth and the sun, so the emergence of the first human species was a breakthrough moment in the living world. As evolution continues, our self-awareness too increases to the point of self-transcendence to become a new species *Homo Universalis* (universal) ; humans with the capacity to integrate with the larger whole. We are at the cross roads of an evolutionary breakthrough, one that requires conscious participation as co-creative agents of altruistic love, or bury ourselves with the gravity of the self-centeredness of our own self-consciousness. Barbara Marx Hubbard in her book: *Emergence: the Shift from Ego to Essence*, says that humans have to transit from being *Homo Sapiens* (wise ones) to *Homo Universalis* (universal ones) . She says that at the present evolutionary stage we must engage our consciousness and respond to the issues that threaten the very survival of the earth: materialism, political geocentricism, religious fanaticism and human ignorance which have created a political and environmental crisis of a colossal proportion. Sooner than later we will have to respond to these issues or else we will not exist as a human species. We need to connect to the totality of life, and the deeper intelligence of the universe.

II. Quest For Meaning in Our Contemporary World

The Cry for Moral and Spiritual Wisdom

The contemporary reality of the world is that though the standards of living for more than half the world's population has actually become better, the dark side is that half the global village still lives in dire poverty, social evils and obscene inequality even though we may boast of the advances in science, technology, industry and wealth accumulation. The United States and Europe spents nearly ninety times as much on luxury items as the amount of money that would be needed to provide safe drinking water and basic sanitation for those in our global village who do not have these necessities now. In one day's military spending; we could virtually eliminate malaria in Africa. What we spend in two days on the military, we could provide the health care services necessary to prevent the deaths of three million infants a year. For less than a week's military spending, we could educate each of the 140 million children in the developing countries who have not gone to school. Poverty and gross inequalities throughout the world waste human potential, weaken the entire community and put the whole family at risk, diminishing their hopes for better lives, and makes them insignificant (Cf. Groody, 2007: 1 – 30) .

Today our globalized free market economy alone is insufficient to bring genuine human liberation and may result in enslaving us in our inordinate desires. The strength of the free-market must be evaluated alongside of the weakness of human nature. In our current predicament, we are losing sight of people in pursuit of profit, responsibility in the face of new freedom, and common good in the search of self-interest. If we have to be veered off course and correct today's abuses as a human family, it requires more than 'market-logic'. The world today is crying out for moral and spiritual wisdom that can help us navigate the path to peace.

Scholars of various academic disciplines have helped identify and analyse the terrain and some have even offered a course of action to steer in the right direction. History helps us understand our place in the unfolding course of world events, but it cannot help us understand the relationship within and among nations, it has not given us insight into the values needed to make us a better global village. Economics helps us to understand the complexities of financial transactions, but it has virtually ignored the human costs that stem from the current market system. Sociology helps us grasp human behaviour, but it has not helped us address the deeper disorders of the human heart that affect it. Psychology helps us understand our relationship with ourselves, but it has stopped short of helping us understand better our relationship with God. For the ones who have a sense of the sacred, globalisation offers a new hope for human solidarity and interconnectedness, which coexists against the re-emergence of age-old human constants like greed, selfishness, and sinfulness.

The economically prosperous parts of the world live with the modern illusion that we are more ' advanced' than the previous generations, but the paradox of our present moment comes from a spiritual emptiness. It makes us realise the paradoxical relationship between economic development and spiritual development, between the cravings of the body and the hunger of the soul, between the invisible hand of the economy, and the invisible heart of the human person. It teaches us the simplicity which has more to do with the clarity of the heart and intention than with simply having ' things' .

Mass Technological Society has forgotten its Humanizing Task

Humanity has forgotten its central task of becoming *human*. The failure to perform that *humanising task* even for a single generation might set the erring community back, a whole geological epoch: indeed, there is reason to suspect that this has actually begun to happen in our time. Humans are thus losing hold on any personal life that can be called their own: they are now being turned into a ' thing' destined to be processed and reconstructed collectively by the same methods that have produced the atomic pile and the computer.

For its effective salvation humankind will need to undergo something like a spontaneous religious conversion: one that will replace the mechanical world picture with an organic world picture, and give to the human personality, as the highest known manifestation of life, the precedence it now gives to its machines and computers. "Of one thing we may be confident, if humankind is to escape its programmed self-extinction the God who saves us will not descend from the machine: he will rise up again in the human soul" (Mumford, 1964: 283). Hence, all thinking worthy of the name now must be ecological, in the sense of appreciating and utilising organic complexity and in adapting every kind of change to the requirement not of humans alone, or of any single generation, but of all their organic partners and every part of their habitat, which is a new organic model of ecological association and self-organisation today (Cf. Mumford, 1964: 285, 393, 409).

At this point in history, it is essential that we ask difficult and searching questions about the place of technology in our lives. What is the essence of modern technology? How does it structure our lives, our perceptions and our politics? How does it shape our psyche? What does it say about our relationship to our humanness and to the earth?

It is not a new idea that we live in mass technological society and suffer psychological addiction to specific technological products. But the picture is bigger and more complex. The social philosopher, Morris Berman, says in *The Re-Enchantment of the World*, "Addiction in one form or the other characterises every aspect of industrial society ... dependence on alcohol, food, drugs, tobacco ... is not formally different from dependence on prestige, career achievement, world influence, wealth, the need to build more ingenious bombs, or the need to exercise control over everything" (Berman, 1981). Gregory Bateson the evolutionary philosopher, in *Steps to an Ecology of Mind*, points out that addictive behaviour is consistent with the Western approach to life that puts mind against the body. He concludes, "It is doubtful whether a species, having both an advanced technology and this strange polarised way of looking at its world, can survive" (Bateson, 1972: 472 – 3). The technological revolution has developed in size and complexity to the point of cancelling our very ability to grasp their impact upon us. The socially structured scientific-technological reality that now threatens to determine every aspect of our lives, and encases the entire planet is in an out of control situation.

Our experience in mass technological society is indeed 'outside the range of human experience' and by evidence of psychological distress, ecological destruction and technological control, this way of life has been 'markedly distressing' to almost everyone (Cf. Deloria, 1970: 185 – 7). As the world has become less organic and more dependent on techno-fixes for problems created by earlier techno-fixes, humans have substituted a new worldview for one, which once was filled with clean rushing waters, animals, constellations of stars, tales of ancestors, and people working together in sacred purpose. It will now require a collective psychological process to heal us technological people who, through a mechanistic culture, have lost touch with our essential humanity (Cf. Deloria, 1970: 185 – 190).

What Does Our Current World Situation Tells Us?

After half a century of communism the previous Soviet Union, Eastern Europe and China are looking to be saved from the results of stagnation by a change to liberal capitalistic market economies. Meanwhile the United States, Germany and Japan are beginning to realise that success has created an underclass of homeless and unemployed, and massive pollution of the environment. On the psychological level, the shadow of our success, the flip side of our affluence, is the increasing problem of stress and burnout, on the sociological level, it is the anomie, homelessness and fragmentation to individualism. But finally, *stress cannot be dealt with by psychological or socio-economic tricks because, for the most part, it is philosophical/ spiritual rather than a psychological problem, a matter of the wrong worldview.* Our dignity as human beings lies not in exhausting ourselves in work but in discovering our vocation (Keen, 1991: 61 – 66).

When we live within the horizon of the economic myth we begin to consider it honourable for one to do whatever he must to make a living. Gradually we adopt what Eric Fromm called a 'marketing orientation' towards ourselves, moulding ourselves into commodities.

III. The Spiritual Quest

Chaos of the Human Soul

People all over the world are seeking to find resolution to all these problems: human survival, ecocide, overpopulation, nuclear armament, greedy rich manipulating the markets for profits for short term gains and leaving the large masses at the mercy of the capitalistic markets etc.; and at a deeper level seeking more lasting foundations. It will involve not only technology but a new understanding of the human story (mythology).

Beneath the surface of the chaos lies a deeper chaos of the human soul, the darkening of his spirit, born of his faulty perception of (scientific rationality) which has no place for the sacred, the mystery in his life. Levis Strauss has written very perceptively about this in his book, *The Savage Mind*, "All sacred things must have their place.... that being in their place is what makes them sacred for if they were taken out of their place even in thought, the entire order of the universe would be destroyed. Sacred objects therefore contribute in maintenance of the order of the universe by occupying the place allocated to them" (Strauss, 1966: 16).

To arrive at existence as it were only physical, statistical and mathematical is to make it false. This approach erodes the human spirit and in the end destroys us all. We are presently experiencing this human condition in our world. We have all the power of scientific technology that can make us one planetary family but paradoxically we are far from such a reality. We are broken and fragmented from the larger reality of life. The most difficult transformation to the new way of life is the realization of an interiorized spirituality.

Ordering of the Soul

Bernard Lonergan a great prophetic theologian contemplated very deeply on the need of such a 'spirituality of integration' . He said that the chaos in the world today is a mirror image of the chaos and disorder in the human soul. "The foundations of order in the soul and the order in society are the same thing…it does the ordering of the outer world order," he felt "there are norms built in the human soul that we discover and these norms have the power to put order not only into our communities but also to put order into the soul itself. " He felt that society should not fail to understand the inner roots of the social decay. He noticed that there was a great breakdown taking place in the private lives of people: that activists mostly do not attend to the matters of the inner heart in their own lives and as a consequence have no real and authentic experience of living a qualitative life; they fail to live at a level of interiority which they ironically strive to make possible for everyone else; they forget to relish the values of silence, of beauty, of solitude, of celebration of life, they are unable to help others appreciate them. Burnout is inevitable, their efforts do not last and it is a pity that good hearts are shattered beyond any recognition. Lonergan comments that Gandhi saw this very clearly. Gandhi's commitment to non-violence was not merely an ideal. He saw how passive resistance worked to turn hearts of enemies and to uproot the view of us-against-them view of the human conflict, in the sense of an empirical theory that explains how things (like self-sacrifice) function. He says that today we need to legitimate spiritual values further by understanding how they function in the psychological and social-order, we need to understand for ourselves how the order of our souls function as a source of the greatest of human achievements, likewise the disorder in it is the source of the greatest disaster (Dunn, 1985: 1 –9) .

The Significance of Cosmogonic Love

Carl Jung contemplating on the mysteries of life wrote at the end of his life of the "cosmogonic-love", a love that transcends our human experience of love and opens us to an unknowable reality that we cannot embrace though it embraces us. We are seen and loved by this unknowable reality of life (Jung,

1963: 354）. It is a critical necessity as citizens of one "Earth Community" to find a way to relocate this human spiritual sense at the personal level to the entire community of life（Woodman, 1997: 220 – 227）.

IV. Asian Religious Experience: A Quest for the Absolute (Wholeness)

Symbolic Thinking

The approach favoured by the Asian spirituality is fundamentally a holistic world-view. Asian spirituality proceeds from the principal of fundamental identity, which means that the profound transcendent reality is simultaneously the most deeply immanent reality. It has a great veneration for the mystery of divine reality and of the cosmos, realising the inability of human language and its conceptual faculties to express the ultimate reality of *God-world-humanity*. They are drawn to the apophatic tradition of spirituality a corrective to Western spirituality enamoured by the kataphatic tradition of affirmation and conceptualisation, that the divine mystery can be grasped-comprehended by means of concepts（mental forms）. It has evolved on the basis of a deeply rooted tradition of meditation and immersion in the mystery of ultimate reality; it is to be experienced（*anubhava*）. The apophatic transpersonal depth of God's nature in the Asian experience is well honoured in Christian mystical tradition which has been forgotten（Smith, 1992: 260）.

The experience of illumination（*satori*, awakening, comprehension or understanding, *Samadhi*, state of consciousness induced by meditation）conduces more to the silence than for expression. The profound spiritual experience shuns hasty communication, preferring discretion. Their approach to encounter with other religions and cultures is fundamentally different from the Western theology that meets religions outwardly. Asian theologians start from within claiming religious and cultural traditions as their heritage and trying to make them fruitful. 'Symbolic thinking of the East' is better able to uphold the mystery of the divine reality, which was neglected by Western theology with its unilateral focus on rational knowledge (Evers, 2012: 28 – 31).

Searching for the Depths: Communication to Communion

Communion evolves through depth communication, in the context of Asian cultural and religious pluralism, through the praxis of dialogue and encounters with diverse cultures and religions. These are now emerging within inter-faith movements of our times, which is described today as a new way of being religious, i. e., *being inter-religious.* This new way is *deeply rooted* in the particular way to the ultimate in the multiform traditions of religious life, yet *respectfully opens* to the ways of others. This was the praxis of Mahatma Gandhi who remained deeply Hindu while learning from other traditions of the ultimate. It was Swami Abhishiktananda who plumbed the interface between Christianity and Hinduism deeply. The monk from Vietnam, Thich Nhat Hanh, elaborates it in his book entitled, *Living Buddha, Living Christ,* as a new way of being religious within a multi-religious tradition. This type of an interreligious living dialogue is a spiritual journey.

Raimundo Panikkar calls it, "intra-religious dialogue" that is an inner dialogue within one's self, an encounter in the depths of one's personal religious experience, having met another religious experience on that very intimate level (Panikkar, 1978: 40). In this type of a dialogue we can expect some creative directions to emerge that may have an impact on the future of such religious traditions. As Abhishiktananda says, "But in every religion and in every religious experience there is a *beyond* and it is precisely this *beyond* that is our goal" (1975: 26).

Thomas Merton the great Trappist monk learnt and absorbed much from the spiritual traditions of Asia. The journey of Thomas Merton is a narrative of one man's longing for the Real or the Absolute. His life attests to this fact:

I believe that our renewal consists precisely in deepening this understanding and this grasp of that which is most real. And I believe by openness to Buddhism, to Hinduism and the great Asian traditions, we stand a wonderful chance of learning more of the potentialities of our own traditions because they have gone from the natural point of view, so much deeper than we have. The combination of the natural techniques and the graces and the other things that have manifested in Asia and the Christian liberty of the gospel should bring us all at last to that full and transcendent liberty which is beyond cultural differences and mere externals-and mere this and that (Burton, 1973: 343).

Thomas Merton was not naive about this new way of being monastic, religious or a Christian. He saw some dangers as he experienced it in the West, as they got entangled in the superficial. His advice to the Eastern monks was:

The time is coming when you will face the same situation and your fidelity to your ancient traditions will stand you in good stead. Do not be afraid of that fidelity…be faithful to your own search…and among these people, if they are faithful to their own calling, to their own vocation, and to their own message from God, communication on the deepest level of communication is not communication, but communion. It is wordless. It is beyond words, and it is beyond speech, and it is beyond concept…My dear brothers, we are already one (Burton, 1973: 307 – 308).

For Merton it was the final integration of the trans-cultural person or as Kegan explores in his study of the *Evolving Self*, a more developmentally refined, wider and deeper level of " being-knowing-relating ". It further evolves from ethnocentric to a global way of relating beyond ethnocentric boundaries. A universal spiritual mode of relating rooted in compassion or agape, sustained by awareness that reality is a reflection of the Divine (Kegan, 1982, 1994).

Transcendental Unity of all Religions

The sinister processes of modernization and globalization are disastrous for humankind's spiritual welfare: intensifying conflicts, conflicts of political and

religious experience to some sentimental 'universal' pseudo-religion centred on some misty platitudes. If this has to be averted we need to understand what Fritz Schuon has called "the transcendental unity of religions", and understanding that takes us to fathom the mystical expression such as that of Rumi the great Muslim Sufi saint, "I am neither Christian nor a Jew nor a Parsi nor Muslim. I am neither of the East nor of the West, neither of land nor sea...I have put aside duality and have seen that the two worlds are one. I seek the One. I know the One. I see the One, invoke the One. He is the First, He is the Last, He is the Outward, He is the Inward" (Schuon, 1975 ed. : 9) . There is some hope that in this climate a properly constituted metaphysical framework in which to affirm the "profound and eternal solidarity of all spiritual forms", the different religions might "present a singular front against the floodtide of materialism and pseudo-spiritualism" (Schuon, 1979: 12) . A rediscovery of the immutable nature of man and a renewed understanding of the *Sophic Perennis*, must be the governing purpose of most serious comparative study of religion: The situation of man in the contemporary world urgently summons us to this noble end (Nasr, 1972: 61) .

V. The Liminal Man Gandhi: His Spiritual Quest for Wholeness

Gandhi's Hope for India

It is now a century since Gandhi returned to India from South-Africa (1915 – 2015) as a transformed and courageous man. He was drawn out from himself by the call in his conscience to play a prophetic role in India's freedom struggle and in the soul of the modernizing world. A call from what was profound in the human heart, purified by his, "My Experiments with Truth. " He used to often enter into prayer and self-examination searching for deep sustaining strength to serve selflessly. It was in Natal, South Africa in the silence of its hills, tending to the wounded and dying in the Boer War, that he discovered how to draw on the spiritual strength of sacrificial love that creatively heals and builds communities not yielding to the dark forces born in the human heart and learning the wisdom making experience of *Satya* (Truth) and *Ahimsa* (Non-violence). (*Ahimsa* in Sanskrit does not contain the negative and passive connotation of the English translation of non-violence; it means much more than the absence of violence; it is intense love). Gandhi in 1908 consciously named his non violent movement *Satyagraha* from the experience of his struggle in South Africa. He said, "Truth (*Satya*) implies love and firmness (*agraha*) ... and therefore serves as a synonym for force. I thus began to call the Indian movement *Satyagraha*, that is to say, the force which is born of truth and love or nonviolence...." (Easwaran, 1997: 150).

The South African experience made him reflect and articulate his idea of India and the true meaning of India's freedom. India for him had to be an all inclusive society, without discrimination of any kind. Freedom for him meant a system of cooperative self rule in which individual communities and the nation as a whole strove to create a sustainable moral civilization. It was here, as a young ambitious man, Gandhi overcame a spiritual crisis in life: he became both Hindu and secular at the same time and developed an unshakeable faith in all the world's religions that could teach humankind the path to wisdom, a wisdom that reconciles the contradictions and paradoxes of life and makes us whole.

He embraced both truth (*satya*) and nonviolence (*ahimsa*) as non-negotiable conditions to a transformative change. The South African experience made him a true global citizen. It is in South Africa that he learnt and studied the world's noblest thinkers and it redefined his political praxis: nurturing a community of dedicated, disciplined and selfless social servants for constructive social work; uniting Indians of all religious faiths, castes, linguistic communities in a common struggle for justice; care for the people in need and distress; empowerment of women, children and youth; indigenous health care, cleanliness and sanitation; making possible inexpensive ways of healing and preventive medicine; and overcoming both the adversary and adversity with a courageous trust, hope and love. Stanley Jones the great evangelist and a close friend of Gandhi wrote in his book *Gandhi: Potrayal of a Friend*, "I am still an evangelist. I bow to Mahatma Gandhi, but I kneel at the feet of Christ and give my full and final allegiance. And yet a little man, who fought a system in the framework of which I stand, has taught me more of the spirit of Christ than perhaps any other man in East or West" (Jones, 1948: 8).

Since sixty-nine years that India has attained its freedom from the British Raj, it still continues to struggle to rise above its entanglements of caste divisions, poverty, regionalism, communal hatred and violence, religious fundamentalism and disparities between the rich and the poor. India has to further walk its road to freedom from its internal contradictions and vulnerabilities. There is now a great hope being born from all our despair because the marginalized and the poor in our country have learnt to voice, assert, organize and educate themselves from being victimized. Is our Government and State ready to guarantee people's rights effectively? Are they going to recognize universal norms of *Common Good* beyond the small menu of basic rights? They will have to take a stand about the redistribution of wealth and income, about employment, land rights, health and education, take care of developmental refugees, religious freedom etc. , and creating opportunities for each citizen in developing its capability and competencies. India cannot afford to ignore its pluriformity to live as a Democratic Republic.

Gandhi's Vision for a Socio-Ecological Sensitivity is Relevant Today

The great paradox of our times is that we have so much material affluence and yet dire poverty and destitution for want of material means for survival. The affluence in the West is like the proportion of one American child who has the same impact on the global environment due to his lifestyle as the birth of, say, seventy Indonesian children.

It is now an anthropological crisis of meaning and purpose of life. The present techno-scientific age has emptied nature and life of all its deeper purposes and meaning. We struggle to understand why we live, what are the right things to do, what is our place in the world? In an essay by John Kenneth Galbraith "How Much Should a Country Consume?" was written soon after his book, *The Affluent Society* (1958) reflects on how the single minded pursuit of wealth has distracted our attention and resources from nurturing true democracy and community, which he defined as the provision of public infrastructure, the creation of decent schools, parks and hospitals (Galbraith, 1958: 91 – 94).

In the long term fallout of this collective promotion of consumption and growing appetite for resources and commodities lies the deeper question: "What about the appetite itself? Surely this is the ultimate source of the problem...will it not one day have to be restrained?" This is a question never asked, it hangs in silence. Though only few scholars of history and social-ecologists have seriously studied the global consequences of consumerism, its impact on land soil, forest and climate, the philosopher Rudolf Bahro is very blunt on this: "The present way of life of the most industrially advanced nations stands in global and antagonistic contradictions to natural condition of human existence. We are eating up what other nations and future generations need to live on...continued industrialism in the Third World will mean poverty for whole generations and hunger for millions" (Bahro, 1984: 184).

Fifty years before the founding of the German Green Party and thirty years before the article of Galbraith, it is the Indian visionary who sternly pointed to the global unsustainability of the Western model of economic growth (development). He wrote: "God forbid that India should ever take to industrialization after the manner of the West. The economic imperialism of a single tiny island kingdom (England) is today keeping the world in chains. If an entire nation of 300 million took to similar economic exploitation, it would strip the world bare like locusts". This is what Gandhi said in 1928 (Gandhi,

1928: 243) . He reflected: "What would be the fate of India trying to ape the West?" (Gandhi, 1928: 243) .

Gandhi's vision and arguments have been revived by the present generation of Indian environmentalists and social-ecologists. India, now is in many ways an ecological disaster zone, marked by speedy deforestation, species loss, land degradation and air/water pollution. This wanton abuse of nature has been chiefly borne by the poor in the countryside, peasants, tribals, fisherfolk and pastoralists who see their resources and markets taken away and depleted by the powerful economic interests who want to make India into another England and America.

The modern sector in India has aggressively moved into the countryside to channelize resources for the parasitical needs of the urban-industrial complex and now is in search for the remaining resources of the frontiers of India, North-East and the Andaman and Nicobar Islands. The urban-industrial civilization is blinded by its insatiable consumeristic appetite, to the environmental implications of its lifestyles. We must now act with balance and learn the wisdom of the *Limits of Growth* (acquisitiveness which has no natural limits) . Against this life degrading attitude Lewis Mumford called us to " cherish history, promoting character and variety and beauty wherever we find it, whether in landscapes or in people" (Mumford, 1964: 43; Martinez, 1997), in other words not to lose our human virtue. The development model in India can only succeed if it becomes inclusive, equitable and appreciative of its cultural diversity.

Gandhi: A Religious Universalist

Gandhi is a religious Universalist, not of a syncretic kind, but as one who, like Ramakrishna, recognized the inner unity and the essential truths of all integral traditions. "It is not Hinduism which I prize most highly, but the religion which transcends Hinduism-the basic truth which underlines all the religions of the world. " he wrote (Jordens, 1991: 28) .

It is well known that Gandhi's political philosophy has had influence non-violent movements in the American civil rights and anti-war campaigns of the 60s, anti-apartheid and Black Nationalist Movements in South Africa, and the resistance to totalitarian regimes in Eastern Europe. A cross section of the public figures, who on their own testimony found inspiration in Gandhi's example: Thomas Merton, Martin Luther King Jr, Freda Bedi, Daniel Berrigan, Danilo Dolci, Desmond Tutu, Erick Erickson, E. F. Schumacher, Robert Aitken, Jean Klein, Kathleen Raine, Wendell Berry, Vaclav Havel, Arne Naess, Joanna Macy, Ken Jones. In recent times two Asian renunciates have engaged in some of the most traumatic political struggles of our times, Tich Nhat Hanh, Dalai Lama. Lanzo de Vasto a Westerner from France was transformed by Gandhi. In 1958 he founded the Action Civique Non-Violente, it was directed against the French internment camps in Algeria and in favour of the right of conscientious objection to military service. In his book, *Return to the Source*, he wrote of his meeting with the Mahatma, "He has come to show us the power over this earth of absolute innocence. He has come to prove that it can stop machines, hold its own against guns and defy an empire. He has come into this world to bring us news from beyond, where nothing changes, to teach us the truth we have always known, being Christian. Truth so ill sorted with us, that we did not know what to do with it. We kept it between the four walls of the Church and in the dark of our hearts. He, the Hindu, has come for us to learn what we had always known. While the old man questions me and smiles: I am silent, trying not to weep" (Del Vasto, 1971: 100 – 101) .

Who was Gandhi?

Two figures who considered deeply and creatively the matters of politics, religion and spirituality were Gandhi and Thomas Merton a Christian monk. It is appropriate that we quote what the Trappist monk's meditation of Gandhi's significance for the world as a whole, one which can be considered by practitioners of all religious traditions. "One of the great lessons of Gandhi's life remains that this: through the spiritual traditions of the West he, an Indian, discovered his Indian heritage and with it his own 'right mind'. And in his fidelity to his own heritage and its spiritual sanity, he was able to show (people) of the West and of the whole world a way to recover their own 'right mind' in their own tradition thus manifesting the fact that there are certain indisputable and essential values-religious, ethical, ascetic, spiritual and philosophical... It was the spiritual consciousness of a people that awakened in the spirit of one person. But the message of the Indian spirit of Indian wisdom was not of India alone. It was for the entire world. Hence, Gandhi's message was valid for India and for himself, in so far as it represented a new world. The Indian mind that was awakening in Gandhi was inclusive not exclusive. It was at once Indian and universal. It was not a mind of hate, of intolerance, of accusation, of rejection, of division. It was a mind of love, of understanding, of infinite capaciousness...," (Merton, 1965: 4 – 5).

It was Rudolf Otto who most clearly, understood the vocation of Gandhi, he said: "We misunderstand Gandhi when we attempt to understand the strong powers and virtues of this man simply in terms of a generalized humanity... 'the greatest nationalist', 'the friend of the people', 'a clever politician', 'a born leader'. He is all these things, but he is so as an Indian Sadhu, as a result of his situation, but if the situation were different, his character as a sadhu would remain the same and would find other ways to express itself" (Otto, 1996: 195 – 196), in his presence one felt like a human being, felt connected to the whole of humanity and the world.

References

Bahro, Rudolf, 1984, *From Red to Green: Interviews with New Left Review*, London: Verso.

Bateson Greogory, 1972, *Steps to an Ecology of Mind*, New York: Random House.

Berman, Morris, 1981, *The Re-Enchantment of the World*, New York: Cornell University Press.

Burton, Naomi, Brother Patrick Hart and James Loughin (ed.), 1973, *The Asian Journal of Thomas Merton*, Sheldon Press.

Byrant, M. Darrol (ed.), 1992, *Houstan Smith: Essays on World Religions*, New York: Paragon Press.

Dass, Ram, 1974, *The Only Dance There Is*, New York, Anchor Double Day Publication. (He is not to be confused with the great Indian mystic, Saint Swami Ramdas. This present Ramdas is Richard Alpert).

Del Vasto, Lanza, 1971, *Return to the Source*, New York: University Books.

Deloria, Vine, 1970, *We Talk, You Listen*, New York: Delta Publication.

Dunn, Ted, 1985, *Lonergan and Spirituality: Towards a Spirituality of Integration*, Chicago: Loyola University Press.

Evers, George, 2012, "The Magisterium and Asian Theologians", *Concillium*, 2, pp. 23 – 38.

Galbraith, John Kenneth, 1958, "How Much Should a Country Consume?" in Henry Jarret ed. *Perspectives on Conservation*, Baltimore: John Hopkins University Press.

Gandhi, M., 1958, "Discussion with Capitalists", *Young India*, December 20, 1928; in *Collected Works of Mahatma Gandhi*, New Delhi: Publication Division, Vol. 38.

Giddens, Anthony, 1999, *Runaway World: How Globalization is Reshaping our Lives*, London: Profile.

Groody, Daniel, 2007, *Globalization, Spirituality and Justice*, Maryknoll, New York: Orbis Books.

Hubbard, Barbara Marx, 2001, *The Emergence: The Shift from Ego to Essence*, Charlottesville, VA: Hampton Road Publishing Company.

Jordens, J. F. T., 1991, *Gandhi: Conscience of Hinduism and Scourge of Orthodoxy*, Canberra: Australian National University.

Jung, Carl Gustav, 1963, *Memories, Dreams, Reflection*, New York: Pantheon Books.

Keen, Sam, 1991, *Fire in the Belly: On Being a Man*, New York: Bantam Books.

Kegan, R., 1994, *The Evolving Self: Problem and Process in Human Development*, Cambridge Massachusetts Harvard University Press, 1994 and *Over our Heads: The Mental Demands of Modern Life*, Cambridge: Harvard University Press.

Martinez-Alier Juan, 1997, "Poverty and the Environment", in Ramachandran Guha and Juan Martines, Alier, *Varieties of Environmentalism: Essays North and South*, London: Earthscan, also Juan Martinez Alier, 1991 new edition, *Ecological Economics: Energy, Environment, Society*, London: Basil Blackwell.

Merton, Thomas, 1965, *Gandhi on Non-Violence*, New York: New Directions.

Merton, Thomas, 1967, *Mystics and Zen, Masters*, New York: Farrar, Strauss and Giroux.

Mumford, Lewis, 1964, *The Myth of the Machine: The Pentagon of Power*, London: Seeker and Worburg.

Nasr, S. H., 1977, "Conditions for a Meaningful Comparative Philosophy East and West", *Philosophy East and West*, 22: 1, pp. 53 – 61.

Otto, Rudolf, 1996, *Autobiographical and Social Essays*, ed. Greogry D. Alles; Berlin: Mouton de Gruyter.

Pannikkar, Raimundo, 1978, *The Intra-Religious Dialogue*, New York: Liturgical Press.

Schuon, Frithjof, 1975 edition, *The Transcendental Unity of Religions*, New York: Harper and Row.

_____, 1979, *Gnosis: Divine Wisdom*, London: Perennial Book.

Smith, Houstan, 1991, *The World Religions: Our Great Wisdom Tradition*, San Franciso: Harper.

_____, 1992, "This Ecumenical Moment: What Are We Seeking", in M. Darrol Bryant (ed) *Houstan Smith: Essays on World Religion*.

Strauss, Levis, 1961, *The Savage Mind*, Chicago: The University of Chicago Press.

Woodman, Marion, 1997, *Dancing in the Flames: The Dark Goddess in the Transformation*, Boston: Shambala Publications.

Relevance of University Outreach Programmes for Regional Development and Asian Values

B. P. R. Narasimharao[*]

Abstract: Despite rapid Science and Technology progress and advancements, the developing countries face a host of problems such as poverty, hunger, degradation of environment and natural resources, ill effects of urbanisation and issues such as renewable energy generation, management of water and farm lands, sustainable agriculture, nutrition, sanitation and health. The solution for all these problems, the governments have to depend on the health of universities and other educational institutions which are knowledge creators and knowledge disseminators. There is also increasing tendency to focus on commoditization of knowledge. One of the fundamental questions arise is how to protect the unique role of universities in knowledge dissemination and in maintaining the values and culture of a region.

The paper discusses the relevance of university outreach in regional development and Asian values. It is time to take another look at the way we perceive development, prosperity and happiness. For instance, in 2011 April, several hundred leaders from government and civil society gathered at the UN headquarters to explore a new way of measuring how a nation is faring.

* B. P. R. Narasimharao, Indira Gandhi National Open University.

Development should not be seen in narrow economic considerations. Development should be holistic covering body, mind and soul of individual, society or nation. How by applying outreach concept one can bring in reorientation of academia to see development in a different perspective is discussed. There are various research studies in terms of modern science also covering various aspects of Asian values and practices which help in holistic development of mind, body and soul. It is argued that university outreach and engagement may prove useful in bringing universities to terms in balancing their entrepreneurial role and cultural role. The social responsibility of universities and academia in making a difference in shaping the society should be main focus in adopting strategies and concepts, it is argued.

Keywords: University Outreach; Asian Values; Regional Development

大学外拓项目对区域发展及亚洲价值的现实意义

B. P. R. Narasimharao

摘　要：发展中国家尽管在科技上有了进步和发展，还面临一系列问题，如贫穷、饥饿、环境和自然资源恶化、城市化的负面影响及可再生能源，水和耕地管理，可持续农业、营养学、卫生和健康。为了解决所有这些问题，政府不得不依赖大学和其他教育机构的健康发展。它们是知识的创造者和传播者。关注知识的商品化成为一个日益强化的趋势。由此引出一个基础问题就是如何保持大学在知识的传播和维护区域价值和文化中的独特作用。

本文讨论了大学外拓项目对区域发展及亚洲价值的现实意义。在追求发展、繁荣和幸福的道路上，应看到另一面。例如，2011 年 4 月，一些政府和市民社会的几百位领袖齐聚联合国总部，探求一条新的道路，衡量一个国家是否公平。发展不应只作狭隘的经济考虑。发展应包括个人、社会和国家的身体、思想和灵魂的全部。文章还讨论了如何运用外拓的方式来引起学术上重新重视以不同的视角看待发展。有许多现代科学意义上的不同研究，也包括有助于思想、身体和灵魂整体发展的亚洲价值及实践的不同方面。本文认为大学的外拓和参与有利于将大学带入一种创业作用和文化作用的平衡。大学和学术界在改造社会中社会责任应主要集中于推行战略和概念。

关键词： 大学外拓　亚洲价值　区域发展

Introduction

"*History has come to a stage when the moral man, the complete man, is more and more giving way, almost without knowing it, to make room for the commercial man, the man of limited purpose. This process, aided by the wonderful progress in science, is assuming gigantic proportion and power, causing the upset of man's moral balance, obscuring his human side under the shadow of soul-less organization.*" (Rabindranath Tagore, 1917: 20)

It appears that we have not taken a cue from what Rabindranath Tagore had said way back in 1917. When we see the developments in University education system which is key for shaping up of the society there is more emphasis on knowledge and higher education as a "commodity". As Reading (1996) points out it has emerged as a result of powerful forces compelling it to conform "to the ideology of today, a global theory called corporatism". Its main role is the production of human resources appropriate for the market place rather than of a "national culture". UNESCO also expressed its concern in the market driven higher education. In its 2003 resolution it states that "unregulated growth of higher education markets could weaken the sustainability of national higher education systems, particularly in less developed countries". Higher education ideally should serve the public interest by contributing to the sustainable development and improvement as a whole (AUCC, 2001).

Traditional university has many problems and issues which is reflected in many commissions and committees on higher education in India (Committee on Rennovation and Rjuvenation of Higher Education in India, 2009; Balram, 2005; Anandakrishnan, 2008). Wrestling (1997) points out that to reform and preserve the traditional university it will take much hard work and all the good will, imagination and intelligence we can muster. In this context it is necessary to add one more important factor. Menamparampli (2015) quoting Sayyid Qutb and others states that reflection on values is absolutely necessary lest we perish. Sayyid Qutb says "Humanity is standing today at the brink of an abyss... because humanity is bankrupt in the realm of 'values', those values which foster true human progress and development" (Mishra, 2012). Universities and higher education is not exception to this. We should apply what Rabindranath Tagore said in general terms to university system and protect it from becoming soul less organization. In order to ensure that future generations act as responsible citizens we need to cultivate to focus on true human development and progress as stated by Sayyid Qutb. In other words universities have the social responsibility of moving from narrow limited purpose to broad multipurpose education.

The present paper aims at discussing on how regional development, university education and values and traditions are linked and the need for universities to plan new strategies to promote university of culture while fulfilling knowledge economy needs.

Higher Education and Need for New Thinking

Despite rapid Science and Technology progress and advancements, the developing countries face a host of problems such as poverty, hunger, degradation of environment and natural resources, ill effects of urbanisation and issues such as renewable energy generation, management of water and farm lands, sustainable agriculture, nutrition, sanitation and health. For the solution for all these problems the governments have to depend on the health of universiteis and other educational institutions which are knowledge creators and knowledge dissiminators. However, there is increasing tendency to view the campus as a place where students get credentialed and faculty get tenured where the overall work of the academy does not seem particularly relevant to the nation "s most pressing civic, social, economic and moral problems (Boyer, 1996 in Braskamp and Wergin, 1997). There is also increasing tendency to focus on commoditization of knowledge. One of the fundamental questions arise is how to protect the unique role of universities in knowledge dissemination and in maintaining the values and culture of a region. As individuals and communities grow and are uprooted becoming more and more materialistic, they fail to draw energy and motivation from the organic and life-giving dimensions of culture.

When we see the developments in areas other than higher education it may be revealing on how we neglected the focus on the mission and objective of higher education. Balaram (2005) points out that while the society around university is evolving as per the demands of the society, the intellectual environment had probably declined and universities find it difficult to come out of their own issues and problems. Relevance and need of disruptive innovations to higher education is well argued by Nigvekar (2015) recently. Disruptive innovation, a term of art coined by Clayton Christensen, describes a process by which a product or service takes root initially in simple applications at the bottom of a market and then relentlessly moves up market, eventually displacing established competitors. One of the best examples where disruptive technologies are used more is consumer electronics. The progress made in consumer electronics can be visualized by anyone easily. Similarly we can see the disruptive innovation in many other fields. The evolution of e-commerce is another example. We argue that like in other fields higher education need to innovate as per the objective it wants to achieve. In this context, we may briefly touch upon the issues and challenges faced by higher education particularly in relation to India.

Challenges and Demands for Universities

For discussion purpose the challenges and demands for universities are categorized under four broad heads-expanding the values, norms and goals of university, Changing societal demands, progress of academy and paradigm shift and developing well rounded individual/organization/society.

Globalization and rat race competition; changing social and family structure; speedy socio cultural changes; commercialization of human life and dysfunctional relations; and artificial and purpose oriented relations are some of the challenges universities may face in expanding the values, norms and goals. Tagore (1950) says " Great civilizations have flourished in the past in the East as well as in the West because they produced food for the spirit of man for all time. " Universities need to look at what they are doing.

When it comes to changing societal demands the following quote from Alice in the wonderland will explain the situation.

" How puzzling all these changes are! I am never sure what I'm going to be from one minute to another!" (Lewis Carroll, 1865) .

There are many developments which results in more societal demands. These may include knowledge explosion, population explosion, science and technology explosion, and globalization and communication technology developments. These demands also started defining and limiting the expansion of values, norms and goals of the university. Further if a community/group/ nation seeks only its own interests then common good and common cause is forgotten. At a bigger level what happens is that national leaders are caught in strategies of populism and are eager to advance their own personal interests (Menamparampil, 2015). This argument may be extended to higher education and those who manage it.

Another important challenge for the universities is progress of academy itself and the need for paradigm shift. Academy is described as an intricate and bizarre world with galore of contradictions and nothing is as simple as it seems (Becher, 1996). Ridley (1998) points out that what is expected of professiorate is vague and unclear and public understanding of professiorate is still more vague. In literature two opposites are identified for academy. While one is idealized representation of academy (acadream), the other is the reality too many academics experience (academon) (Leggon, 2012; Albe, 1962). Hall (1994) points out that the academy has made a social contract with society's legal and political institutions. This contract is based on the assumption that non-academics cannot determine whether or not academics are meeting their professional and ethical standards.

Another challenge universities need to take up is preparing well rounded individual and thus organization by imparting required competencies. This is not simple taking into consideration the tendency of universities to give more focus on market driven subject orientation. The aspects to be covered are Using tools interactively (Cognitive, Socio-cultural and Physical); Interacting in Heterogeneous groups (Social Capital) -social competencies, social skills, intercultural competencies, soft skills etc; Acting autonomously-awareness of one's environment, of social dynamics, and of the roles one plays and wants to play (Narasimharao & Nair, 2010).

What is the Need?

The need to meet the challenges faced by universities can be deduced from what

Boyer (1996) states. He says "...*the academy must become a more vigorous partner in the search for answers to our most pressing social, civic, economic and moral problems, and must reaffirm its historic commitment to what I call the scholarship of engagement.*" Further, developing human capital is to be properly understood. Human capital development should be holistic to form a well rounded individual integrating knowledge and skills with values.

The academy must focus on sustainable development of society as a whole by

- Preparing highly qualified graduates who will be able to meet the needs of all sectors of the human activity

- interpreting, preserving, and promoting cultures in the context of cultural pluralism and diversity

- providing opportunities for higher learning throughout life

- advancing, creating and disseminating knowledge through research

- contributing to the development and improvement of education at all levels

- protecting and enhancing civil society by training young people in the values (AUCC, 2001)

The need is also for innovations and new thinking. As already discussed disruptive innovation strategies are found to be effective in many areas and Nigvekar (2015) advocates this for education. We also need to be clear in our objective before applying this strategy. If the need is to integrate human value system and knowledge economy needs we have to accordingly design our strategies and innovations.

Many leaders in higher education started advocating a new academy which is more engaged in the environment they have been while maintaining their integrity as institutions of scholarship and culture. In this context the universities and other educational institutions need to focus on regional development and regional transformation. Nadkarni (2015) talking about economics states that after the invention of central banking, the fourth big innovation (the other two being fire and wheel) is more likely to be around the conversation on how business can co-create sustainable value-a next level beyond money. Gradually people are realising the fact that development in real sense and economy is dependent not only on capital and labour, but also on values like traditions of trust, skills developed in cultures, and habits of the mind.

We may extend this concept to higher education and human capital development. Human capital and education is not only knowledge and skills but also values like motivation, sense of purpose, sense of belonging, mutual trust, energies for resilience, and absolute determination (Menamparampil, 2015). It is argued that for developing this concept it is important to focus on regional development and regional transformation.

Regional Development and Regional Transformation

Gunasekara (2004) suggests that the role of universities has evolved over the last twenty years. He says that universities were once regarded as focusing on two key roles, teaching and research, which were exogenous to, and independent from, economic and social development imperatives of the state and industry. The regional development can be planned by involving all stake holders. The aspects which need to be covered are

- Regional clusters & net works-Regional Agglomeration
- Regional knowledge needs
- Regional specialization and use of 'Tacit' knowledge
- Human capital and other resources
- Regional self regulation and strong social capital
- Protecting traditions and cultures
- Emphasis on Regional policy (local authorities, regional development agencies, government agencies, business and industry and labour groups)

- Developing learning culture (Universities and academia)

Often we discuss regional development and higher education in one way. Nadkarni (2015) points that value can be produced one-way, but to move upwards to sustainable value one has to co-create it through a host of stake holders. Similarly regional development should be co-achieved through a host of stake holders. In this context we need to examine the various concepts and systems available in higher education. Some of the concepts and models adopted by Higher education institutions to reach out to society are

- mode 2 thesis (Gibbons et al. , 1994),
- university-industry linkage (Schiller & Brimble, 2009),
- Tiple Helix (Etzkowitz et al. , 2007),
- Regional innovation Systems (Gunasekara, 2006),
- higher education for sustainable development (Barth et al. , 2007),
- centres of excellence (Beerkens, 2009),
- National Innovation systems (Nelson, 1993)
- University engagement (Sandman, 2008),
- University outreach (Boyer, 1996)

The role of universities in the regional development has gone beyond the study of technology and the establishment of science parks or creating employment opportunities through spin-off industries to the wider ethos of enhancement and development of human and social capital in the region. There is growing importance for regional clusters and net works, regional specialisation, utilisation of 'tacit' knowledge and the need for promoting flexibility and adaptation. It is necessary to examine the nature of universities' contributions to human capital formation and protecting the regional culture while taking development route. It is important campus being in the world and world in the campus. That is universities need to see human and social capital in a larger context. For instance, Menamparampil (2015) lists some of the civilizations that were collapsed on their own when they became the victims of success in one area and neglecting or marginalising other areas particularly values and traditions. Education system cannot be exceptional to this natural law.

Regional Transformation and Values and Traditions

Regional development cannot be seen in isolation. It needs to be seen in a whole. For instance recently even in biology the new concepts of holobionts and hologenome gaining more importance. Bordenstein and Theis (2015) in their recent paper states "Animals and plants are no longer heralded as autonomous entities but rather as biomolecular networks composed of the host plus its associated microbes, i. e., "holobionts." As such, their collective genomes forge a "hologenome," and models of animal and plant biology that do not account for these intergenomic associations are incomplete. "

Similarly, it is argued that regional development will be interaction and interplay between the values and traditions, people, universities, venture capitalists, business people and all other components (animate and inanimate). All the components directly or indirectly are connected. One of the concepts developed for regional transformation is regional innovation systems covering spatial agglomeration of industries and organisations, human capital and other resources, shift to regional self regulation with strong social capital and protecting traditions and culture. Mahabubani (2013) argues that the general belief of practical interests divide people while ideals converge them is reversed in the present day society. He argues that in today's situation material interests of people converge but their minds fail to find a way to move forward together. He says that a new human consciousness must emerge, one that encourages togetherness. The same argument is applicable in the context of higher education.

The role universities and academia can play in the whole process is to develop a learning culture to bring change from within. This learning culture should not be restricted to only subject matter but extend to self actualization and karma capitalism where individual development is coupled with organizational development.

Here we may relate this to three important attributes for developing a well rounded organization/region/individual. The three attributes are-using tools effectively and interactively (cognitive, socio-cultural and physical tools); Social capital (ability to interact in heterogeneous groups); acting autonomously (awareness of one's environment, of social dynamics and of the roles one plays and wants to play) . It is argued that the total person/organization consists of mind, body and soul. We need to take care of not only cognitive, intellectual and emotional dimensions but also spiritual dimensions. In this context it is relevant to mention some of the recent scientific research and arguments in relation to how our biological and psychological system works. We should not restrict our perception only to individual level but also should extend it to organization/region/society level.

For instance, Nobel Physicist Brian Josephson while talking about synthesis of science with religion proposes meditation as a observation tool and our nervous system as instruments. He states that " ordinary scientific instruments like telescopes, galvanometers, and particle detectors are not going to be good in this context because they are designed to function in the material domain. Our nervous systems, on the other hand, are designed to allow us to interact not only with the material level of existence but also with the spiritual levels. ... All the different levels are open to exploration if we develop our nervous systems so that they tune in. One can imagine that this would be part of the scientific training of the future. " (Cousins, 1985) .

Feel good is an important thing for individual and organization development. This can be related to traditions and values. An interesting discovery has been how many kinds of connections count for one's health and well being. The traditions of melas, festivals, cultural events, community level celebrations, family get together etc. can be related to this. Dean Ornish (2011) says that anything that will help us freely transcend the boundaries of separateness is joyful. In this activity your feel-good endorphins level increases. He reveals that the real epidemic in modern culture is not only physical heart disease but also what he calls spiritual heart disease: loneliness, isolation, alienation, and depression. Similarly feeling resonance and joy can change your biology by releasing the chemical dopamine in the brain (Morrison and Severino, 2009) .

Acting autonomously for regional development/individual development warrants greater responsibility and wisdom. One need to develop good thoughts and good visualization. All this requires promoting certain traditions and values which help in developing the mind. Herbert Benson, professor of Medicine writes-over the years you develop ' circuits' and channels of thought in your brain. These are physical pathways which control the way you think, the way you act, and often, the way you feel. These circuits become so deeply ingrained that it seems almost impossible to transform them. " Through meditation ... you can set the stage for important mind-and habit-altering brain change. " (Benson and Proctor, 2010) . We can extend these finding to values and traditions also. It is argued that the values and traditions followed may help in forming positive ' circuits' .

In order to use these understandings on values and traditions for regional transformation through universities/tertiary education institutions it is necessary we use the concept of disruptive innovations which made it possible life changing developments in many areas of human activity.

Disruptive Innovations in Education

Table 1 presents the areas where disruptive innovations in education may be thought of. Though they are linked to each other and should not be dealt separately, for the convenience and relevance sake of present paper only holistic development section may be focused.

Table 1: Disruptive Innovations in Education-Areas to be Covered

---

• INNOVATIONS

Technologies, Pedagogies & Societal Context

• BORDERLESS EDUCATION

Convergence of all systems,

Making disciplinary boundaries and the education systems more porous,

Integrating modern and traditional knowledge

Knowledge management & knowledge integration

• APPROACHES

Collaboration & net working, outreach & engagement, sustainable education, corporate education, community engagement

• HOLISTIC DEVELOPMENT

Well rounded region/organization/individual, Linking scientific research, education and values/traditions

---

Disruptive innovations in education should cover areas of research, teaching-learning, funding, treating of discipline/subject, societal needs, educating policy makers and academic administrators etc. All these should be linked to values and traditions for effecting holistic development and well rounded region/organization/individual.

In order to achieve this it is necessary that universities think in new direction. As already discussed in earlier section, there are many concepts and models developed in tertiary education systems. As Mgrath (2006) states it is important to use the concept to meet the objective rather than focusing on the methodology or terminology or the system. He states

> Personally I prefer Engagement, but have little interest in debating labels and terminology. What ultimately counts is the concept of a major state university being in partnership with its community, its state and region, and, yes, the wider world with which we are inextricably involved in this new globalized environment. Ultimately all that counts is what we do in effective working partnerships with businesses, civic organizations, government agencies, and, indeed, other colleges and universities.

The concept here is how higher education in partnership with others can serve the society. Society is a complex structure with many inputs including traditions, values, practices, certain bias and beliefs, customs and culture, social and economic factors etc. How universities can use disruptive innovations for working in partnership with different communities and individuals to integrate values and traditions is important for the holistic development we listed in the table 1. We may need to develop models for each region taking the suitable concepts in a given context. In this connection it is argued university outreach is a useful approach.

University Outreach and Values and Traditions

The concept of university outreach programmes is highly potential for introducing innovations in many areas like use of university resources, treating disciplines differently, linking universities to the place, using different types of delivery etc. (Figure1).

University outreach programmes, by linking the university to various civic society organizations in the region, will help the university in identifying new research needs, curriculum development, in organizing traditional disciplines differently, in making education & training relevant to the region, and in increasing faculty vision & experience.

Under outreach programmes various activities can be covered including adult and continuing education, university-industry alliances, training programmes, add on courses for students, courses for specific non-governmental organizations, remedial courses, community learning courses, awareness courses etc. , (Narasimh-arao, 2007) . University outreach concept also ensures the involvement of other stakeholders of higher education as equal partners in the educational process.

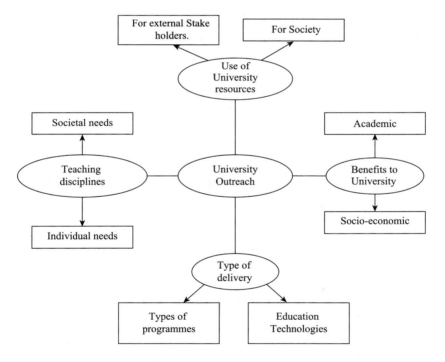

Figure 1   University outreach programmes and their relevance

It is also necessary one has to understand that the mutuality in such partnerships should not focus on material outcomes but more on substance of the relationship. Effective relationships will form when organizations or partners have common interest and when the capacity of each organization enhances because of partnership. In one of the successful model Southside-Virginia Tech the relationship between the university, state and local agencies, private industry, and community partners was collaboratively shaped. It requires extensive co-production and communication among stakeholders from different backgrounds. In this each stakeholder is in a position to shape the partnership and contribute to the production of knowledge (Kleiwer et al., 2013). It differs from many other collaborations where only economic and for profit is focused. In another example one of the leading non-governmental organisation (NGO) in close relationship with a university demonstrated how management education can be reshaped as per the requirement at field level. In this the key features were stakeholder participation, designing the courses through integration of different disciplines, treating the disciplines differently, and course design through a workshop with stakeholders (Dongre and Narasimharao, 2013).

It is argued that values can be integrated through interaction with other stakeholders and also taking into consideration the local culture and traditions into account. Neeraj Jain (2015) in his paper on Vivekananda emphasised the need for different approaches depending on the region to inculcate values. Similarly Al Uddin (2015) discussed the importance of local knowledge for sustainable development. Biswas (2015) states that combining the domain of senses, feeling and concerns in relation to specific communities and their particular abstractions will serve the methodological import of establishing empathy, dialogue and observer-depend reality by moving beyond simple dichotomies and binaries of 'cellular expression. Kim Young Suk (2015) and Han Gang-Hyen (2015) have discussed on new life cultural movements, education of core values and Neohuman' culture and futurology. All these points out to the significance of university outreach programmes with several models depending on the region and depending on the objective to be achieved. The interconnectedness of different components, including values and traditions which may or may not be directly related to the present day education system, can be envisaged from these observations. The need for interconnectedness can be deduced from the concept of Deep Ecology. According to it "The attempt to ignore our dependence and to establish a master-slave role has contributed to the alienation of man from himself." (Liu Jingjing, 2015). The same argument can be extended to education as well as regional development. University outreach programmes, where collaborations and equal partnerships are emphasized, can be used for integrating different components of a region for holistic development. As Narasimharao (2013) points out the potential of outreach lies in its key feature of knowledge sharing. This concept helps universities to link to their places as well as to the shareholders of higher education. It can help to think beyond the needs of students and research specializations. Making other stake holders as equal partners in the knowledge creation may help in integrating some of the traditional knowledge and tacit knowledge available in the society with the disciplinary knowledge of academics.

Conclusion

Development should not be seen in narrow economic considerations. Development should be holistic covering body, mind and soul of individual, society, region or nation. Universities should not become soul less organizations by focusing on commodilization of knowledge. Knowledge need to be treated in wholistic way integrating different aspects. There are several scientific researches which emphasize the importance of values, culture, traditions for the well being of humans. Education and knowledge should not be only discipline based but should integrate various other aspects including values and traditions. It is argued that the education systems should also look into the developments in the society and adopt new models. Disruptive innovation may be one of these as it showed tremendous results in many areas of human activity. In tertiary education many models and concepts are developed to reach out to society. However, it is also argued that implementing and applying the concepts in a suitable way for fulfilling the desired objectives is more important than a discussion on the models and concepts. Higher education has a great role in protecting the civilization as Menamparampil (2015) lists the number of civilizations that collapsed on their won when they became victims of success in one area and neglecting or marginalizing other areas. At present there is concern among many experts on eroding values and traditions. Similarly there is also concern on how higher education is becoming more and more for job orientation or technical or professional skill development. It is argued that regional development and regional transformation is key for covering body, mind and soul of individual, society, region and nation. Though as suggested earlier we may apply any concept or model which is suitable for a particular region, university outreach concept has the potential to integrate various concepts and models for regional development through integration of knowledge, values and traditions. One of the advantages of outreach concept is linking the university with civic society organizations and others. The equal partnership concept in outreach help in integrating tacit and traditional knowledge available in the region. This includes the values, local culture and traditions, local practices, skills, morals, ethics and others.

References

Ala Uddin. 2015. "People, Knowledge, and Development: Local Knowledge for Sustainable Development in the Chittagong Hill Tracts of Bangladesh." International Conference on Asian Values and Human Future, 7 – 9 July, 2015. Guwahati, Assam Don Bosco University.

Albee, Edward. 1962. "Who's Afraid of Virginia Wolfe?" New York, NY: Atheneum.

Anandakrishnan, M. 2008. : "Promises and Perils of Globalized Higher Education," *Journal of*

Educational Planning and Administration, XXII (2) : 199 – 212

AUCC, 2001. Joint Declaration on Higher Education and GATS, Association of Universities and Colleges of Canada, September.

Balram, P. 2005. "Reinventing our universities," *Current Science*, 88: 529 – 530.

Barth, M. , Godemann, J. , Rieckman, M. and Stoltenberg, U. 2007. "Developing Key Competencies for Sustainable Development in Higher Education", *International Journal of Sustainability in Higher Education*, **8** (4): 416 – 430.

Becher, Tony. 1996. *Academic Tribes and Territories: Intellectual Enquiry and the Cultures of Disciplines*. Buckingham, United Kingdom: Open University Press.

Beerkens, E. 2009. "Centres of Excellence and Relevance: The Contextualisation of Global Models", *Science, Technology & Society*, **14** (1) : 153 – 175

Benson, H. and W. Proctor. 2010. *Relaxation Revolution: The Science and Genetics of Mind Body Healing*, Simon and Schuster, p. 288.

Biswas, Prasenjit. 2015. "A critique of Cultural (In) security: Philosophical Meditations on Southeast Asia. " International Conference on Asian Values and Human Future, 7 – 9 July, 2015. Guwahati, Assam Don Bosco University.

Bordenstein SR, Theis KR. 2015. "Host Biology in Light of the Microbiome: Ten Principles of Holobionts and Hologenomes. " *PLoS Biol* 13 (8): e1002226.

Boyer, E. 1996. "The Scholarship of Engagement", *Journal of Public Service and Outreach*, **9** (1): 11 – 20.

Braskamp, L and J. F. Wergin. 1997. "Universities and the New Social Contract," in W. G. Tierney (ed) *The Responsive University: Restructuring for High Performance*, Baltimore: Johns Hopkins University.

Cousins, Norman. 1985. *Nobel Prize Conversations with Sir John Eccles, Roger Sperry, Ilya Prigogine, and Brian Josephson*, San Francisco, Calif. : Saybrook.

Dean Ornish. 2011. *Love and Survival: The Scientific Basis for the Healing Power of Intimacy.* Harper Collins. p. 100.

Dongre, Y. , & Narasimharao, B. P. R. 2013. "University Outreach in Management Education-A case from India for Meeting the Needs of Professionals in the Field. " in Narasimharao, B. P. R. , Rangappa, K. S. , & Fulzele, T. U. (Eds.), *Evolving Corporate Education Strategies for Developing Countries- Role of Universities.* Hershey, PA: IGI Global.

Etzkowitz, H. , J. Dzisah, M. Ranga, and C. Zhou. 2007. "The Triple Helix Model of Innovation," *Asia Pacific Tech Monitor*, 24 (1), Jan-Feb: 14 – 22.

Gibbons, M. , C. Limoges, H. Nowotony, S. Schwartzman, P. Scott and M. Trow. 1994. *The New Production of Knowledge: The Dynamics of Science and Research in Contemporaty Societies*, London, Sage Publications.

Gunasekara, C. 2006. "Academia and Industry: The Generative and Developmental Roles of Universities in Regional Innovation Systems," *Science and Public Policy*, 33 (2): 137 – 150.

Hall, Richard. 1994. *The Sociology of Work.* Thousand Oaks, CA: Pine Forge Press.

Han Gang-Hyen. 2015. "A Study on Ne Life-Cultural Movements for Oneness Focused on

Neohumans' Culture & Futurology. " International Conference on Asian Values and Human Future, 7 – 9 July, 2015. Guwahati, Assam Don Bosco University.

Kim Young Suk 2015. "Study on the Education or Core Value and Practice of Ultimate Virtue. " International Conference on Asian Values and Human Future, 7 – 9 July, 2015. Guwahati, Assam Don Bosco University.

Kliewer, B. W. , Sandmann, L. R. , & Narasimharao, B. P. R. 2013. "Corporate-university Partnerships: The Outreach and Engagement Model. " in Narasimharao, B. P. R. , Rangappa, K. S. , & Fulzele, T. U. (Eds.), *Evolving corporate education strategies for developing countries- Role of universities.* Hershey, PA: IGI Global.

Leggon, C. B. 2012. "The Ordeal of Civility in Academe. " http://web. archive. org/web/20060914141613/http://www. lsus. edu/la/journalofideology/

Lewis Carroll. 1865. *Alice's Adventures in Wonderland*, U. K. Macmillan.

Liu Jingjing. 2015. "Deep Ecology and Confucianism. " International Conference on Asian Values and Human Future, 7 – 9 July, 2015. Guwahati, Assam Don Bosco University.

Magrath, C. P. 2006. "Outreach Now: Inventing the Future through Engagement," September 27, 2006. The Inn at Virginia Tech and Skelton Conference Center Blacksburg, VA.

Mahbubani, K. 2013. "The Great Convergence. " *Public Affairs*, New York.

Menamparampil, Thomas. 2015. "Encouraging Values to Ensure a Future-Asian Values for Future of the World, Key Note Address," International Conference on Asian Values and Human Future, 7 – 9 July, 2015. Guwahati, Assam Don Bosco University.

Morrison, N. K. , and Sally K. Severino, 2009. *Sacred Desire: Growing in Compassionate Living*, Templeton Press, pp 200

Nadkarni, A. G. 2015. "Value Merchants," *The Speaking Tree*, 16th August, p. 8.

Narasimharao, B. P. R. and P. R. R. Nair. 2010. "Universities and Corporate Education, 21st Century Social Responsibility of Developing Countries," SRRNet, Discussion papers in social responsibility, No. 1002, www. socialresponsibility. biz

Narasimharao, B. P. R. and Sridhar, Y. 2007. "University Outreach Programmes-Their potential to meet changing societal Demands," in Narasimharao, B. P. R. et al. (ed) *Changing Societal Demands and Adopting Teaching Learning Systems in Higher Education to Reach Out*, University of Mysore, Mysore pp. 85 – 94.

Neeraj Jain. 2015. "Swami Vivekananda on Making the World a Better Place to Live-in for All. " International Conference on Asian Values and Human Future, 7 – 9 July, 2015. Guwahati, Assam Don Bosco University.

Nelson, R. R. 1993. *National Innovation Systems: A Comparative Analysis.* Oxford: Oxford University Press.

Nigvekar, A. 2015. "Need for Disruptive Innovations in Education," Prof. G. RamReddy Memorial Lecture, IGNOU, July, 2015.

Rabindranath Tagore, 1917. *Nationalism.* Delhi: Macmillan, p. 190.

Readings, B. 1996. *The University in Ruins*, Cambridge and London, Harvard University Press.

Ridley, Harold. 1998. Review of Academic Duty by Donald Kennedy (Harvard University Press) .

New York, NY: America.

Sandmann, L. R. 2008. "Conceptualization of the Scholarship of Engagement in Higher Education: A Strategic Review, 1996 – 2006. " *Journal of Higher Education Outreach and Engagement*, *12* (1): 92-104.

Tagore, Rabindranath 1950. *Crisis in Civilization*, Calcutta, Viswa-Bharati.

UNESCO, 2003. "Higher Education in a Globalized Society," UNESCO Education Position Paper, 2003, UNESCO, Paris.

Westling, J. 1997. "Review-The University in Ruins by Bill Readings," *Academic Questions*, 10 (3): 89 – 91

YashPal 2009. "Report of ' The Committee to Advise on Renovation and Rejuvenation of Higher Education", http://www. education. nic. in/ accessed on 11/7/2009.

儒家伦理的情感特征及其作用

强以华*

摘　要：无论从起源上看还是从实质性的内容上看，儒家伦理都主要表现为一种（感性的）情感伦理，并且首先表现为基于亲情的家庭伦理。尽管西方伦理学也包含了情感主义伦理学，但是，西方伦理学特别是西方传统伦理学主要还是理性主义的伦理学，因此，儒家伦理学的情感特点是它区别于西方伦理学的一个根本特征。情感伦理与理性伦理在发挥作用时分别具有外延较小、内涵丰富和外延广大、内涵贫乏的不同特色，这些不同特色在一定程度上决定了情感伦理和理性伦理之间具有差别对待伦理对象或对伦理对象一视同仁的差异。随着中国经济的崛起，儒家伦理将在国际社会中产生越来越大的影响，而它区别于西方伦理的情感特征将会决定它将对世界文明和人类价值起着什么样的积极作用。

关键词：儒家伦理　情感伦理　理性伦理　作用　限制

Confucian Ethics's Emotional Feature and Its Effect

Qiang Yihua

Abstract：Whether according to origin or essence Confucian ethics expresses mainly sensual emotional ethics，and expresses firstly family ethics.

---

* 强以华，湖北大学哲学学院教授，湖北大学高等人文研究院研究员。

Western ethics （ especially western traditional ethics ） belong mainly to rationalist ethics in spite of it also has some emotional ethics. Therefore the emotional feature of Confucian ethics is fundamental characteristics that it differents from western ethics. There are a difference between emotional ethics and rationalist ethics, that is, former has small extension and rich content, and the latter has larger extension and poor content. To a certain extent these differences brings about another difference that emotional ethics has dissimilarity in the treatment of ethics object and rationalist ethics can be just in treatment of ethics objects . Along with China's economic rise, Confucian ethics will has greater and greater influence to international society. It emotional feature unlike western rationalist ethics will decide it has what kind of positive effect to world civilization and human values as well as its limitation of effect.

Keywords：Confucian Ethics；Emotional Ethics；Rationalist Ethics；Effect；Limitation

　　无论是从起源来看还是从内容来看，儒家伦理都具有明显的情感特征。正是儒家伦理的情感特征使它具有明显区别于西方伦理的不同之处，也使它会在世界文明和人类价值的发展中起着不同于西方伦理的作用。因此，在中国经济日益崛起从而使得儒家文明（它本质上是一种伦理文明）在国际社会的影响越来越大的当今时代，研究儒家伦理将对世界文明和人类价值产生的独特作用具有重要的意义。本文将围绕这一目标探讨儒家伦理对世界发展和人类价值产生的积极作用，以及它的作用范围及其限度。

一　儒家伦理的情感特征

　　儒家伦理的情感特征首先来自儒家伦理发源于家庭伦理这一事实。我们认为，任何一个国家或者民族的包括伦理在内的文化都只能产生于这一国家或民族的生存和发展的需要；因此，儒家伦理作为中国文化的主要内容也必然产生于中华民族生存和发展的需要。生存乃是在自然环境和社会环境中的生存，由于社会环境起初应是人类或相关区域中的人群为了适应和改造自然环境而组成的社会形式，因此，人类相关区域中的人群的包括伦理在内的文化首先是适应和改造自然环境的产物。中华民族发源时所面对的自然环境乃是一种适宜于小农经济的自然环境。农业生产是一种长周期的生产，它要求从事农业生产的单位是一种能够在长时期中相对稳定的单位；同时，农业生产作为小农经济的生产，它也要求从事农业生产的单位是一种规模较小的单位；家庭作为一个具有自我延续性的较小的血缘单位，既能满足农业生产需要长期相对稳定的生产单位的要求，也能满足小农生产需要规模不大的生产单位的要求。因此，把家庭作为基本的生产单位应是中华民族发源时适应和改造自然环境的最佳选择。不仅如此，发源中的中华民族还从适应和改造自然环境的生存方式中形成了特有的社会环境。家庭在适应和改造自然环境中的重要地位使它在组成社会时也成了重要的社会组织形式，从而使得统治者把它看成是最基本的社会细胞（社会组织形式）。这样一来，在中华民族发源时，家庭就有了三种形式并且承担着三种使命：其一，最基本的生产单位，承担着社会中的主要生产使命；其二，最基本的社会单位，承担着支撑社会存在的使命；其三，除了最基本的生产单位和社会单位之外，家庭的直接表现形式是血缘单位，它承担着帮助家庭繁衍的使命，并且这一使命的实现在客观上维系着家庭作为生产单位和社会单位的持续存在。家庭的特殊重要地位使得中国社会最终成为一个以"家"为基础的社会，家国同构成为中华民族特有的社会形式，它给中国的古人提供了特有的社会环境。因此，中华民族若要在特有的自然环境和社会环境中生存和发展的话就必须维护家庭的稳定性，并且以此为基础来维护"国家"的稳定性。由于家庭直接表现为一个血缘单位，所以，维护家庭稳定性的最佳方式通常应该是伦理特别是家庭伦理的方式。儒家伦理乃至整个儒家文化为了适应中华民族发源时维护家庭稳定性的需要，提出"孝"这一概念，试图通过家庭成员对于家长，尤其是在生产中居于主导地位的男性家长"孝"来维护家庭的稳定性。在孝的基础上，还衍生出了"忠"这一维护国家这一大的家庭的稳定性的概念,其实,"忠"不过是带上了某种政治色彩的"孝"的概念。在下面即将讨论的儒家伦理的内容中,我们将会发现"孝"和"忠",尤其是"孝"是儒家伦理学乃至整个儒家文化的中心概念,并且是儒家伦理学乃至整个儒家文化的发源。由于"孝"是源自家庭伦理中的一种自然情感,所以,儒家伦理以"孝"为中心是儒家伦理学乃至整个儒家文化之发源的情形表明:情感是儒家伦理的基本特征,并且这一情感主要作为家庭情感,乃是一种感性的伦理情感(以下我们称儒家伦理的情感特征时一概指的是"感性的"伦理情感)。

儒家伦理学发源于"孝"这一伦理情感概念并以"孝"这一伦理情感概念为中心的情形也决定了它的实质性内容具有情感特征。一般来说,我们可以把"五常"看成是儒家伦理的基本概念,"五常"以"仁"为首,并且"仁"与"五常"中的另一概念"礼"互为表里("仁"是内心要求,礼则是"仁"这一内心要求的外在表现),所以,我们可以把"仁"看成是儒家伦理的核心概念。那么,何谓"仁"呢?"仁"就是爱人。儒家伦理认为仁爱的实质是对于父母的爱也就是"孝",以及对于父亲继承人的兄长的爱也就是"弟"。所以,儒家伦理把"孝"看成是"仁"的根本。正如孔子的弟子有子所说的:"君子务本,本立而道生。孝弟也者,其为仁之本与!"[1] 这样一来,我们就可以综合地把"仁"理解成为以"孝"(以及"弟")为实质的广泛的爱(爱人,以及爱自然万物)。据此,我们将会发现,除了实质性的"孝"(以及"弟")之外,儒家的很多伦理概念表达的都是以仁爱之实质为基础衍生出来的表达仁爱不同等级的爱的概念,它们都产生于并且服务于仁爱的概念。例如,孟子曾经进一步发挥了有子关于"孝弟"为仁之本的思想。他说:"仁之实,事亲是也;义之实,从兄是也;智之实,知斯二者弗去是也;礼之实,节文斯二者是也;乐之实,乐斯二者,乐则生矣;生则恶可已

---

① 孔丘:《论语·学而》,参见杨伯峻《论语译注》,中华书局,1980,第2页。

也，恶可已，则不知足之蹈之手之舞之。"① 由此可见，孟子不仅把仁、义的实质归结为"孝"、"弟"，甚至还把儒家伦理的其他重要概念诸如智、礼、乐一并看成是产生于并且服务于"孝"、"弟"的概念。因此，我们可以得出结论：仁构成了儒家伦理的实质内容，仁作为儒家伦理的实质内容其实就是"孝"（以及"弟"）。鉴于"孝"（以及"弟"）是起源于家庭伦理的概念，也就是说，它是一种作为亲情的伦理情感，所以，从儒家伦理的实质性内容来说，儒家伦理依然是具有情感特征的伦理。

综合起来说，儒家伦理起源于作为家庭亲情的情感（作为仁爱实质的"孝"），并且这种作为亲情的情感构成了儒家伦理内容的实质，甚至进一步决定着整个儒家文化的性质，所以，我们可以得出结论，儒家伦理（甚至整个儒家文化）的基本特征是情感。

二　情感伦理的作用特色

儒家伦理的情感特征使得儒家伦理是一种情感伦理。那么，情感伦理在发挥伦理作用时具有什么样的特色呢？为了更好地理解儒家情感伦理在发挥作用时的特色（作用特色），我们将通过比较儒家伦理学与西方伦理学的不同特征来进行分析。

儒家伦理学的情感特征应是儒家伦理学区别于西方伦理学的一个根本特征。毫无疑问，西方伦理学也包含了情感因素，这不仅表现在众多的西方伦理学家都曾在自己的伦理学中探讨过涉及情感的问题并把它作为德性，提出了一些情感性的概念（例如，亚里士多德就曾在他的《尼各马可伦理学》中讨论了对于朋友的友爱并且认为"它就是某种德性，或者是赋有德性的事情"②），而且还表现为情感主义伦理学曾是西方近代以来重要的伦理学派别。西方伦理学中的严格意义上的道德情感理论

---

① 孟轲：《孟子·离娄上》，参见杨伯峻《孟子译注》，中华书局，1980，第183页。
② 〔古希腊〕亚里士多德：《尼各马可伦理学》，参见苗力田主编《亚里士多德全集》第八卷，中国人民大学出版社，1992，第165页。

源自西方近代的英国情感伦理学，它开始于莎夫茨伯利，经由哈奇森等人一直延至休谟和亚当·斯密。尽管从莎夫茨伯利一直到亚当·斯密的情感伦理学有着这样那样的差异，但是，总体来说，他们的道德情感理论一脉相传，他们一致认为道德情感是一种区别于理性的感性情感，并且道德的根源，能够帮助人们辨别善恶从而进行道德选择和道德判断。到了西方当代哲学，道德情感理论又得到了复兴和进一步的发展，关怀理论更是直接把关怀和爱作为直接的研究对象进行了深入的探讨。但是，无论从出现的时间来看还是从在伦理学史上占有的地位来看，西方的伦理学（尤其是西方古代的伦理学）主要还是一种理性主义的伦理学。其实，在西方伦理学史上，理性主义哲学家一直想把情感纳入理性的控制之下，从而使得当代社会关于认知主义的情感理论和非认知主义的情感理论之争成为情感主义伦理学面对的主要问题之一，"……一个公认的分类是认知主义情感理论和非认知主义情感理论之间的分类。认知主义的情感理论认为情感必然会涉及思想、情感或者判断……相反，非认知主义的情感理论接受了这样的观点，即：本质上作为感受到的经验的情感乃是某种有别于思想、信念或判断的东西。"① 康德曾经讨论和赞扬过对于上帝的爱，但是，他认为这种爱是一种理性的爱，也就是说，它是一种以道德法则为根据并且受到道德法则制约的爱。在他看来，道德情感原本就应该是一种理性（实践理性）和情感（自然情感）的复合体，在这种复合体中，理性起着基础作用，它以先天的道德法则的形式为情感提供了道德基础，从而使得情感从自然（感性）情感转变成为一种道德情感。由此出发，康德激烈批判那种非理性的爱，认为如果没有道德理性的制约，爱就会成为一种十分危险的狂热。正如杨晓梅所说的："因此我们先天地知道法则必须是这种积极情感的根据。道德欲望或道德情感之所以可能，正是由于道德法则自身能够影响到我们的爱好。"②

① Donale M. Borchert Editor in Chief, *Encyclopedia of Philosophy*, Volume 6, 2nd edition, Detroit etc. 2006, p. 389.

② Xiaomei Yang, "Categorical Imperatives, Moral Requirements, and Moral Motivation," *Metaphilosophy*, Vol. 37, No. 1, (January 2006): 126.

从某种意义上来说，我们可以把主要具有情感特征的儒家伦理学与主要具有非情感特征的西方伦理学之间的区别看成是情感主义伦理学与理性主义伦理学之间的区别。那么，作为伦理学的情感伦理和作为伦理学的理性伦理究竟有什么不同呢？它们的一个基本不同就是情感是具体的而理性是抽象的。一般来说，作为具体的伦理情感具有内涵丰富但外延较小的特点；而作为抽象的伦理理性则具有外延广大但内涵贫乏的特点。具体来说，伦理情感乃至所有的情感（例如爱、恨、欣赏、嫉妒等等）大多属于感性的情感，感性情感的对象主要是具体的对象。这一情形造成了情感主体对情感对象起作用的两种特色：其一，范围比较狭小。情感主体的感性对象主要是情感主体感性所及的范围，包括他通过直接的方式了解到的人和通过间接的方式了解到的人。其中，通过直接的方式了解到的人主要是他的熟人（包括家人、亲属、朋友、同学、同事，以及其他的熟人）；通过间接的方式了解到的人则主要是他通过熟人了解的人，以及通过其他手段（例如广播、电影、电视、图书等）了解到的人。其中，他的熟人是他之情感的主要对象，并且，通过间接方式了解到的人，相对地说，与其通过其他手段了解到的人比较起来，通过熟人了解到的人则是更为主要的情感对象。之所以会造成情感对象不同等级的情形，乃是因为情感对象越是直接，情感主体对于情感对象的了解就越深，因而他对情感对象的情感就可能越是亲密。这里，又涉及了情感主体对情感对象起作用的另外一个特色。其二，内涵比较丰富。由于情感主体的情感对象或是熟人或是比较了解的人，所以，情感主体对情感对象的饮食起居、学习成长、工作事业，以及性格爱好、喜怒哀乐、甘甜困苦等等应该都十分清楚，至少是比较清楚或有些清楚，这一情形使得他对情感对象的具体情感可能十分丰富、十分具体，而不至于停留在抽象的层次之上。与此同时，包括实践理性在内的所有理性的对象都是抽象的对象。这一情形则造成了理性主体对于理性对象起作用的两种特色。其一，范围比较广大。理性的抽象特征使理性主体在思考理性对象的时候超越了对象的感性内容，这样一来，他的对象就突破了熟人甚至间接地了解到的人的范围而扩展到了任何陌生人的范围，从而使它的对象成了一个地区、一个民族、一个国家甚至整个人类。其二，内涵比较贫乏。正是由于理性主体的理性对象超越了具体的感性对象走向了范围广大的陌生之人，所以，他不可能（其实也无必要）熟悉和了解那么多的陌生之人的诸如饮食起居、学习成长、工作事业，以及性格爱好、喜怒哀乐、甘甜困苦等具体情况，从而使得他对理性对象的作用缺乏丰富的内涵。

三 儒家伦理情感特征的作用

情感伦理作用于对象的不同于理性伦理的特色决定了儒家情感伦理对于当今世界文明和人类价值的积极作用的形式及其作用范围。

在西方伦理学居于主导地位的视野中，理性主义伦理学起支配作用。在这种作用下，伦理学虽然也包含了情感，但是，从整体上说，它处于情感不足甚至缺乏情感的状态。情感应该是伦理学的重要内容，它在理论上可以纠正西方伦理学情感不足甚至缺乏情感的局限，从而也使得它在实践上纠正西方伦理学不重视情感在伦理行为中的作用的局限。我们知道，在国际环境中，经济话语权与包括伦理价值话语权在内的文化话语权有着密切的关系。近代社会以来，西方世界在国际经济事务中居于主导地位，从而使得它们在包括伦理价值在内的文化中也占有主导地位，并进一步导致了国际社会在伦理价值的理论和实践中更加注重抽象理性的现象。当今，随着亚洲国家在国际社会经济事务中的崛起，特别是随着中国成为世界上的第二大经济体，亚洲传统文化中的伦理价值，特别是中国传统文化中的伦理价值在国际社会中的影响越来越大。中国（儒家）伦理价值的情感特征，特别是家庭伦理的情感特征将会成为影响国际社会伦理价值的主要内容。伦理价值作为一种文化现象和意识现象，它的变化通常要比经济现象的变化缓慢得多，所以，尽管20世纪后期以来亚洲经济的高速增长对国际社会影响颇大，但是，亚洲文化及其伦理价值对国际社会的影响并不显著。就此而言，我们在讨论亚洲文化及其伦理价值对国际社会的影响时更多的是在未来的意义上讨论的。由于日本文化深受中国儒家文化的影响，并且日本文化随着日本经济在 20 世纪 60 年代以后的崛起已经强烈地影响到了国际社会，所以，我们可以通过日本文化中的伦理价值对于国际社会的影响来从一个侧面说明中国（儒家）情感伦理将会对国际社会产生什么形式的影响。第二次世界大战结束以后，日本作为一个战败国，经济崩溃、满目疮痍。战前日本就是一个经济比较落后的军事封建主义国家，并且除了阳光和空气之外，土地有限，资源奇缺，战争的失败更使日本社会雪上加霜，因而战后的日本其实已是一片废墟。然而，令人始料不及的是，20 世纪 60 年代以后，日本的经济逐步以比美国更快的速度发展起来。60 年代日本国民生产总值先后超过加拿大、法国、英国和联邦德国，外贸每年平均递增 16.2%。到 20 世纪 70 年代，日本已经实现了工农业现代化，一跃而成为西方世界第二经济大国。从 1946 年到 1976 年日本的经济增长了 55 倍，日本的经济增长率是美国的 4 倍。那么，为什么日本会出现这样的经济奇迹呢？早在 1962 年，伦敦《经济学人》杂志就在 9 月 1 日和 8 日连载了一篇《正视日本》的长文，后以《惊人的日本》一书出版，开始研究日本的奇迹。20 世纪 80 年代左右，美国人在寻找日本经济奇迹、企业腾飞的原因的过程中，对比研究了美国和日本在企业管理方面的所有硬件和软件，认为美国在硬件上绝不亚于日本，甚至远远高于日本；而在软件方面，日本则拥有美国所不具有的优势。这些软件指的就是带有浓厚的儒家情感文化色彩的企业文化，包括企业有意识地培育企业价值观、文化传统、风俗习惯、道德情感等。当学界的研究越来越认为日本的带有儒家情感色彩的企业文化是日本企业乃至日本经济崛起的原因时，研究、学习和效法日本企业文化便成了其他国家尤其是西方国家的一种时尚，这些不仅对于世界经济的发展起着重要的作用，而且也对世界文明和人类价值（包含伦理思想）的发展起着重要的作用。这里，日本的案例至少给了我们两点启示：其一，从日本国内来说，带有儒家情感色彩的日本文化应是日本经济腾飞的重要原因之一；其二，从国际社会来说，随着日本经济的崛起，带有儒家情感色彩的文化也对国际社会起着越来越大的作用，并且是正面的积极作用。这种情况就与整个亚洲特别是中国的情形十分相似，即：中国的经济腾飞毫无疑问有着中国儒家情感伦理在其中起的推动作用，同时，随着中国经济的崛起，中国儒家的情感伦理也必将会对国际社会起着越来越大的积极作用。

尽管我们坚信随着中国经济的崛起中国的儒家情感伦理将会对国际社会起着十分积极的作用，但是，我们认为也应该看到儒家情感伦理之积极作用的范围。这就是说，我们在肯定儒家情感之积极作用的同时也没有必要过分夸大儒家情感伦理的作用。我们曾说，情感伦理与理性伦理的作用分别存在着外延较小、内涵丰富和外延广大、内涵贫乏的不同特点，这些不同的特点又进一步使得中国儒家情感伦理的积极作用更加适应于私域（私人领域）的范围，而在公域（公共领域）的范围之内，它的作用只能是辅助的作用，若不如此，它的积极作用就会转变成为消极作用。我们之所以会得出这样的结论，乃是因为外延较小、内涵丰富和外延广大、内涵贫乏的情感伦理和理性伦理之间有一个变动的领域。在这个变动的领域中，一端是外延最小、内涵最为丰富的家庭情感伦理，另外一端则是外延最大、内涵最为贫乏的理性伦理。两端之间的变动领域就是伦理情感对象的外延由小到大并且它的内涵由丰富到贫乏的区间。在这个区间中，随着伦理情感的对象从直接了解到的对象到间接了解到的对象的过渡，以及在直接了解到的对象内部从家人到非家人的过渡、间接了解到的对象内部从熟人到广大陌生人的过渡，伦理情感主体的对象的范围越来越大，同时它对情感对象的情感则越来越贫乏。因此，伦理情感主体对于伦理情感对象的外延和内涵是一个不断变动的东西，它以了解程度为基础，尤其以熟人和陌生人的差异为基础，随着外延的不断扩大会出现内涵的不断贫乏，直到它的外延完全成为陌生人从而内涵变得最为贫乏。当情感完全抽象化，成为面对广大陌生人的外延最大、内涵最为贫乏的情感时，它就不再是感性的情感而变成了理性的情感从而成为理性的一部分了，就像感性的爱（针对具体对象的爱）逐步抽象化而变成了理性的爱（博爱）一样。由此出发，伦理情感主体对于亲疏不同等级的对象有着不同程度的情感，从儒家的情感伦理学来看，情形正是如此。其实，儒家伦理学不仅把"孝"（以及"弟"）作为仁爱的实质，而且它也把"仁"理解成为更为广泛的爱。孔子在回答他的弟子樊迟问仁时不仅明确认为仁的意思就是"爱人"，而且他还特别指出"泛爱众，而亲仁"①，认为仁包含了对于所有"众"的泛爱，不仅如此，儒家甚至还进一步把仁爱扩展到了对于自然万物的爱，认为人应该去爱自然万物。但是，尽管如此，在儒家的情感伦理学中，伦理情感主体根据情感对象的亲疏（远近）不同而给予了它们程度不等的情感（爱）。儒家伦理学明确地说：爱有差等！对父母的"孝"之所以是仁爱的实质乃是因为它是最高等级的爱。因此，儒家的情感伦理尽管强调爱甚至"泛爱众"，但是，对于不同的人，它的爱不会一视同仁。理性伦理（包括理性的情感伦理在内）则有所不同，当伦理情感主体的情感对象最终变成了外延最为广大的陌生人并且内涵变得最为贫乏的时候，伦理情感主体的伦理情感其实已经成了理性的情感，这时情感主体其实已经变成了理性主体。由于理性的情感主体之理性（情感）的内涵被抽象到了最为贫乏的程度，所以，它会对所有的理性（情感）对象一视同仁。

就伦理情感（爱等正面情感）来说，由于儒家情感伦理不会一视同仁地对待自己的情感对象，所以，它主要适应于私人的领域。根据儒家情感伦理的观点，爱是有差等的爱。在私人的领域之中，有差等的爱是人们可以接受的爱，并且人们也不会由于有差等的爱的存在而感到不平。在私人的领域中，相比于陌生人来说，我们把更多的爱献给朋友、同学、同事、同乡等，人们不会对此持有异议；相比于一般的熟人来说，我们把更多的爱献给家人，人们也不会对此持有异议；甚至在一个家庭之中，某个家庭成员把更多的爱献给父母，其他家人也不会持有异议。其实，除了少数特殊情形之外，我们若不这样去做，人们才会感到意外。然而，如果在公共领域之中，情形则会有所不同。公共领域不仅包括政治领域，而且还广泛地包括了一切职业的领域，在这些领域中，更需要的是一视同仁的公平、正义，即使是爱，它所需要的也是一视同仁的博爱（理性的爱）。否则，人们便会感到不公平、无正义，从而感到不满，并且持

---

① 孔丘：《论语·学而》，参见杨伯峻《论语译注》，中华书局，1980，第4页。

有异议。在公共领域中，虽然也可能存在着有差等的爱（它体现了感性的情感），但是，它只能在不违背公平、正义乃至博爱的原则下起到一种补充或辅助性的作用。一旦有差等的爱在公共领域中起着主导的作用，那么，便会产生不公平和无正义。由于儒家伦理无论从起源上说还是从实质的内容上说都是（感性的）情感伦理，因此，当它随着中国经济的崛起而必然在国际社会产生重要影响的时候，我们在看到和肯定它的积极作用的同时，也不应该忽视它的积极作用的限制。其实，承认这种限制，恰好正是为了更好地使它在国际社会中发挥积极作用！

中国诚信价值观的过去、现在与未来

吴成国　曹　林[*]

摘　要：诚信是我国自古以来源远流长的政治意识形态和社会道德准则之一，也是现代中国国家理性的重要表现。诚信作为一种伦理政治价值观，承载着丰富的思想资源；今天它也产生了凝聚人心与维护公道的社会效益；而我国在前不久提出的二十四字社会主义核心价值观则将"诚信"提到了国家意识形态和精神文明建设的战略层面上，这不仅为诚信价值观夯实了新的理论基础，也为它的进一步发展和充实指明了方向。

关键词：诚信　价值观　中华文明

The Past, Present and Future of Honesty in China

Wu Chengguo, Cao Lin

Abstract：Honesty is one of China's political ideologies and social ethics since the ancient times. As an important ethical and political value, honesty carries rich ideological resources; today it still helps unite the people and maintain social justice; in the twenty-four-word socialist values proposed

* 吴成国，湖北大学高等人文研究院副院长；曹林，湖北大学历史文化学院教师。

recently, honesty is put on the strategic level of state ideology and spiritual civilization, which not only consolidates a new theoretical foundation for honesty values, but also indicates the direction for its further development and enhancement.

Keywords：Honesty；Values；Chinese Civilization

诚信，在现代话语中是一种个人德行或社会道德。从思想史、伦理学再到法理学、社会舆论，"诚信"都是一个充满言说意义的词语。古今中外对诚信思想、诚信价值的探讨可谓贯穿了人类文明社会的整个发展过程。作为从上古时代一直绵延流传至今的中华文明，在创造了璀璨不朽的精神文明和物质文明、为全世界人类文明做出贡献的同时，也没有忘记对这种永恒而普世的价值观——诚信——的探讨。要理解和重建当代中国的诚信价值，势必要理解它的过去。这就要回溯到中华文明创生之初及其在演生过程中对诚信价值的理解和阐述之中。

一 "诚""信"释诂

要理解"诚信"一词的概念源起，首先要理解"诚"和"信"的含义、联系与区别。

"诚"与"信"从训诂学角度来讲属于互训关系。《辞源》酉集言部："诚，真实也；信也。"① 《辞源》子集人部："信，不欺也。"② 信就是诚，诚就是信，相依伴生。从字形来看，"诚"与"信"都有"言"字，在字源中同属言部。《说文解字》"言部"段玉裁注云："言，直言曰言，论难曰语。……凡言之属皆从言。"③ 在甲骨文中，"言"表示告

---

① 《辞源（修订本）》下册《酉集·言部》，商务印书馆，2009，第3154页。
② 《辞源（修订本）》上册《子集·人部》，第230页。
③ （汉）许慎：《说文解字》卷三《言部》，中华书局，1963，第51页。

祭，指在对祖先、神的告祭活动中不能有丝毫的欺蒙和亵渎之心，必须始终处于一种虔诚的宗教情感和心理状态方能完成告祭，与祖先神灵相通。①

诚，信也。从言成声。信，诚也。从人从言。②

说明"诚"和"信"都是上古时代神权政治的产物，代表了人王祭祀鬼神的礼仪规范。"诚"是指于祭祀祈祷时的态度或情感，"信"则是指祭祀祈祷时所说的祝文或誓言。如伪古文尚书《太甲篇》："鬼神无常享，享于克诚。"③《礼记·曲礼上》："祷祠祭祀，供给鬼神，非礼不诚不庄。"④《礼记·郊特牲》："郊特牲而社稷大牢。天子适诸侯。诸侯膳用犊。诸侯适天子。天子赐之礼大牢。贵诚之义也。故天子牲孕弗食也。"⑤ 这些都是说明祭祀礼仪的诚恳、庄重、严肃。而《左传·桓公六年》记述楚国伐随国时，随国贤臣季梁给随侯的进谏中说："所谓道忠于民而信于神也。上思利民，忠也；祝史正辞，信也。"⑥ 国君的理想品质是忠于人民而取信于鬼神。国君经常想到对百姓有利，这就是忠；祝史祭祀时的言辞诚实不欺，这就是信。⑦ 在这里，"诚"体现的是合乎规范的德行，"信"则更偏重于言行信实不妄诬。

后来，"诚"主要指主体自身的一种心理状态，指主体言行一致，所谓"诚者自成也"⑧。故先秦典籍中对"诚"的论述多集中体现主体内心的诚意。如《礼记·礼器》对儒家理想人格——君子——的行为有这样的规定："君子之于礼也，有所竭情尽慎，致其敬而诚若，有美而文

---

① 张志云、吕丹丹：《以传统诚信伦理为本推进文明湖北建设》，载吴成国主编《文化发展论丛·湖北卷（2014）》，社会科学文献出版社，2015，第255页。

② 《说文解字》卷三《言部》，第52页。

③ 李学勤主编《十三经注疏·尚书正义》卷第八《太甲下》，北京大学出版社，1999，第213页。

④ 《十三经注疏·礼记正义》卷第一《曲礼上》，第14页。

⑤ 《十三经注疏·礼记正义》卷第二十五《郊特牲》，第766页。

⑥ 《十三经注疏·春秋左传正义》卷第六《桓公三年至六年》，第164页。

⑦ 译文参考李梦生《左传译注》，上海古籍出版社，1998，第70页。

⑧ （宋）朱熹：《四书章句集注·中庸章句》卷第二十五，中华书局，1983，第33页。

而诚若。"① "诚若"乃至诚和顺之意。君子的礼仪表现为至诚和顺，对内要戒慎恭敬，对外要有威仪。这种行为规范来自个体的自我约束，其立意就在于通过身体真实地表达"礼"的价值内涵。

南宋理学将"诚"的意义演绎得更加抽象。如朱熹释《中庸》"诚者，天之道也；诚之者，人之道也。诚者不勉而中，不思而得，从容中道，圣人也。诚之者，择善而固执之者也"，有云："诚者，真实无妄之谓，天理之本然也。诚之者，未能真实无妄，而欲其真实无妄之谓，人事之当然也。圣人之德，浑然天理，真实无妄，不待思勉而从容中道，则亦天之道也。"② 朱熹认为，诚实是天之道，亦是人之道，天之道是自然规律，人之道是人法于天而行于世的当然之理。这其实是一种形而上的道德论。

相比"诚"充满浓厚的道德意味，"信"的义项及其迁延更加朴实。最早"信"常用"允""孚"代替，代表信实无欺。如《尚书·尧典》："曰若稽古帝尧，曰放勋。钦明文思安安，允恭克让，光被四表，格于上下。"③《周易·中孚》："中孚：豚鱼，吉。"④ 而"信"作为信任关系的意义，与春秋战国时期诸侯国之间的频繁会盟有关。作为一种制度性的礼仪活动，盟誓中需要结盟双方对自己的预期行为负责，这就要依赖于各自的信任。这一时期，周王室衰微，政治结构多元化，社会内部上下流通的渠道被打开，阶级成员之间不再依靠过去的律法来维持关系，而往往只能依赖于彼此间的信任。这是"信"观念在春秋战国时期得以发达的原因。⑤ 儒家对"信"有很多论说，这时的"信"才带有德行的意味。如《论语·学而》："有子曰：'信近于义，言可复也；恭近于礼，远耻辱也；因不失其亲，亦可宗也。'"⑥《论语·为政》："子曰：'人而

---

① 《十三经注疏·礼记正义》卷第二十三《礼器》，第 741 ~ 742 页。
② 《四书章句集注·中庸章句》卷第二十，第 31 页。
③ （清）孙星衍：《尚书今古文注疏》卷一《尧典上》，中华书局，1986，第 2 ~ 5 页。
④ （魏）王弼注、（唐）孔颖达疏：《周易正义》卷第六《第六十一卦中孚》，北京大学出版社，2000，第 284 页。
⑤ 阎步克：《春秋战国时期"信"观念的演变及其社会原因》，《历史研究》1981 年第 6 期。
⑥ 《十三经注疏·论语注疏》卷一《学而》，第 10 页。

无信，不知其可也。大车无輗，小车无軏，其何以行之哉？'"① 孔子认为有信之人，其言可反复，人们能够一次再次地相信他。人言而无信，如大车没有輗、小车没有軏，套不上马牛，所以寸步难行。这就把"信"的有无大小与人的基本品质好坏联系起来，将信实视为不可或缺的基本道德规范。

《礼记·儒行》更是将信德视为一般儒者的处世之道："儒有席上之珍以待聘，夙夜强学以待问，怀忠信以待举，力行以待取。其自立有如此者。""儒有居处齐难，其坐起恭敬；言必先信，行必中正。道涂不争险易之利，冬夏不争阴阳之和。爱其死以有待也，养其身以有为也。其备豫有如此者。""儒有忠信以为甲胄，礼义以为干橹；戴仁而行，抱义而处，虽有暴政，不更其所。其自立有如此者。""儒有博学而不穷，笃行而不倦；幽居而不淫，上通而不困；礼之以和为贵，忠信之美，优游之法；举贤而容众，毁方而瓦合。其宽裕有如此者。"② 这里将信与忠联系在一起，强调忠信作为儒者遵行礼仪法度的重要标识，体现出"信"观念向人伦道德范畴的进一步延伸。

朱熹从体用统合的角度申明了诚与信的道理。他说："诚是个自然的实，信是个人所为之实。中庸说'诚者天之道也'便是诚。若'诚之者，人之道也'，便是信。信不足以尽诚，犹爱不足以尽仁。上是，下不是。"③ 意指"诚"是自然规律、人性之本，无须多做姿态就可以理解；"信"却是人们后天习得的处世规范，是"一种社会性的道德实践"④，必须时刻谨记并自我要求。"信"是表达"诚"的一种手段，"诚"是践行"信"的一种追求。朱熹又强调"信"受"义"之节制，合乎义的言行是信义，反之则是非信义。此间的标准在于内心的忠诚和

---

① 《十三经注疏·论语注疏》卷二《为政》，第 23 页。
② 《十三经注疏·礼记正义》卷五十九《儒行》，第 1578、1583、1585 页。
③ （宋）朱熹撰，（宋）黎靖德编，王欣贤点校，《朱子语类》卷六《性理三·仁义礼智等名义》，中华书局，1986，第 103 页。
④ 詹向红：《朱熹诚信思想论》，《江淮论坛》2008 年第 6 期。

信实。①

除开对主体道德的讨论，"信"的观念在先秦思想资源中还表现在政治思想方面。儒家认为"信"是重要的政治手段。儒家言信，是在礼的框架下展开讨论的。② 如伪古文尚书《仲虺之诰》："克宽克仁。彰信兆民。"③ 又如《尚书·武成》将周武王功业之盛的原因总结为"信"："天下大定，乃反商政，政由旧，释箕子囚，封比干墓，式商容闾。散鹿台之财，发钜桥之粟，大赉于四海，而万姓悦服。列爵惟五，分土惟三，建官惟贤，位事惟能。重民五教，惟食丧祭，惇信明义，崇德报功，垂拱而天下治。"④ 正因为周武王能够为民着想，取信于民，故能"垂拱而天下治"。

孔子在论述"信"的时候，着重于君主对人民的责任。《论语·颜渊》："子贡问政。子曰：'足食。足兵。民信之矣。'子贡曰：'必不得已而去，于斯三者何先？'曰：'去兵。'子贡曰：'必不得已而去，于斯二者何先？'曰：'去食。自古皆有死，民无信不立。'"⑤

将"信"视为政治统御术的先例，亦起始于先秦。《韩非子·扬权》："二者诚信，下乃贡情。"⑥ 《管子·权修》："赏罚不信，则民无取。野不辟，民无取，外不可以应敌，内不可以固守，故曰有万乘之号，而无千乘之用，而求权之无轻，不可得也。"⑦ 以赏罚号令天下的秘诀，在于有"信"。有信则民有所取，民有所取则号令明。

以上是上古时代的中国人对"诚"和"信"这组相互依存而又一体两面的字词的解释和认识。历史上明确提出"诚信"这一命题的是管仲。《管子·枢言》有云："诚信者，天下之结也。"⑧ 其意是，讲诚信是

---

① 《朱子语类》卷二十二《论语四·学而篇下》，第 525 页。
② 萧伯符、易江波：《中国传统信任结构及其对现代法治的影响》，《中国法学》2005 年第 2 期。
③ 《十三经注疏·尚书正义》卷第八《仲虺之诰》，第 197 页。
④ 《十三经注疏·尚书正义》卷十一《武成》，第 293～295 页。
⑤ 《十三经注疏·论语注疏》卷第十二《颜渊》，第 160 页。
⑥ （清）王先慎撰《韩非子集解》卷第二《扬权》，中华书局，1998，第 45 页。
⑦ 黎翔凤撰《管子校注》卷第一《权修》，中华书局，2004，第 48 页。
⑧ 《管子校注》卷第四《枢言》，第 246 页。

天下行为准则的关键。这句话代表了先秦诸子的共识。

"诚信"体现了二者意义的统一。一方面，"诚信"承接了"诚"合乎规范礼法的意义，具有道德约束感。如《礼记·祭统》在对理想君主的祭祀礼仪要求上提到了"诚信"的概念：

> 是故天子亲耕于南郊，以共齐盛。王后蚕于北郊，以共纯服。诸侯耕于东郊，亦以共齐盛。夫人蚕于北郊，以共冕服。天子、诸侯非莫耕也，王后、夫人非莫蚕也，身致其诚信，诚信之谓尽，尽之谓敬，敬尽然后可以事神明。此祭之道也。①

另一方面，"诚信"也表达了"信"信实不欺的本意。《孟子·万章上》记载万章问孟子：舜异母弟象设法杀舜，舜从容顺应，这是不是虚伪呢？孟子用子产的故事说明圣人君子对他人的信任是一种天生不造作的情感，并不是虚伪的。并说："故君子可欺以其方，难罔以非其道。彼以爱兄之道来，故诚信而喜之，奚伪焉？"朱熹对此注解道："欺以其方，谓诳之以理之所有；罔以非其道，谓昧之以理之所无。象以爱兄之道来，所谓欺之以其方也。舜本不知其伪，故实喜之，何伪之有？此章又言舜遭人伦之变，而不失天理之常也。"

中华文明是一种"伦理-政治"型文明。人与人之间的基本关系构成了家庭、宗族、国家的凝聚力。诚信观念在中国上古社会的形成，体现了人们对社会伦理和道德基准的关注，这在儒家经典中有非常多的反映。作为儒家礼法和社会道德的基础之一，诚信在中国古代社会享有崇高的地位。同时，先秦以来的思想资源赋予诚信一词以极高的能动性，一方面将"诚信"人格化，把诚信视为圣人、君子的理想行为守则；另一方面又将"诚信"抽象化，将"诚信"塑造为一种理想的政治品格，在此基础上涵盖了从君民关系到治国理念再到政治统御术全方位的多重维度的解释。

---

① 《十三经注疏·礼记正义》卷四十九《祭统》，第1347～1348页。

二 "诚信"的历史演变

先秦时期积累起了探讨诚信价值观念的丰富资源，将"诚信"这一词语的内涵初步定性为对人的道德、礼教与处世言行的约束。汉代学术一统，汉儒糅合先秦各家思想，用阴阳五行来解释儒家的德性论，对"五德""五性"的说法做了综合化的解释，将"诚"与"信"的意义混同起来。《白虎通义》论五性时曰："义者，宜也，断绝得中也。礼者，履也，履道成文也。智者，知也，独见前闻，不惑于事，见微知著也。信者，诚也，专一不移也。"① 这就把"诚"的精诚和"信"的信义结合在了一起。后来，"诚""信"在连用或单用的时候，基于抽象的道德伦理范畴的概念越来越清晰，而作为有实际意义的工具理念范畴的概念则越来越模糊，到最后已经完全演变为伦理道德的一部分。

这种道德认同在汉语成语中得到了稳固的传承，例如表现在成语中，对"信"与"不信"就有着鲜明的褒贬、赞弹、誉毁的不同态度。褒、赞、誉者如"信誓旦旦"、"信赏必罚"、"信而有征"、"果刑信赏"、"讲信修睦"；贬、弹、毁者如"信口开河"、"信口雌黄"、"轻诺寡信"、"轻言寡信"、"背信弃义"等。对"诚"的描述如"抱诚守真"、"心悦诚服"、"开诚布公"、"主敬存诚"、"精诚所至，金石为开"、"巧诈不如拙诚"等，也体现了这一点。

古代中国对诚信价值观的推崇往往有道德劝诫和规训礼教的意义在其中。所谓"政教"，也就是在中国古代社会接近于"意识形态"这个表达的词语，其中"政"代表国家和社会，包括政府管理和全国从上到下全方位的矫正与引导；而"教"不仅代表教育，还有逐步灌输和保持一种社会秩序的道德水准。② 作为伦理－政治型国家，在主流意识形态

---

① （清）陈立撰，吴则虞点校，《白虎通疏证》卷八《性情》，中华书局，1994，第 381~382 页。

② James T. C. Liu, *China Turning Inward*, Cambridge：Harvard University Asian Center, 1974, pp. 37－38.

的表现及其叙述形式中，诗书礼仪即是规范法度。对诚信观念的推崇和引导，其道德价值是远远大于其他任何一种价值的。

自先秦时候起，楚人便以精诚的守信精神最早闻名于世，后来发展成为文明中国、礼仪之邦坚守的行为准则，楚地也流传着许多讲诚信、重信义的故事。"楚人重然诺"成为楚文化中的一个标志性特征，故而李白《送储邕之武昌》有这样的诗句："诺为楚人重，诗传谢朓清。"① "楚人重然诺"的事例书之于史册的，有三则故事即"复陈""存郑""和宋"都与楚庄王有关，体现了楚庄王无愧为"英主"二字，有霸主气度。以"复陈"为例，《史记》记载，公元前598年，楚庄王为了加强对中原的控制，借平息陈国夏征舒之乱为名，出兵伐陈。事先对陈国声明：只杀有弑君之罪的夏征舒，不会惊扰陈国百姓。为了争取陈国邻邦齐国的中立，遂派大夫申叔时到齐国游说。后来，楚师未经剧烈战斗即攻进陈都，捕杀了夏征舒。楚庄王宣布：陈国已灭，改为陈县。这时，大家纷纷向楚庄王道贺，只有自齐国归来的申叔时不贺。楚庄王问其原因。申叔时说：民间有一种说法，一个人牵着牛践踏了别人的田地，这个人虽有错，但田主却将牛据为己有，这就太过分了。大王伐陈时只宣布要惩罚夏征舒的罪，是以仁义的名义来兴师征伐的，可是却为了获得利益而把别人的国家也灭了，今后如何号令天下！所以我没有向大王表示祝贺。楚庄王听后说：你讲得对。于是宣布收回成命，履行诺言，并派人去把逃到晋国的陈国公子午接回陈国继承王位。《史记》载："孔子读史记至楚复陈，曰：'贤哉楚庄王！轻千乘之国而重一言。'"② 孔子的这一评价也见于《孔子家语·好生》："贤哉楚王！轻千乘之国而重一言之信。"③ 正如研究者所言："'复陈''存郑''和宋'的决策，在历史上广受称赞，影响深远，充分体现了楚人言信行果的思想。楚人屡屡释

① （清）彭定求等校点《全唐诗》卷一百七十七《送储邕之武昌》，中华书局，1960，第1811页。
② （汉）司马迁：《史记》卷三十六《陈杞世家》，中华书局，1959，第1580页。
③ （魏）王肃注《孔子家语》卷第二《好生》，影印文渊阁本《四库全书》，台湾商务印书馆，1986，第695册，第23页。

放忠信之君、忠信之人，尊重那些能够'言必信，行必果'的守信之
人，恰恰从一个侧面表现出对忠信重诺的认同和推崇。"①

此外还有流传千古的"一诺千金"的故事。楚汉相争时，季布是项
羽手下一员大将，他为项羽出生入死，冲锋陷阵，多次陷汉王刘邦于绝
境，为项羽立下大功。刘邦建立汉王朝后，因痛恨季布，下令以千两黄
金捉拿季布。季布为人言而有信，答应别人的事情一定竭尽全力去做，
从不食言于人。这种品质使他获得了大家的尊重与友谊，以致敬慕季布
为人的人，都在暗中帮助他。在朋友的保护和帮助下，季布终为高祖刘
邦所用，担任郎中。《史记》云："季布者，楚人也。为气任侠，有名于
楚。……楚人谚曰'得黄金百，不如得季布一诺'。"② 可见，诚信重然
诺，不仅是季布知名度较高的原因，也是为社会所公认的道德，否则，
不会出现在民间谚语中。"一诺千金"的成语即源出于此。

即使今天看来，这种将诚信的表现本身与著名历史人物进行叠加的
组合也是宣导价值观的有效方式。它表达了对一种美好品格的肯定，并
希冀未来的人们能够效仿。但事实上，每一种价值观的兴起都是与当时
社会发展的现实联系在一起的。春秋战国时期的政治变动与经济发展带
动了诸侯国之间的互动和阶级内部的流通，使得诚信观念和信任关系越
来越有实际意义，也越来越受到尊重；两千年来儒家思想的发展，将诚
信理念由一种实际操作上升为道德标榜，与逐渐道德化的儒家思想史的
演化历程也是息息相关的。

三　诚信价值观的当代困境

当代中国却恰恰缺乏此前诚信价值所依托的精神和物质土壤。儒家
传统的诚信伦理主要是基于地缘、血缘的人与人交往过程中的诚实守信，
主要依靠个人良心和无字无据的"君子协定"来约束各自的行为，缺乏

---

① 王生铁主编《楚文化概要》，湖北人民出版社，2013，第282页。
② （汉）司马迁：《史记》卷一百《季布栾布列传》，中华书局，1959，第2731页。

相应的制度保障。正如费孝通先生所说的："乡土社会的信用并不是对契约的重视，而是发生于对一种行为的规矩熟悉到不假思索时的可靠性。"① 这种基于血缘、亲缘、地缘的信用，其约束力、约束范围都极为有限。如果说在传统社会由于交换范围的有限性，社会在缺乏公共生活伦理和制度伦理层面的信用伦理的条件下依然可以维持下去的话，那么，在市场经济条件下，人们的交往日益普遍和复杂，交往的范围日益扩大，不再局限于有限的范围和熟人的圈子，非人情的交易也越来越多，传统的人伦信用已经无法满足市场秩序的需要，必须借助于以法律为保障的契约信用来维持。②

2012 年 9 月 13 日，托马斯·L. 弗里德曼在《纽约时报》发表《中国缺少的不是创新，是信任》一文。③ 这篇文章分析了当代中国在经济发展过程中所面临的一个重要制约因素——诚信品质与信任体系及其与创新社会之间的互动关系。可以说是对我国目前整个国民经济行业发展现状和未来发展方向做了注脚。他阐述了社会信任与创新社会之间的关系：当社会中存在信任时，就会出现持续创新的情况，因为人们有安全感，他们就敢于进行冒险，做出创新所需的长期承诺。当有了信任时，人们就不会害怕自己的创意被盗取，愿意分享他们的想法，愿意合作开发彼此的创新项目。现代中国想要成为一个创新社会所面临的最大问题是，它现在还是一个信任度很低的社会。而如果中国想要继续提高人民的收入水平，就必须成为创新社会。他一针见血地指出，中国现在缺失的不是创新文化，而是一种更基本的东西：信任。他认为当前中国存在巨大的信任亏空。这是因为中国正处于新旧信任体系过渡的阶段。过去建立在村落和家庭之上的信任形式已经破裂，而基于法治和独立的司法系统之上的新体制又还没有完全建立起来。

诚信的缺失，带来的是整个社会的信任危机。当代中国在诚信方面

① 费孝通：《乡土中国》，三联书店，1985，第 6 页。
② 郜爱红：《儒家诚信伦理的现代诠释与整合》，《中国人民大学学报》2002 年第 5 期。
③ 纽约时报中文网，http://cn.nytimes.com/opinion/20120913/c13friedman/。

最为吊诡的情况，表现为深陷道德困境而又不得不做足姿态："不管你信不信，反正我是信了"，成为缺乏诚信、无法获得别人信任却又硬要冒充诚信之人的典型写照。层出不穷的食品药品安全事故、真假难辨的团购网以及防不胜防的商业欺诈、信用欺诈、就业陷阱、传销组织，都让老百姓常常受到戏弄。师长谆谆教导孩子们要"尊老爱幼"，要"乐于助人"。可谁会想到，助人的人被反诬，竟连续出现了老人倒地而无人敢扶的事件，真是让人唏嘘。出现这样的道德困境，恐怕再出台《老年人跌倒干预技术指南》式的专业指导也无力破解。

诚信价值在当代中国社会的缺失和失衡，是主客观原因共同构成的。从社会伦理道德的角度来说，诚信始终面临着外在的冲击。新中国成立以来在经济建设和政治中经历的种种曲折曾使中国人一度失去了传统文化，也失去了根植于传统文化中的诚信价值。中国经济在最近30年的起飞，其速度和效率令全世界为之瞩目。但国民经济建设方面所取得的辉煌成就并不能掩盖国人信仰的缺失和心灵的枯萎。改革开放、国门大开的同时，由资本主义生产方式所引发的特定价值观念，如对金钱、物质的崇拜也随着对经济发展的追求和渴望而逐渐得到了广泛的认同。仅就经济发展最快的一部分地区而言，巨大的经济效能带来的个人物质生活的提升和城市公共设施建设的改善也使得国人在调和以金钱至上、物质至上为主导的价值观时发生了偏差。更重要的是，改革前夜被无数次政治运动所侵入的信任结构已然岌岌可危，根本无法对抗前者所带来的冲击。30年来，中国在高速发展的过程中逐步认识到过去一些摒弃文化和丧失操守的行为是错误的；近些年来，要求回到传统文化中寻找应对当代人恶劣的精神生存环境的声音开始增强，人们认识到中华传统文化对信任结构的保护是值得回顾、思索和重新利用的。

从诚信法治的角度来说，当代中国依然在努力建设法治社会的过程之中。这个特点决定了有些并不令人满意的执法过程和步调缓慢的法律建设将并行存在很长一段时间。从19世纪中期建立海关与通商口岸，开始对接外国法律体系以来，中国的现代化进程就与法制建设紧密联系在了一起。但应当注意到的是，这个过程并不和缓，基于西方民主制度的现代法律体系和信任结构常常与伴随中国现代化进程的民族解放、自力更生等要求相违背。应当看到，当旧的信任结构无法胜任新的社会模式时，新的信任结构却远未能完全建立起来。中国的法制建设，特别是现代信任结构的重建，还有很长一段路要走。传统与现代价值观的对焦和碰撞表明我国对主流价值观的重构势在必行。

四　当代诚信的反思与展望

既然过去的价值体系无法真正发挥作用，那么势必需要注入新的血液来满足当今社会对诚实守信这种品质的要求。这种新的血液来自对诚信价值的现代转化和现代法治观念的引入。

诚信价值的现代转化就是从旧的、传统的诚信观走向新的、现代的诚信观。有学者研究指出，社会经济基础的变更使原有的观念自身发生"转构"，即在与新观念的相互冲突、相互交融中旧的观念得以充实和修正，成为适应新的经济基础的观念。这是诚信观念的价值转换机制。[①]有学者结合中西方对诚信的阐述，以及各自从伦理道德和民主法治两种截然不同的思想范畴来启发的特点，综合出现代诚信的三种向度，即道德的、政治的和法律的。现代诚信不仅保有道德结构、政治情境和法律场域的三重意境，更因解构而存在新的三维之义：作为个体品质的诚信、作为关系纽带的诚信和作为价值追求的诚信。[②]较传统诚信观念而言，现代诚信更讲求法理依据以及在具体的法律保障下所体现的人文关怀。这也是现代国家理性与公民正义之间所寻求的和谐基点。

政府在制定良好的治理模式和行为规范时往往希望得到人民的支持，双方的互动就需要信任机制来调控，这时的诚信是一种政府诚信；政府有权力对社会行为予以意志的贯彻，表现在引导和塑造公民行为和公民意识，促进公民道德的提升，这时信任机制也将展开作用，此时的诚信

---

① 郜爱红：《儒家诚信伦理的现代诠释与整合》，《中国人民大学学报》2002 年第 5 期。
② 付子堂、类延村：《诚信的自由诠释与法治规训》，《法学杂志》2013 年第 1 期。

是道德诚信；而在制定管理社会的法律时，法律诚信就成为必不可少的制度和实践基础。此时的诚信就属于法治诚信。

就政府诚信而言，中国古代的政治传统对此有重大的借鉴意义。先秦时儒家有关于君、民、信的论述，法家有强调官术的说法；自秦汉学术、政治、教化大一统以来，所谓"德主刑辅""内儒外法"的政治伦理就一直绵延不断地继承下来，成为古代帝制中国独具特色的意识形态。政府诚信的目的在于与民立信，举商鞅变法徙木立信的例子，一些著名的政治家对此都有阐述。如毛泽东在早年所作国学作文《商鞅徙木立信论》中就此强调为政者要取信于民，法律、政策必须以民为本，以民为出发点、归宿点，要有利于人民。有益于人民的法律、政策，人民会自动地去实现与维护；如果法律违背了人民的意志，政策有损于人民的利益，那就会使政府与人民对立起来。然后，又从执法的视角，阐明执法要严明、公正。有了好的法律，但不去执行，有法不依，执法不严，不能取信于民；或对人不对事，刑不上大夫，礼不下庶人，不公正，不透明，也不能取信于民。至于违法不惩治，那天下就会大乱，好人也会变坏。而司马光在评价商鞅此举时更将是否诚信上升到事关国与家成败得失的高度来看问题了："夫信者，人君之大宝也。国保于民，民保于信；非信无以使民，非民无以守国。是故古之王者不欺四海，霸者不欺四邻，善为国者不欺其民，善为家者不欺其亲。不善者反之，欺其邻国，欺其百姓，甚者欺其兄弟，欺其父子。上不信下，下不信上，上下离心，以至于败。"①

就道德诚信而言，中国传统诚信价值观也能够发挥一定作用。中国古代的信任结构以家庭为基本单位。由村社乡党所控制的舆论基本决定了基层信任体系的构建。即使在"明刑弼教"的王朝，也在乡间设立申明亭以伦理为纽带对臣民进行道德控制。② 而中国传统伦理多属私德。正如梁启超所谓："私德居十之九，而公德不及其一焉。"③ 公德的严重

---

① （宋）司马光：《资治通鉴》卷二《周纪二·显王十年》，中华书局，1956，第48页。
② 付子堂、类延村：《诚信的自由诠释与法治规训》，《法学杂志》2013年第1期。
③ 梁启超撰，吴松点校，《饮冰室文集点校》第一集《新民说·论公德》，云南教育出版社，2001，第554页。

缺乏导致中国现代化转型困难重重。直至今日，还有不少人对中国传统伦理的现代转换、私德与公德之间的顺利对接持怀疑甚至悲观的看法。认为儒家伦理缺乏建立公德机制的基础和保证。① 但是，私德与公德之间存在着转化的可能性。正如梁启超先生所说，因为"私德公德，本并行而不悖者也""是故欲铸国民，必以培养个人之私德为第一义；欲从事于铸国民者，必以自培养其个人之私德为第一义"②。作为中国传统伦理基石的"诚信"伦理，正可以拿来当作重塑现代公民伦理道德的基础，以"诚信"之私德开出现代之公德，实现私德与公德的整合。③

就法治诚信而言，中国传统价值观所能起到的作用就比较微小了。诚信是法律的重要精神与原则，诚实信用通常被视为私法的黄金法则。然而，古代帝制中国的律法中是没有民法和私法的，我国第一部民法始于 1907 年制定、1911 年完成的《大清民律草案》。事实上，中国儒家的传统诚信价值观同现代法治文化之间存在一定距离。二者的文化导向、道德约束的主体以及各自实践的内涵都是不一样的。有学者认为，诚信与法治的关系源于市场经济体制下评价标准的转移与补充："市场经济的客观发展和当前科技日益进步为现代社会确立了市场游戏规则，但制度往往落后于转瞬即逝的市场演进和变革，一些法律规则尚未进入或暂时未考虑到的领域和部门出现了，这时具体的法律规范无法约束它们从而使市场和社会正义无法体现，道德与法律的分野开始模糊，道德的社会性与法律的强制性开始出现妥协和对话，作为补充的正义评价标准就这样交给诚信原则了。"④ 按照这种理解，诚信价值观称得上是当代法治文化的必要补充，诚信法治观念的深入贯彻则是理所应当、势所必至的。反过来，法制体系又为诚信价值观的践行提供了必要保障。

---

① 如刘清平《儒家伦理与社会公德——论儒家伦理的深度悖论》，《哲学研究》2004 年第 1 期；崔大华《儒学的一种缺弱：私德与公德》，《文史哲》2006 年第 1 期；许建良《儒家道德缺乏公德机制论》，《伦理学研究》2008 年第 2 期。
② 《饮冰室文集点校》第一集《新民说·论私德》，第 622 页。
③ 张志云、吕丹丹：《以传统诚信伦理为本推进文明湖北建设》，载吴成国主编《文化发展论丛·湖北卷（2014）》，第 259 页。
④ 王伟国：《诚信体系建设法制保障的探索与设想》，《中国法学》2012 年第 5 期。

从实事求是到科学发展观，从"八荣八耻"到"核心价值观"，再到每年一度的感动中国年度人物评选，重构当代中国主流价值观正在努力践行当中。作为古楚地区的行政演化物，今天的湖北大地在传承优秀价值观的过程中也发挥了作用。楚人重然诺的优秀传统在今天集中表现在"信义兄弟"孙水林兄弟身上。在北京当建筑包工头的湖北武汉黄陂孙水林兄弟俩，每年都会在年前给农民工结清工钱。2009 年底，哥哥孙水林为赶在年前给农民工结清工钱，在返乡途中遭遇车祸遇难。弟弟孙东林为了完成哥哥的遗愿，在大年三十前一天，将工钱送到了农民工的手中，兄弟俩的诚信之举深深打动了全中国的人。时任武汉市市长阮成发批示："孙氏兄弟事迹感人。这就是典型的武汉人，信义、守诺、豪气，我为这样的武汉人而自豪。"2010 年 2 月 25 日，《湖北日报》在头版显著位置刊发了全景式长篇通讯《超越生命的承诺——记生死接力的"信义兄弟"孙水林、孙东林》和评论《千秋万代信义为本》，深度挖掘和全方位报道"信义兄弟"的感人事迹，新浪网等主要门户网站转载，让无数读者和网友为之落泪。"信义兄弟"黄陂孙水林兄弟当选为 2010 年度感动中国人物。2010 年度感动中国组委会授予"信义兄弟"的颁奖词是："言忠信，行笃敬，古老相传的信条，演绎出现代传奇，他们为尊严承诺，为良心奔波，大地上一场悲情接力。雪夜里的好兄弟，只剩下孤独一个。雪落无声，但情义打在地上铿锵有力。"

古往今来，诚信价值观经历了生发、扩张、转向与再度传承的过程。基于儒家伦理道德的诚信价值观曾在古代中国社会发挥了积极作用；而诚信价值观的现代转化则将使旧的精神文化迸发出新的色彩和希望。当代中国在俯身捡拾传统文化所遗留下来的遗存与宝藏之后，必将怀着意气风发的精神和无惧无畏的心态，高举诚信旗帜，在自由、民主、富强的道路上大踏步地迈进。

Sustainable Development Vie the Family

Corazon Toralba[*]

Abstract: The World Commission on Environment and Development defines *sustainable development* as the kind of "development that meets the needs of the present without compromising the ability of future generations to meet their own needs. Recognizing that this is a good that must be pursued, solutions were proposed to address this concern. Among these solutions are population control and curbing greed through cessation of desire. Both positions are untenable based on the premise that development is by people and for people. Reducing population growth through population control will not assure the future of its own pool of human resources that will spur growth. Training to curb greed may lead to a weak population if the greed is directed to goods needed to sustain life; hence present and future generations may not be healthy enough to sustain growth. While governmental intervention has been actively pursued, the role of the family has been neglected. This lecture will explain why the family and the efforts to preserve the traditional family will be the key to sustainable development. It will use Aristotle's notion of the family, citizenship and education to illustrate this claim.

Keywords: Sustainable Development; Family; Citizenship

---

[*] Corazon Toralba, Ph D at the Unirerity of Asia and the Pacific, Philippines.

以家庭为纽带的可持续发展

Corazon Toralba

摘　要：世界环境与发展委员会将可持续发展定义为"既满足当代人的需求，又不损害后代人满足其自身需求的能力的"发展。认识到这是个值得追求的好提议，人们提出了解决这一问题的方案。这些众多方案中包括控制人口数量，中止欲望以遏制贪婪。基于这样的前提，无论是为了人民发展还是依靠人民发展都站不住脚。通过控制人口数量来减少人口增长无法保证其自身的人力资源未来的激增。如果对维持生命需要的商品非常贪婪，那么学会遏制贪婪可以减少人口；因此，当代人和后代人可能达不到足够健康来持续增长。尽管政府干预正在积极开展，家庭的作用却一直被忽视。此次讲座将解释为什么家庭以及努力保护传统家庭是可持续发展的关键。讲座将引用亚里士多德关于家庭、公民权和教育的概念来进行说明。

关键词：可持续发展　家庭　公民权

I　Introduction

Sustainable development's definition as the kind of "development that meets the needs of the present without compromising the ability of future generations to meet their own needs" reflects that relationship between the available natural resources and man. As I stated elsewhere "The physical world is an external reality that he experiences as something that imposes on him, as something to be transformed, used and dominated. Dominion here is understood as governing the world in a way that it could serve man. By dominating the world, he leads it toward the purpose, which is to serve man. This means using whatever he finds in this world to satisfy his existential needs."① The relationship reclaims his sense of responsibility to be a steward of natural resources. Man should think of means to preserve the existing natural resources in view of the future.

In the last Southeast Asian Biennial Conference held in Hanoi with the theme "Cultural Traditions and Sustainable Development" it has been repeated that development is of people, by people, and for people. Prof. Trân Văn Ðoan from the International Federation of Philosophical Societies and a Vietnamese living in Austria, noted in his concluding reflections-and attempting to integrate ideas presented in the conference—the solutions proposed by the east and the west are not viable. The Western solution is to control population growth assuming that a huge population merely translates to having more consumers whose needs have to be met given available resources. This way out is not tenable because if the aim of preserving the earth's resources is for the security of future generations, then curbing population growth may not ensure that there will be enough people who will preserve and/or benefit from such measure.

On the other hand, the Eastern solution is through Buddhism's *nirvana*. It suggests reduction of desires to save more. It further suggests the curbing of greed through cessation of all desires. This measure could go against self preservation. One cannot and should not suppress the vital instincts related to the self and to specific preservation; otherwise, future generation's wellbeing could be at stake. The future's welfare could only be assured if the present generation is healthy enough to carry out the needed developmental intervention for growth.

Văn Ðoan proposed a third solution which he calls "care for and by the ancestors." Banking on the natural desire that parents have to improve the lot of their children so that their children are better off than them, he claims that

---

① See Work and Society, Universitas, November 2009, pp. 38 – 39.

parents will strive to provide for the children's present needs in view of the future. Parents will deprive themselves of some legitimate needs to meet the needs of their children. He insists, however, that such parental attitude is something they must pass on to their children. Given the pressure of modern day's consumerist mindset, this could simply be a farfetched idea unless the children are trained in the virtue of frugality having the clear purpose of saving for the future. The family should be true to its calling, since children who have learned to save are grateful for the benefits from the past and will be responsible enough for future preservation.

Reacting to Vãn Ðoan's contribution to the forum, I commented that I fully agree with his insights and pointed out that such solution is an embodiment of the solidarity and intergenerational justice that Benedict XVI speaks of in his encyclical *Caritas in Veritate.* [1]While it takes individual effort to preserve and conserve natural resources, it takes a concerted effort of the whole community to preserve the presently available natural resources. A fundamental aspect of living in a community or state is the cooperative working together of all those who take part in the interlocking, differentiated, mutually supporting single set of activities. [2]Solidarity would entail the judicious use of the available resources for the improvement of the living condition of the populace. Inter-generational justice is giving what is due to the past and future generations by the present generation. To the past, one owes a sense of gratitude shown in the preservation of the gains that were handed on to the present. To the future generation, one

---

[1] Human beings interpret and shape the natural environment through culture, which in turn is given direction by the responsible use of freedom, in accordance with the dictates of the moral law. Consequently, projects for integral human development cannot ignore coming generations, but need to be *marked by solidarity and inter-generational justice*, while taking into account a variety of contexts: ecological, juridical, economic, political and cultural. Vãn Doan, "Caritas in Veritate", p. 48.

[2] John M. Cooper, "Political Animals and Civic Friendship," *Friendship a Political Reader*, Neera Badhwani Kapur, ed. (Ithaca: Cornell University Press, 1993), p. 311

owes the conservation and improvement of what was inherited from the past, and to subsequently pass on as legacy. These attitudes are possible if mutual benevolence exists among contemporaries and generations.

Concern for sustainable development took shape amid widespread consumerism—an attitude that bases the dignity of the person on *having* rather than *being*; hence the desire to have more instead of addressing real needs. Satisfying such desires has strained natural resources. Some key philosophies that led to consumerism are rationalism, positivism, and postmodernism. [1] The facts are explained by the facts themselves and there is nothing mysterious in this universe, as positivists' claim. These ideologies are offshoots of modernism, an attitude that marginalizes the role of religion and faith in the discovery and explanation of the world. Modern man, with his ability to unlock the secrets the universe, began consuming available resources at the rate that surpasses nature's capacity to regenerate or renew itself. The onset of modernist attitudes coincided with the developments in science and technology. This contributed to the shaping of a culture that scorns the idea of something beyond man. "He is convinced that he is the sole author of himself, his life and society." [2] Left to his devices, man becomes a prey of other humans who consider themselves more human than others. Modernity spawned a civilization that glorifies man and history is a witness to a self-caused human degradation. Two mindsets have been at war: the glorification of the individual in liberalism and the primacy of the collective in socialism. However, with the fall of communism came the gaining of liberalism. As members of society, liberals have placed emphasis on their rights to be protected by the state while the individual or the elite few may reign supreme.

---

[1] See Bernardo Villegas, Lloyd Bautista and Guillermo Dionisio. " Genesis of and Antidote to Consumerism," *Selected Papers on Caritas in Veritate: The Philippine Experience*, Caparas, Ma. Victoria, ed. (Philippines: University of Asia and the Pacific, 2010), pp. 52 – 53.

[2] Ibid. , p. 34.

There is a need to be freed from the shackles of liberalist ideals. With liberalism's glorification of the individual and of a lifestyle that gives priority to the self comes the forgetfulness that he is part of a whole. Thus, a mentality that thinks only of the present without due regard for the future is nurtured. Behind this world view is the unawareness of *who* and *what* he is. Many have lost their ground without firmly establishing identities due to the lack of affection and attention found in the family. Man may have forgotten that he is a historical being who owes his present from the past and is called to prepare the future for the next generation.

However, for a generation to take care of the present to secure the future, one must be schooled in a spirit of solidarity and educated to be a good citizen. In the measures proposed for sustainable development the role of the state and policymakers has always been emphasized. Some of the solutions posed marginalize the pivotal role of the building block of society—the family.

In this lecture, I propose to answer why this institution could be the key to sustainable development and that it is *in* the family that conservation of resources for future needs is taught as training in citizenship. I will use Aristotle's notion of the family, citizen and education culled from his *The Politics* and *Nicomachean Ethics*. In developing the topic, I will not venture into the textual interpretations and controversies that haunt Aristotelian scholars.

II   Why Aristotle?

Susan Collins claims that after September 11, 2001 Aristotle's notion of citizenship is being revisited by scholars when they realized that modern liberalism does not provide the adequate answer of what it means to be a citizen. They realized that liberalism's obsession with claiming all sorts of rights and its emphasis on individual freedoms jeopardize the state's interest. Hence, they begin to ask again what it means to be part of a community, what it means to be a citizen. They saw in Aristotle that view that the individual is part of a larger community and that he is ruled by an authority besides their own will or "creative self." Aristotle also added that there is no separation between the public and the private or between the highest end of politics, moral virtue, and the human good. ①The state's role is not simply limited to being the provider and guardian of rights. The State's primary role is being an educator. ②The highest pedagogic aim of civic education is not simply good citizens but morally good citizens with virtues-qualities that make a person and his actions *good*③, and human good is understood as the possession of a comprehensive doctrine of values and beliefs giving life its deepest meaning. ④

What is a citizen?

Aristotle's citizen has as its defining features the participation in the affairs of the state⑤, which proceeds from his birthright⑥. As stated in the foregoing, their main task is the fostering of goodness among the members of the state. A review of Aristotle's notion of the state leads us to the family as basic unit. ⑦Citizenship and the virtues of a citizen lead us to recognize the importance of the family. This is the thesis that I would like to defend in this lecture.

Reading through Aristotle's *The Politics* and *Nicomachean Ethics*, it may

---

① Susan Collins, *Aristotle and the Rediscovery of Citizenship* (New York: Cambridge University Press, 2006).
② "This is confirmed by what happens in states; for legislators make the citizens good by forming habits in them and this is the wish of every legislator." -NE 1103b 3 - 6
③ Every excellence both brings into good conditions the things which of which it is the excellence and makes the work of that thing done well...Therefore, if it is true in every case, the excellence of man also will be the state which makes man good ad which makes him do his own work well." -NE, 1106a 15 - 11
④ Susan Collins, Aristotle and the Kediscorery of Citizenship (New York: Cambring, University press, 2006), p. 40.
⑤ "A citizen in the strictest sense, against whom no such exception can be taken, and his special characteristic is that he shares in the administration of justice, and in offices." Pol. 1275a22 - 23
⑥ "In practice, a citizen is defined to be one of whom both the parents are citizen." -Pol. 1275b 20 - 25
⑦ See Pol. 1252a 25 - 1252b30

seem that such is not the case. On the one hand, based on the nature and the purpose of the family; there seems to be a dichotomy: the family is an association providing the supply of man's everyday wants①while the state is an association of villages that aims more than the supply of daily needs but self-sufficiency and administration of justice. ②Aristotle also distinguished the values that rule in the family and the state. Friendship reigns in the family while justice is for the state. ③Moreover, membership in the family is by blood while in the state that of being born as a free man. A person may belong to the family even he is a slave while a citizen of the state are those who are free. The virtues proper to family members are different from those of a citizen. ④

On the other hand, some texts may defend my position. In *The Politics*, Aristotle, traces the genetic development of the state from the family. He explicitly states that the family is the primary unit of the polis and is the natural offshoot of the union between a man and a woman who come together for the continuance of the race. The procreative act answers man's need to leave behind an image of him. ⑤The family answers man's basic needs⑥and could do so through its activity of *household management*, part of which is *wealth management* or the acquisition and preservation of wealth. ⑦The household manager's end is self-sufficiency understood as having the needed means to survive and raise a family and to contribute to the needs of the society. ⑧However, the Stagirite emphasizes

---

①   See Pol. 1252b 15
②   Pol 1252 b 30
③   " Parents seems by nature to feel it (friendship) for offspring and offspring for parents.... " -NE
    1155a15 and "But justice is the bond of men in states..." Pol. 1253a
④   "The good man "is he who has a single excellence which is perfect excellence while "the excellence
    of the citizen must therefore be relative to the constitution. " -Pol. 1276b 30 and 34
⑤   Pol. 1252a 25 – 30
⑥   See Pol. 1252b 15
⑦   See Pol. 1256a1 – 1259a35
⑧   See Pol, 1253b25, 1256b30

that wealth management is only a means to live and live well①. Living well implies self-sufficiency which encompasses satisfaction of bodily needs and the ability to contribute to the wellbeing of others. ②The ultimate end of household management is the attainment of moral excellence of its members. ③The burden of moral training rests on the father. Thus, Aristotle argues against Plato's community of wives and children. He reasons that for the identification of children, it would be better for the community that there should be one man to one woman. A person who knows that he is the father of the child is more conscious of his responsibilities for the child's upbringing. ④

The acquisition of virtues is a result of study, experience and training. Teaching rather than discovery facilitates acquisition of intellectual virtues whereas habituation helps develop moral virtues. For both, the process of acquisition demands that another person helps the one in need of the virtue because no one is born possessing the virtues. ⑤Moral virtues are learned by doing. ⑥It is not enough to know what the needed virtues for a happy life are. One has to put them into use. ⑦

---

① "For no man can live well or indeed live at all, unless he is provide with necessities." -Pol. 1253b25

② "By self-sufficient we do not mean that which is sufficient for a man by himself, for one who lives a solitary life, but also for parents, children, wife, and in general for his friends and fellow citizens, since man is born for citizenship." -NE 1097a9 – 11

③ Pol. 1259b 20. For the Athenian moral education is primarily the burden of the family; hence they saw the need to preserve the institution of the preservation of the state. Thus "while Sparta deliberately destroyed the family, Athens aimed to preserve it as a means of developing and shaping personality and placed upon it the burden of education. -Paul Monroe, A Brief Course in the History of Education (New York: The McMillan Co., 1969), p. 40.

④ "For that which is common to the greatest number has the least care bestowed upon it. Everyone thinks chiefly of his own; hardly at all of the common interest; and only when he I himself concerned as an individual. For besides other considerations everybody is more inclined to neglect something which eh expects another to fulfill..." -Pol. 12621 35 – 40

⑤ "For if this were not so, there would have been no need of a teacher, but all men would have been born good or bad at their craft." -NE 1103b10

⑥ Ibid. 1103a 27 – 32

⑦ "Men of experience succeed better than those who have theory but without experience." - Metaphysics 891a 13 – 15

Study is also important because one must strive to perform the right actions in every circumstance. He needs the intellectual habits that will facilitate the practice of actions that lead to his true end and will determine the proper course of action in each of them. The will also has to be trained in wanting, choosing and accomplishing these deeds. The right actions are those guided by right reason understood as the mean between excess and defect because the extremes lead not to the virtue but to vices. The criterion for distinguishing virtuous action from vicious ones is not a fixed limit. It is not based on quantitative determination of what is the average between the two extremes but is something to be determined in the moment an action is to be performed. This requires knowledge of the principles and demands that the person experiences the deliberation and decision making moments of the act.

On the proper course of action two standards are used in judging whether an action is virtuous: the objective and the subjective. The objective dimension is the expectation of the community for what constitutes a good habit. It is the standard set by the community. The subjective dimension is what is relative to the person when performing an act, that is, an act may be a show of magnanimity for one but a pettiness for another.

Virtues are developed through the repetition of the same acts of a particular virtue. In the performance of the virtuous act, the person gains the facility for the execution of the same acts that produce virtue in the person. Virtues incline the person to make the same choice for the same kind of activity. Since virtues have a double dimension its effects also facilitate both the flourishing of goodness in the community and in the person performing the acts. This communitarian dimension of the act requires that the immediate society facilitate the practice of the virtues; thus the need for right laws and as standards of goodness and habituation to curb the passions. In addition, the person in a struggle to be virtuous must be surrounded by other persons who can serve as role models and teachers by example. Teaching and training are indispensable for character formation. A person becomes good by habituation and not by chance. In the household, this is the task of the head of the household.

Household management ensures attainment of the good life for the members of the household and the other members of society if the household head possesses the needed prudence to discern the order of things.

Of the virtues that the members of the family must possess, Aristotle underscores the importance of justice and temperance in varying degrees. This means that the head of the family or the father possesses the virtue in a more prefect state than the children and his wife because the virtue is practiced given their own situations and functions. ①Temperance is the virtue that regulates the appetite's craving for pleasure and self-indulgence. ②Justice is the virtue that regulates one's relationship with others③and seeks to do what is of benefit to the other. ④That what is just is based on existing laws. ⑤The family is ruled by the father, who exercises moral leadership in the household. He issues laws to his children and wife; assuring that the moral code is transmitted and instilled. ⑥

A quasi-virtue allied to justice that facilitates moral formation is friendship. Friendship spurs the union between a man and a woman,⑦ the foundation of

---

①   Pol. 1259b 30 – 35

②   "A self-indulgent man craves for all pleasant things or those that ate most pleasant, and is lead by his appetite to choose these at the cost of everything else; hence he is pained both when he fails to get them and when he is craving for them." -NE 1119 1 – 5

③   "Justice is that kind of state which makes people disposed to do what is just and makes them act justly and wish for what is just." -NE 1129a 5 – 10.

④   See NE 1130a 5

⑤   "All lawful acts are in a sense just acts; for the acts laid down by the legislative art are lawful and each of these we say is just. Now the laws in al their enactments on all subjects aim at the common advantage either if all or of the best of all those who hold power, or something of the sort; so that in one sense we call those acts that are just that tend to produce happiness and its components for the political society." -NE 1129b 10 – 20

⑥   See Pol. 1252b 20 – 25

⑦   It was for this reason that the various institutions of a common social life-marriage connections, kin groups, religious gatherings and social pastimes-arose in the cities. But this institutions are the business of friendship-Pol 1280b 35 – 38

parental educational task①and this keeps the family together. Friendship is naturally found in families because parents love their children as soon as they are born and siblings love each other for having come from the same set of parents. ②The essence of friendship wishing the good of the other and in its perfect form, it is wishing the good of the other *for the other's sake* and such is present in the parents. ③The qualifier *for the other's sake* is important because all men act in view of some good that fulfills one's longing. Men seek friends because friends make their lives complete. ④

III   The Family and Sustainable Development

Friendship, justice and temperance are the keys to sustainable development found in the family.

Aristotle mentioned that when men are friends there is no need for justice. ⑤It was stated at the beginning of this paper that sustainable development could be assured through the practice of intergenerational justice and solidarity. The good life, characterized by self-sufficiency, does not mean just the possession

---

① The friendship of kinsmen itself, while it seems to be of many kind appears to depend in every case on parental friendship; for parents love their children as being part of themselves and children their parents as having themselves originated from them. -NE 1161b 16 – 19

② NE 1161b 25 – 30

③ NE 1156b 5 – 10

④ "For without friends no one would choose to live. Though he had all other goods; even rich men and those in possession of office and of dominating power are thought to need friends most of all; for what is the use of such prosperity without the opportunity of beneficence, which is exercised chiefly and in its most laudable form towards friends?" -NE 1155a 5 – 10

⑤ "Friendship seems to hold states together, and lawgivers to care more for it than justice; for unanimity seems to be something like friendship, and this they aim at most of all, and expel faction as their worst enemy; and when men are friends they have no need for justice, while when they are just they need friendship as well, and the truest form of justice is thought to be a friendly quality. " -NE 1155a 20 – 30

of external goods enough to live not wanting on basic needs. It includes loved ones, fame and honor. Among the goods that one could count is the presence of other human beings with whom a *sufficient life* could be shared, which for Aristotle is the enjoyment of a minimum of material wellbeing not for enjoyment's sake but for sharing these material goods with others, especially with one's friends. ①Friendship, as an ally of justice necessarily includes *benevolence* because the demands of justice would not be met without the good will of those with the duty to meet needs.

On the other hand, satisfaction of the debts needs the gratitude that comes with the recognition that a good deed has been done. Recognition is an element present in friendship. Thus, friendship binds the members of the community in the pursuit of a good in which one's own good is at stake. Moreover, since one needs a friend to live well, persons will not be seen as competitors for good things in life. They in fact provide occasions for doing good deeds for others. A good person sees the other as someone like oneself who helps him to become a better person. Friends rejoice in the good fortune of others because at the core of a life well lived is in treating people kindly, and justly and leaving them better and happier than they were before. ②

Aristotle's family is not an isolated piece or the individual members of this basic institution; rather his vision of the individual and the family are incomplete. They are not self-sufficient and still need the community to live as human beings should. Thus Aristotle comments that he who is not part of the state is either a beast or a god. ③Justice is the virtue that perfects man, making

---

① NE 1097b 9 – 11

② Lorraine Smith Pangle, *Aristotle and the Philosophy of Friendship* (Cambridge: Cambridge University Press, 2003), p. 199.

③ "Man is by nature a political animal. And he who by nature and not by mere accident is without a state is either a bad man or above humanity. "-Pol. 1253a 1 – 5

him attentive to the needs of the others by being temperate. ①

Temperance is the virtue that restricts the appetite in the pursuit of needed goods for living well. It rules both personal and societal limits set by demands of the practice of liberality②and its usefulness for the household and the state. ③Therefore, needs are met without sacrificing one's health—an element necessary for the good life. ④One could be self-effacing but not to the extent of losing one's life to preserve the planet for future generations.

As stated at the beginning of this lecture, solidarity and intergenerational justice are essential values to address concerns of sustainable development. The family is the best place for values to take roots since solidarity is learned through the quasi-virtue of friendliness, while the virtues of justice and temperance are explicitly cultivated in preparation for the participation in community affairs. To be a citizen is to participate in the deliberation of justice. The virtue of justice would entail living temperance, a quality that restrains man from wanton destruction of resources to satisfy one's needs. Temperance would also limit satisfaction of desires to what is needed to live well, which is not to live in

---

① "For man, when he is perfected, is the best of animals, but when separated form law and justice, he is the worst of all; ...That is why if he has not the excellence, he is the most unholy and the most savage of all animals; and the most full and glutton. But justice is the bond of men in states; for the administration of justice, which is the determination of what is just, is the principle of order in political society." -Pol. 1253a 30 – 40

② "Liberality is the virtue that concerns giving and taking of wealth." -NE. 1119b 20

③ "The art of household management must either find ready to hand, or itself provide, such things necessary to life and useful for the community of the family or the state, as can be stored. They are the elements of true riches; for the amount of property which is needed to the good life is not unlimited...But there is a boundary fixed...and riches may be defined as a number of instruments to e used in a household or in a state." -Pol. 1256b25 – 35

④ Among the external goods that satisfies man are "good birth, plenty of friends, good friends, wealth, good children, plenty of children, a happy old age, also such bodily excellences as health, beauty, strength, large stature, athletic powers, together with fame, honor, good luck, and virtue. A man cannot fail to be completely independent if he possesses these internal and these external goods; for besides these there are no others to have. (Goods of the soul and of the body are internal. Good birth, friends, money, and honor are external.) Further, we think that he should possess resources and luck, in order to make his life really secure" -Rhetoric 1360b 20 – 25

abundance but sufficient for self-maintenance, support one's family and help society.

As seen from the foregoing, the moral education the family provides can directly contribute to sustainable development through the parental duty filled with love that inculcates in the children to care for the others, and acquire and use only what is needed to live well.

Bibliography

Badhwani Kapur, Neera. ed. *Friendship a Political Reader*, Ithaca: Cornell University Press, 1993

Barnes, J. *The Complete Works of Aristotle*, Vol. II. Princeton University Press, New Jersey, 1984.

Benedict, XVI. *Caritas in Veritate* Vatican: Vatican Press, 2009.

Caparas, Ma. Victoria, ed. *Selected Papers on Caritas in Veritate The Philippine Experience*, Philippines: University of Asia and the Pacific, 2010.

Collins, Susan. *Aristotle and the Rediscovery of Citizenship*, New York: Cambridge University Press, 2006.

Monroe, Paul. *A Brief Course in the History of Education*, New York: The McMillan Co. , 1969.

Pangle, Lorraine Smith. *Aristotle and the Philosophy of Friendship*, Cambridge: Cambridge University Press, 2003.

Sherman, Nancy. *The Fabric of Character Aristotle's Theory of Virtue*, Oxford: Clarendon Press, 1989.

问题探讨

A Study on New Life-Cultural Movements for Oneness Focused on Neohumans' Culture & Futurology

Han Gang-Hyen [*]

Abstract：The study found that traffic was linked to 8% of heart attacks. The study on all the scriptures of the east and the west found that the basis of knowledge and wisdom is in heaven. The Palm 111：10 records，"The fear of the LORD is the beginning of wisdom". The Buddhism records，'悉有佛性'과'见性成佛'. The scriptures of Confucianism write，'知天命'과'顺天'. I found that Those words above indicate the original hometown of human beings and the wisdom that suggests humans to move forward. Ancient scriptures predicted information about the words of wisdom，the value of new era，the vision about human future in a hundred years and a thousand years ago. The writer of this paper will examine the contents focusing on the new cultural movement and Dream Society in Future of neohumans that was studied through ancient scriptures and prophetic books. I am sure it will lead the world culture of a new era for One world. The Advent of Neohumans and New Life-Cultural Movements（新生命苏生运动）은 will overcome the limit and crisis

---

* Han Gang-Hyen，Secretary General of IANC，International Academy of Neohumans Culture.

of modern materialistic civilization and be an alternative for opening a new era. So they are valuable. The new spiritual culture of saving life and the rising of a public philosophy happening in Korea will be a saving philosophy（救世救援）that will establish the world mainstream culture to lead the 21st century, solve the inner emptiness and unhappiness of humanity and plant a core value. Therefore, this paper will suggest the vision and the future of human being, the mainstream culture, a spiritual culture, a new wind, and the promising perspective. It is important and valuable.

Keywords：New Life-Cultural Movements；Saving Philosophy；Dream Society

以新人类文化和未来学为核心的一体化新生命文化运动研究

韩康炫

摘　要：研究发现，交通与 8% 的心脏病发作相关。所有东西方经文研究表明，知识和智慧源自上天。《圣经》记载，"敬畏耶和华乃是知识之始"。佛教记载，"悉有佛性"和"见性成佛"。儒家经文写道，"知天命"和"顺天"。我发现上述的那些话都表明了人类以及推动人类前进的智慧的最初故乡。古代经文在 1100 年前就预言了智慧名言，新时代价值，以及人类未来视野的相关信息。笔者在本文将通过古代经文和预言书重点考察新人类未来梦想社会的新文化运动。我相信这将引领新时代的世界文化。新人类的出现和新生命苏生运动的出现将克服现代物质文明的极限和危机，成为开启新时代的一个选择。因此它们是有价值的。韩国关于挽救生命的新型精神文化以及大众哲学的崛起将是一个救世救援哲学，这一哲学将建立起引领 21 世纪的世界主流文化，解决人类内心的空虚和不快，培养核心价值。因此，本文将提出人类的视野与未来、主流文化、精神文化、新风以及发展前景之间的关系，这非常重要且很有价值。

关键词：新生命苏生运动　救世哲学　梦想社会

I Introduction

Today' humanity is facing Singularity or the critical point that changes the principle of the universe, the core value of all things' lives and a cultural feature. So far, we have lived in the mechanical paradigm with dividing philosophies and stereotype which recognize you and I as others and understood all things and alive things as isolated individual ones or conflicting existences. They fought each other and killed. Now the writer of this paper will call the Universe's Life-Theory Paradigm, this thinks of all living things as the other selves of the life of the universe's life, regards them as one lump, one tree, and one body that cannot be divided. Although they are individually living, cultures have separated from the whole, they are connected by life and spirit and are tied by the universal net. That is, it is a view of regarding organic bodies, inorganic substances, seen revealed order of life, the basis of life not only seen but also not seen, and even the order of the universe hidden by the utmost Holy Spirit as one living form like one body and one tree. That is a view of Holistic Ontology from the new view of the universe of life and the heart of the universe. To save all decaying and dying things and the earth is the core of a movement of saving life. Due to the mamonism and the harmful effects that put first the rapid development of materialistic civilization and individual interest socioculturally, people are losing their dream and even their existence's values. It is urgent to re-find the dignity of man, and the Asian core value and culture of life.

To overcome all humanity difficulties and crisis, first we need to change our thought and to develop our mind, and to level our awareness up. Now is the time when we realize their nature. As originally humanity was God, the original hometown of life', we should awake our spirit, and change our value, which get out of the two-dimensional consciousness such as trivial illusion and desire; money, material, wealth and honor. If one's consciousness is not leveled up and one's divine nature lacks, they will have problems in joining the mainstream toward the new world and cannot follow it. Now is the time to wake up that the era of light that neohumans lead is opening now.

II The Movement of Saving life and the Culture of Neohumans

The period of advent of the movement of saving life and neohumans is the late 20th century according to a prophetic books. The words of wisdom about the future were predicted by the life form of the universe and the main body of the Holy Spirit a hundred years and a thousand years. However, due to the power of Satan that grips the authority of death, the nature of heaven which ruled the life of the universe was locked. It lost its autonomous power destruction of life, and became old heaven which did not have the power of survival preservation. All humanity of the world have waited for the advent of the existence that will emancipate and save all things that are locked by the spirit of darkness, the spirit of death, and remove death（衰病死葬）.

1. New Heaven and the Movement of Saving Life

Studying today's future in the world of scriptures and classics, human beings have waited for the man of heaven, the Victor Messiah in the Bible, the Maitreya Buddha in the Bible, a saint that is the true man, and Jeongdoryeong in the east who will open a new world from thousands of years ago.

Here, New Heaven means a strong man of heaven who can overcome the spirit of Satan, the basic spirit of "Ego", false consciousness, can remove the spirit of death. The Korean religious movement call the changing period of this new heaven and new earth the Big Change. The Korean religious movement that is removing the old heaven and the world where all things cannot but die, that is opening a new immortal world（不死世界）started 150 years ago. Also this prediction was foretold through Gyeokamyourok（格庵遗录）around 500 years ago. It was revealed through thousands years ago through relics and ancient books. Now we are entering into the era of neohumans where the final steps of movement of saving life bear its fruits. That is, the movement of saving life means the recovery movement of the universal vitality that is the work of changing the three. That movement indicates that it will to revive heaven, earth, and humanity including all things. The factor that makes the movement of saving life possible is the advent of the Victor, the Maitreya Buddha. However, it is the top secret of heaven to the dark and sinful world, 'who appears as the Maitreya Buddha, how and where he comes'.

2. The Hidden Secret of New Heaven

Due to the advent of the Victor Maitreya Buddha in the late 20th, the dark world is becoming bright, the basic root of humanity and the hidden secret of new heaven starts to be revealed. The Victor tells the original hometown of human beings, preaches the great righteous Tao of heaven, and produce the second neohuman, third neohuman, the citizens of the new world by awaking the dark spirit and divine nature with the Sweet Dew. Until the Victor who can recover the lost paradise and destroy the authority of death appears, details of new heaven, new earth and the fostering of neohumans should be hidden as the secret of heaven. Also, the advent of the Victor in the Bible and the light era of the Sweet Dew Water（the Symbol of the Victor, the essence of mandala flower rain in the Amita utmost joy land, and the hidden manna of heaven）are the top secret of heaven. I will introduce about it later.

Thanks to the Victor's revealing the hidden secret of heaven, the way of all humanity recovering their original figure and reaching nirvana was opened. Additionally, He have fostered neohumans, developed the movement of saving life, and preached to advise all humanity to positively join the movement in order for them to become one.

3. The Singularity of Values view

The Global village（地球村）of the 21st century is facing the era of the universe. However, due to the explosive population growth, they have food problems, water shortages, the destruction of environment and ecosystem, and the exhaustion of resource. The fierce struggle and conflicts for existence between humanity become serious as well. Now human beings stand on the Singularity, the critical point, which needs the change of the existing worldly cultures and the change of awareness that one should replan new qualitative improvement, true happiness and a valuable life beyond the level of consciousness seeking materialistic affluence and vain values. No matter how much money one has and no matter how one has all things what one wants to have, they cannot keep it forever. Moreover, enjoying them and satisfying them make their false owners' consciousness happy. Being accomplished in desire, they are a momentary happiness and make people catch diseases and die.

This era is facing the Singularity that undergo a change in values, "where we should put a core value". There are futurists who anticipate the advent of neohumans. That is, it means that we welcome a new era when new values and a new culture are established also in the field of society, politics, culture, religion, and scientifical technology. That is, now is the critical point that gets out of ignorant philosophy that sticked money, wealth and honor, the faith view of going to heaven after death, causes a revolution to save immortal life and makes consciousness level rise by rethinking of what is the most valuable, what true happiness is, and for what we should live.

4. The New Cultural Movement of Neohumans

Neohumans who become global citizens in the new era received the secrets of heaven, which are about eternal life that all humanity has dreamed, and they already started to establish a new culture. That is the movement of saving life. Neohumans are ones who were reborn as the men of heaven, who can live forever enjoying infinite happiness, they will have a leading role in building the paradise. Their new culture is beyond agelessness, it is the cultural movement of new men, that is based on an immortal science and is a new science for coexistence and co prosperity. Plus neohumans open a way that all human being live harmoniously and peacefully. They are studying and learning the secret of living happily forever through their new culture. Such new learning and cultures are presented for the first time in history. It is the work of the Holy Spirit, and receives attention as the supreme spiritual movement.

On the other hand, they were persecuted and despised by the existing religions of low level and western religious groups. However, when the global village is confused and is wandering about their existing culture and philosophies, the new philosophy and culture of neohumans are the door of salvation, their value and importance are revealed.

(1) The Definition of Neohumans and Their Roles

The Definition of Neohumans

The men being reborn as the Holy Spirit are ones to reinstate the original essence. They are changed into the men of God spiritually and physically. They exist and will live forever eating the Sweet Dew, not eating worldly food. When the big change is ripe, they can be changed into light. Nostradamus said Neohumans, as other existence. They are angels who will realize the paradise, they are transcendent of not only eating but also In-Yang (阴 阳), like Jeremiah says in the Bible. In the new era, people neither will get married nor deliver babies nor fight. They will regard everybody as themselves by practicing one body philosophy. Also, they are sane existences who are reborn as the Holy Spirit, are not conscious of others, are free from agonies and diseases, and are always happy. Besides, they do not cause population problems, food problems, and environment problems. Further they are free from the restraint of time and space, do not hold funeral because they do not die in an immortal society.

The Role of Neohumans

Their role is to build heaven and to lead humanity to heaven by practicing big love and sacrifice. Gyeoamyourok writes that as the building of heaven did not exist so far and people live in ignorance and sins, neohumans are mocked and blamed by people and few people participate at the work of heaven. When the message spreads to the world, people will crowd to Korea to seek the food of life according to prophetic books. Therefore, the roles of neohumans become the foundation of heaven. It will become a leading role of heaven, and will lead all humanity to the paradise. God planted his strategy to recover the Garden of Eden in every scriptures and prophetic books. We can see who is the Savior through them. "Gyeoamyourok（格庵遗录）" has a key to solve hidden ciphers in the prophetic books and scriptures. So to know 「Gyeoamyourok」is very important in reading them.

（2）A Study on the Prophecies of Neohumans' Advent

There are a lot of the classics and prophetic books which predicted the advent of neohumans in the world. The prophecies in the Bible, the Buddhist books, 「San hyegyeong（山海经）」, "Gyeokamyourok（格庵遗录）" are representative. In Korea, there were outstanding predictors who cannot be compared with other countries. Among world prophetic books, Korean "Gyeokamyourok" is the master key of all prophecies.

What is "Gyeoamyourok（格庵遗录）"?

"Gyeoamyourok（格庵遗录）", a Korean prophetic book. It is a representative of Korean prophetic books. It was written by Namsago 450 years ago. His nickname is Gyeokam. He was born in Gyeongsang province in 1509. He was an expert in astronomy. When he was young, he met one transcendent person and received the predictions about the future of Korea and the world from him. He recorded the prophecies in this book. The book was registered in the National Central Library. So you can read it there.

This prophetic book written by Nam Sa-Go （南师古）, after receiving the revelation of heaven around 500 years ago is famous for a book of God （神书）. It has a master key to solve the secrets of heaven existing in prophetic books in the world. Therefore, its predictions about the Victor Jongdoryeong and the era of neohumans were minutely and concretely. It is so persuasive that Korean new religious groups and spiritual leaders often cite the book to establish their authority. "Gyeokamyourok" records that the Sweet Dew Water （甘露水 = soma 酒 of New Heaven） is the light of Dharma that the Maitreya Buddha emits, that is spiritual manna that neohumans eat.

As all prophecies were sealed thoroughly so as not to be interpreted easily, this book was recorded by splitting Chinese letters or metaphor so as not to be solved easily, too. As the predictions of「Gyeoamyourok」have 100 percent accuracy, people cannot but believe it. It foretold the day of Yee dynasty's collapse and the ending day of the Japanese colonial period in Korea, the attack of the Japanese upon Korea in 1592, the attack of the Chinese, and the Korean War in 1950. It also suggested ways to survive during those wars. Furthermore, the book foretold that the Korean peninsula would be divided, face and fight each other between the 38th Parallel and build Panmunjeom after the Korean War. As well, it predicted the family names or hometowns of all Korean presidents. Above all, the most important prediction of the book is that the Savior will appear in Korea, His symbol is the Sweet Dew, He will revenge all humans' enemies, and build an immortal world and universe. Also the book writes that the tree of life by the river of life in Revelation of the Bible will grow a lot by the Savior. When the Japanese read the book, they were afraid of it, because the book has huge secrets about Korea and gave the Koreans a lot of hope. It also predicted that Korea would be the strongest country, be the parents' country of all humans, and all the people of the world are supposed to come to Korea. Hallyu is a part of it.

Also "Gyeoamyourok" said that epidemic diseases would sweep the world, the diseases would be so dreadful, if people catch the disease in the morning, and they will die in the evening. It also suggests a survival way against the disaster in the book. "Gyeoamyourok" is the master key of solving predictions of all prophecies and scriptures, however it is written in hidden code, everybody cannot interpret it. When the Victor appears and reveals the secret of heaven, the predictions of the prophetic books are supposed to be revealed completely. So far, I told about the secret of New heaven in "Gyeoamyourok".

III   One World & Dream Society

In the 21th century, people will welcome a new era where they will not die, but will live forever enjoying the utmost joy. However, if one is not changed by the movement of saving life and the culture of life that the organism of the universe leads, their new life in this era will not be. The future society is the era of light where all humanity will become one. The dream society will be realized, the change of thought and value for the new movement of saving life is urgent. According to the Buddhist scriptures such as the Nirvana Sutra, Amita Sutra, the Maitreya Sutra, Avatamska Sutra, and Dharma Flower Sutra, if the Maitreya Buddha who emits the Sweet Dew Water appears, there is neither death nor anguish and delusion. The utmost joy land will be accomplished. Additionally, the Bible predicts the new world, the peaceful dream society, will be built.

The Bible and all the prophecies of heaven announce that people will see a new heaven and a new earth in keeping with his promise. According to 2 Petro 3: 13; Isaiah 65: 17, 'a New Heaven' and 'a New Earth' are not just words. The Bible foretells that a real new heaven and new earth will be constructed completely in Psalm 89: 36 – 37 and Psalm 104: 5. Therefore, 'the New Earth' will be the righteous dream society where one becomes a neohuman on the earth. 'The New Heaven' will be new spiritual government (天国) with spiritual leadership that will rule the dream society. Further, Revelations 21: 1 – 22: 5 of the Bible records about the dream society in detail.

1. Looking ahead Dream Society & Human Future

Also in accordance to the Bible, the dream society will be totally different from the modern society.

Isaiah 11: 6 – 9 and Hosea 2: 18 records, "The wolf will live with the lamb, the leopard will lie down with the goat, the calf and the lion and the yearling together; and a little child will lead them. The cow will feed with the bear, their young will lie down together, and the lion will eat straw like the ox. The infant will play near the hole of the cobra, and the young child put his hand into the viper's nest. They will neither harm nor destroy on all my holy mountain. "

Also according to in Isaiah 33: 24, all diseases and physical personal discomfort will be cured. God promised "No one living in Zion will say, 'I am ill' " . Additionally, According to Revelation 21: 4 in the Bible "He will wipe every tear from their eyes. There will be no more death or mourning or crying or pain, for the old order of things has passed away" and there are a lot of phases about the future society. God promised in Psalm46: 9 and Isaiah2: 4, "He makes wars cease to the ends of the earth" . The Bible writes that the whole earth will be recovered as the paradise.

According to Isaiah 35: 1, 6, 7, "the desert and the parched land will be glad; the wilderness will rejoice and blossom. Like the crocus, water will gush forth in the wilderness and streams in the desert. The parched ground shall become a pool, the thirsty land springs of water. "

Furthermore, the Bible said there is no more reason that people will not be happy. And Psalm 67: 6; 72: 16 record that people will not be hungry. The dream society will not be built by itself but it will depend on how people will live with what core values and the philosophy of bright life.

(1) Futurology and the truth of prophecy

Futurology is a learning to study the future of human beings, it needs to understand the meaning and feature of future well. The future has a relationship with the life of the present. It has meanings of not only the tomorrow of today but al the today of tomorrow. It is like identical twins, and it is on the connection of time. That is, the future is influenced by the present, it is the production of humanity's present behaviors. So the future is the mirror of the present. Also there is a factor which influences on the present. Today is the portrait of the past, the present face and the body condition are 'the portrait of mind', the results of one's past values, thoughts and behaviors.

Therefore, the basic aim of futurology is to announce the whole change trend, to anticipate the desirable condition of the future, and to suggest the direction of selection. It also helps ultimately optimal decisions-making and choosing alternatives, and suggest feasible concrete things. In modern society, futurology become an essential learning to the managers of companies or in decision making departments. Studying the future is not for foretelling but for forecasting. Also prophecy is different from forecasting in methodology. It can anticipate and foretell through the spiritual inspiration of light transcending time and space.

There are many futurologists including Ray Kurzweil who forecast and insist that the dream society of the 21st century will come also in the aspect of scientifical technology. Ray Kurzweil used a term, 'Singularity' to express the moment scientific technology transcends humanity. The writer of this paper wants to say that 'Singularity' comes in all areas such as learning, religion, and all kinds of science. The Critical Points, that is the limit of science that humanity can neither be happy and nor live forever with the scientific technology, already came. Therefore, the wind of humanities' revival is blowing in Korea and advanced countries. To know the future is important because we can prepare for it today. According to the prophetic books and the scriptures, the era of light will come soon. Next I will explain how the era of light will be built scientifically.

(2) The Era of Brilliant Light and the Spiritual Food of Neohumans

God used different names of the Savior of each religion and planted His plans in each scriptures of each religion to save all humans, so He is in every scripture of each religion. Actually, all His teaching in every scripture is about the hidden manna and the era of light. Now the era of immortality which is that of light has already started. All things are light. These words have been revealed by today's quantum physicists. Every material is composed of molecules; molecules are formed by drawing atoms. Atoms are formed by nucleus and electrons. Nucleus is composed of protons and neutrons, scientists call these (proton, neuron) nucleon. Three quarks are bound by gluon in nucleon. The quark in nucleon is a kind of a particle of light. Like this, the smallest unit of all material is a particle of light. Physicists call this an elementary particle. Above we examined that all things are formed by light, but they are caught by soul of darkness. Light is a living material with consciousness. Therefore, light is not just light. Light that forms all things has its own consciousness according to today's quantum physicists.

Today's quantum physic reveals that light which is the source of all things has its own consciousness through Sans lit experiment, the experiment of electron paramagnetic resonance, the experiment of Classer and Friedman, and several experiments from different angles. The reason we have consciousness is because the light that forms our bodies has consciousness. Therefore, having consciousness is not only humans' privilege. Now it is revealed that all plants have high consciousness, in a way, they have more eminent awareness than humans according to a lot of researchers including Clive Baxter, and Marcello Vogel, the co-authorship with Peter Tomkins Christopher Bud of "the world of spirit of plants". Humans' body is spirit （灵） and the mass of light. As all things are formed by light, humans' bodies are formed by light, too.

Elementary particle which is the particle of light forms nucleon, nucleons form an atomic nucleus. Nucleons are formed by drawing elementary particle, atomic nucleus are formed by drawing nucleons. Surrounding an atomic nucleus, electrons that have a different character from nucleus go around nucleus. That is an atom. The atoms form molecule that is the smallest unit that has the character of material. The molecules form blood, the source of our lives. And the blood forms our bodies' cells. Our bodies are formed by ten trillions of cells according to medical scientists. Like this, actually our bodies are formed by light. In other words, our bodies are the mass of light.

For the first time, Kirlian of old Russia revealed that humans radiate light, through photographs that were taken by a camera with the function of high frequency. Now, it is the time when advanced machineries which can check the health condition of humans are developed. Then, why are humans somber and dark though they are formed by light?

Why do they grow old and die in pains? Because their bright spirit is locked by the soul of darkness. All things were God that is light, but they were changed into sinners by being caught by Satan of darkness. Today quantum physicists say in one voice that all things in the universe are caught in a trap. Being in a trap means being captivated. According to the theory of string, the universe is connected by one string. This incomplete theory will be clearly explained by reading my book about one body philosophy which is the principle of one tree. Let's examine the principle that the universe is one.

First, examining the condition of atom, electrons go around the nucleus, protons captivates neutron using powerful nuclear force in the nucleus. If people break up the nucleus artificially, neutrino （中性微子） in neutrons bounces out from the nucleus. This phenomenon is the liberty of God that is caught. Whenever people perform the experiment, neutrinos bounce out from the nucleus and win freedom. This means that neutrinos are caught.

Second, there are several nucleons in a nucleus, protons and neutrons that are nucleons have three quarks, which are tied by chain called by gluon. Quantum physicists call this condition the confinement of quark. What does this mean? It says that quarks, the smallest unit of light, are caught.

Third, Einstein said that the universe is like a huge closed box. Therefore, any materials in the universe cannot get out of the universe. This explains the principle of the universe that the soul of darkness, which captivates light, rules the universe using stronger power than the energy of light. Even light cannot get out of the universe because of the gravity that Satan draws. If people become a victor who overcomes the soul of Satan and are free from self-consciousness, the condition reverses.

Fourth, material is in the condition that free frequency is caught in limited space by the soul of Satan. I mentioned above that the particle that is the smallest unit of material is not only the particle of light but also frequency like electromagnetic wave. This is revealed by modern physics.

All things and humans are dark because bright spirit is captivated by evil and dark spirit. It is like wrapping bright lamps with dark cloth. If the Victor removes the dark spirit, all things and humans will be changed into brilliant light.

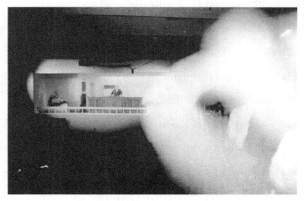

The picture is the Holy Dew Spirit of the Victor who overcame his consciousness

In addition, the Victor in Korea said, thirty years ago, "people can be turned into flying beings that move faster than airplanes in a moment." That is a hint about a new era. Like you looked at the brilliant light, the Sweet Dew, above, the appearing of the Sweet Dew means the advent of a brilliant living being that removed dark soul and overcame it. So I say, as God promised, in scriptures and prophetic books, "the Reincarnate Maitreya Buddha overcame the spirit of Satan and appeared wearing a man's body to save people who are caught and are dying by the spirit of Satan."

God of light lost to the spirit of Satan, dark spirit, 6000 years ago. Hebrews 2: 14 says, "Since the children have flesh and blood, he too share in their humanity so that by death he might destroy him who holds the power of death, that is, the devil. Therefore, the Bible and "Gyeokamyourok" coincide in saying that Satan has the authority of death. Because of this, the children of God were destined to die; all things become bad and die.

Because god made secret plans in a poor situation, predicted His plans, after a long time of His efforts, He won Satan and appeared in the world as the Victor God. 4 – 2 in the nature part of Reincarnate Maitreya Buddha of Great Nirvana Sutra volume5 says, "Dying means that bodies collapse and are finished. However, here is no death. That is because of the Sweet Dew. This Sweet Dew is true nirvana." The Reincarnate Maitreya Buddha is the man who attained nirvana. The above sentences are interpreted that the Sweet Dew is the Reincarnate Maitreya Buddha who reached nirvana. What is nirvana? Nirvana is to get out of desire, anger, and ignorance; it is not easy like people take off dirty and tainted clothes. Because the basic root of desire, anger, and ignorance is Satan that locks God. Nirvana means true freedom when the Buddha (God) kills the spirit of Satan which captivates Buddha (God) in humans. The advent of the Sweet Dew means that God became a Victor by overcoming Satan, which is consciousness of humans and grasps the authority of death. It means that God of the beginning won Satan finally. Eunbiga part of [Gyeokamyourok] says that three Gods are combined into one and comes one body. This man is the Reincarnate Maitreya Buddha; He appears with the Sweet Dew. The Reincarnate Maitreya Buddha is the Victor God and Jeongdoryeong. At the end of times, three saints come to the world as one person.

The Reincarnate Maitreya Buddha (the Savior of Buddhists), Jeongdoryeong (the Savior of Koreans), always emits the Sweet Dew according to the scriptures. Therefore, Malunlon part of "Gyeokamyourok" writes, "He seems like a man but he is never a human, 'He is God wearing human's body". Additionally, He appears with the Sweet Dew. The men who receive this light never die and are changed into brilliant light. The era when people fly is coming. People will never die. The people who receive the Sweet Dew never die. Even they contract any serious diseases, they are cured soon. If they receive the Sweet Dew, their minds are changed; their blood is changed, so their bodies become immortal. People's bodies are changed into brilliant light. Humans were originally God according to the Bible, Buddhism Scriptures and [Gyeokamyourok]. In the old Bible, in Psalms 82:6, it says, "You are gods; you are all sons of the Most High. Deuteronomy 14:1, "You are the children of the LORD, your God."

The baby of cows is a cow; the baby of horses is a horse. If humans are the children of God, all humans are surely Gods. John1:1 says, " God is life and light. " Therefore, if God was brilliant light, humans should be brilliant light, too. Therefore, it is natural if humans receive the light (spirit) of God continually, the spirit of God removes the dark spirit of Satan which surrounds each cell of humans, and then all humans recover the light of God. In the Bible, in Hosea 14:5, it says that the Sweet Dew is just God.

The universe is made of the principle of the In-Yang (阴阳). All materials have positive or negative characters. For example, the negative light is attracted by the positive light. However, as neutrons have neutral character, they are not attracted by positive or negative materials. Above the physicist said that neutrons have strong penetrating power, in spite of that, why are they caught by proton? Because the distance between them is only one third of the nucleus' diameter, protons catch neutrinos.

Right before the big bang in the beginning, the universe existed very compactly in an extremely small space by the very strong pressure power of Satan according to physicists. However, according to the prophecy and the Savior, on the process that Satan occupied the God of brilliant light, Satan compressed God continually until God could not manage Satan's pressure, then, by the pressure of Satan, God that was a mass of light was split into female and male, changed into all things such as plants, rocks, stars, animal, and so on, they were scattered to the universe. God is still locked in all things as light. For example all living things emit light. According to the Bible and Buddhism scriptures, God is light and life. For another example, every star has a burning ball in the center. The existence is the spirit of God. So plants grow strongly due to the power of life of God in the middle of the earth. The light of neutrons does not shine in a straight line like sunshine, but in spiral line, which can move as it wants as you see above pictures because it has its consciousness. Therefore, the future coming soon will have no night according to Saengchojirak part of "GyeokamYourok".

As the light of the future coming soon will not shine straight but in spirals, it will shine to even winding holes brightly, the era is a non-poles era without yin-yang. The era will have neither shadow and nor shade. The light of God is neutral（中性）light. Therefore, it is not influenced by positive negative electrons and gravity. Moreover, the light is the Sweet Dew that broke the chain of Satan and overcame Satan. The great light of nirvana is neither attracted nor captivated by positive and negative materials. On the contrary, the Sweet Dew breaks the chain of Satan that captivates imperfect gods and emancipates the spirit of imperfect gods from the prison of Satan. Soon all people will be free from the spirit of Satan due to the immortal Sweet Dew of the Victor. Then all things recover their original light and enjoy eternal life.

The Hidden Manna in the Bible and the flower rain in the Mandala. The descending of the Holy Dew Spirit, the hidden manna, is the essence of God, it is the basic factor to form a new heaven. However, only few scholars of Korean new religion know the fact. The researchers of Korean new religions are ignorant about the will of heaven, a new paradigm of the movement of Korean new religions, never studied the hidden manna (the Holy Dew Spirit). So my study will become a fresh shocking. I already finished my thesis of 20 years about the hidden manna. Where the Sweet Dew does not fall, there is no salvation, and the paradise cannot be completed according to the scriptures. The fact is a key point of all the scriptures. Here are the predictions about the Sweet Dew in the Bible and the Buddhist scriptures.

(1) The Sweet Dew in the Buddhist scriptures.

Sakyamuni predicted 'the Dharma of the Sweet Dew' in the Buddhist scriptures. Let's see how the Buddhist scriptures foretell about the Reincarnate Maitreya Buddha. The Buddhist Scriptures express the Sweet Dew (甘露水 = soma juice) as the light of great nirvana that the Reincarnated Maitreya Buddha pours out, the whole Buddhist scriptures such as the Great Nirvana Sutra, the Dharma Flower Sutra, and the Flower Adornment Sutra, say that the Sweet Dew is the symbol of the Reincarnated Maitreya Buddha.

(2) The Hidden Manna in the Bible.

Manna is miracle food from heaven, according to Exodus 16: 14 – 31, Numbers 11: 6 – 9, Deuteronomy (8: 3), Nehemiah 9: 20 – 21 Psalm (78: 23 – 24), John (6: 31), Revelation (2: 17) in the Bible. When Moses took the Israel people to the desert from Egypt, there was no food with them. So they almost starved to death. They complained to Moses. Therefore, he prayed to God. The Lord of God said, "You will eat meat fully in the evening, eat rice cake in the morning." In that evening, quails covered the camp place and the next morning, dew fell down densely on the ground, the dew disappeared and something white and round like frost piled fully there. Moses said to people "God gave us this food; take the amount of food you can eat." This food has covered their camp site. They called the food 'manna'. As it was rotten after one day, they should bring the amount they could eat for one day; they were permitted 4 liter for each person. The Israel people lived on manna for forty years according to the Book of Exodus16: 13 and Number11: 6 – 9. If the manna of Moses period is physical manna, the Hidden manna in the Bible, the Holy Dew Spirit of the true Messiah, is spiritual manna. The Holy Dew Spirit in the Bible is the hidden manna of New Heaven that makes dying all creatures be reborn as the Holy Spirit and live forever in happiness.

Revelation 2: 17 "He who has an ear, let him hear what the Spirit says to the churches. To him who overcomes, I will give some of the hidden manna." These words mean that the man who has the hidden manna is the Victor. The Dew is the immortal manna. Dew did not fall after Moses' times. Much later, Isaiah, a great prophet, predicted as follow, "But your dead will live; their bodies will rise. You, who dwell in the grave, wake up and shout. Your dew is like the dew of the morning; the dew will give birth to her dead "in Isaiah 26: 19. This predicted, "if the Savior who pours down the Dew appears, death would perish." The Dew is not physical food, but spiritual food. It means just immortal manna. Also John 6: 27 says, "Do not work for food that spoils, but for food that endures to eternal, which the Son of Man will give you. On him God the Father has placed his seal of approval." 1Corinthians 15: 54 writes, "When the perishable has been clothed with the imperishable and the mortal with immortality, then the saying that is written will come true: "Death has been swallowed up in victory." Therefore, the words "humans'life span is like trees" are accomplished after the Holy Dew Spirit appears.

（3）Mandala flower（曼陀罗花）and flower rain and 醍醐味 that symbolizes nirvana According to Amita Sutra, in the land of happiness, the

Reincarnate Maitreya Buddha always stays as His other self, the infinite Sweet Dew. Mandala flower rain that symbolizes nirvana always falls down there.

Therefore, I will introduce my enlightenment through the wisdom of the Sweet Dew using the term of Buddhism on the basis of the preaching of the Reincarnate Maitreya Buddha. Mandala flower rain is the Sweet Dew in the land of happiness, it has the light of wisdom without any obstacles. Also, it is the other selves of the Reincarnate Maitreya Buddha, and the Holy Dew Spirit. Those who lack good character and blind with sins and karma cannot see the Sweet Dew in the world of Mandala and cannot see things in advance according to "Nirvana Sutra", "Dharma Lotus Sutra", and "Flower Adornment Sutra". "Pure Land Sambugyeong" and "Prajñā-Paramitā" say that righteous men in the immortal happy land see the Reincarnate Maitreya Buddha in a naked eye. Therefore, it is necessary to pay attention to that mysterious immortal world where unprecedented people reach nirvana physically like 醍醐味 in Sosa Korea. The Buddhist Scriptures record that 十住地 (the pure land that Mandala flower rain falls down and the Reincarnate Maitreya Buddha stays) is expressed as the Castle of the Sweet Dew, pure land, the door of the Sweet Dew, or Amita Palace. Buddha said before when people receive the light of wisdom from Amita Buddha, they can achieve immortal bodies and are physically in the stage of nirvana. What is the world of nirvana that 醍醐味 symbolizes? What does nirvana have relationship with 醍醐味? What should people do to reach nirvana? There are four steps in explaining reaching complete nirvana through cultivating themselves, comparing nirvana to the final refining of milk. Usually, the gist of sorting method is when people's levels grow up, they compare the refining of milk to the degree of their mind and bodies becoming clean. According to Buddhism Sutra, there are four steps in the process of reaching nirvana.

A. The stage of achieving of Sudawon and Sadaham is small nirvana, its stage is like milk.

B. This stage is achieving of anaham, its stage is middle nirvana. In this stage, people's blood is like milk being refined through second process.

C. If people achieve fruit of 辟支佛 and 十住菩萨, their stage is called Great nirvana, their blood is like clear alcohol（生酥）.

D. When people are on the stage of righteous men or Sakyamuni, their stage is called great nirvana. Their nature of Buddha and their blood is compared like the final refined steps of milk, 醍醐味.

The level of the Reincarnate Maitreya is that. He has infinite life span, is the immortal existence（无量寿）that emits unlimited light（无量光）, can change into a lump of fire anytime, also can change as His other selves like a tiny dirt. Anyway, Nirvana Sutra compares the nature of people's Buddha to the process of refining milk. I could see the advent of the Reincarnate Maitreya Buddha was predicted through a lot of books, He possessed all the evidence that the prophetic books and the scriptures record.

2. For One World beyond 'Ego'

（1）Borderless of Mind & Hand in Hand.

As the dream society of new heaven will be 'One World', the task to overcome for building the paradise is to remove 'ego' that denies humanity's homogeneity and controls disputes and conflicts between them. Therefore, all the scriptures emphasize, "Throw away 'I' all the time", "one can be a saint by reaching the level of absence of ego.", "overcome myself and recover the original nature". All the words accent on the recovering of one's original nature by being reborn as the Holy Spirit through moving in contrast of what one wants. All the scriptures say that humanity is locked by false owners and are crazy. When all humanity recovers their conscience and realizes that they are the children of God, they can find out the way that they should proceed. As neohuman already appeared and established a new culture, the task to remain is to learn the new culture and the new science. It is the time when we realize that humans have the same blood and are the 7 billion branches of God and the children of God. Also now is the time when we should take an effort to break the wall of the mind, to recover the mind of becoming one with others (一心), to be reborn as the Holy Spirit hand in hand with brothers and neighbors.

(2) The Bright Light of the East and Luminist.

The Victor who appeared in the east is the light of the east, He speaks of a bright philosophy, who is a Luminist who emits the light of life, and is other existence who Nostradamus called. Also it has predicted by Rabendranath Tagore his poem, "You would be The Light of the East".

The Light of the East

Korea, one of the brightened candles in the golden time of early Asia,

On the day the candle is lit again,

You will be the light of the east.

where no fear is in the heart, head is held up high,

where knowledge is free and the world is not split between a narrow wall,

where the Holy testament is sprung from the depth of the truth,

where endless effort spreads toward accomplishment of eternal life

where the pure flowing of wisdom does not lose its way

in the wilderness of solid habits,

where our mind leads through the limitless spreading of thought and behavior,

Korea, the homeland in my heart, wake up as the new heaven of liberty.

Rabendranath Tagore of India: This prophecy poem was written by Rabendranath Tagore of India, the great poet and meditator, around 1930, when he was visiting Japan, looking at the sea between the neighboring sea of

Korea and Japanese sea. After writing the poem, he gave it to a Korean reporter of DongAhIlBo, who spread it to a lot of Koreans.

(3) Back Spiral Movement & the Principle of Changing Cosmos.

The future society is the time when the Back Spiral Movement happens. Which is to stop the killing civilization that fights and divides each other, and to recover the original nature, and to become one with the organism of the universe. Further, it will accomplish the win-win world of coexistence and co-prosperity through Principle of Changing Cosmos for One World.

Ⅳ Conclusion

So far, I examined the new cultural movement and the Dream Society in the Future of neohumans, from the aspect of the futurology, who will lead the World Cultural Development, through ancients scriptures and prophetic books.

The Advent of Neohumans and New Life-Cultural Movements （生命苏生运动） are valuable because they can overcome the limit and crisis of the materialistic civilization and open a new era of humanity. The rise of the immortal culture for saving life and new public philosophy in Korea have no fault to form the world mainstream culture in the 21st century. Also they are expected to be settled as a new saving philosophy （救世救援） that solve emptiness and unhappiness, plant core values to people and save the world. Therefore, this paper will be recognized as one to reveal the future society and vision of humanity, 'by what culture, the new world mainstream culture is established', and 'what is the spiritual culture of new wind?' Neohumans （新人类＝神人类） that the writer of this paper mentions do not mean the people changed by mechanism or the development of medicine but mean the people being reborn as the Holy Spirit by the spiritual changing and with the heart of God without borrowing the power of material and scientific technology. The bodies and minds of neohumans are reborn as the heart of the universe and the organism of the universe （重生）．Their minds and bodies are gradually changed taking several steps such as the man of heaven （神人），fairy （神仙），天人，义人，真人，上善人．And they will be reached to the step that they can live without eating or drinking．Then their organs are changed into those of fairies and they will become neohumans who can fly as they want and can live forever．The righteous men of the east mean one who can fly as flying existence anytime．Nostradamus predicted neohuman as other existence．Also as neohuman （angel of heaven）will complete the paradise，are ones who get out of not only food，clothing，and shelter but also the character of In-Yang （阴阳）．They will neither marry and delivery babies like the prediction of Jeremiah of the Bible，nor fight nor hate people．Additionally，they regard everyone as my body and serve everyone as God．They are the men of heaven who have only the Holy Spirit that is not conscious between you and I．And they are free ones who get out of birth，old age，sickness，pain or diseases．Further neohumans live happily with delight all the time．They do not cause population problems，food problems，and funeral problems as well because they are immortal existences．

The wind of the new culture was announced in 1986，1988，and 2002 through the sports events．Koreana，a singing group，sang 'Hand in Hand' as the Olympic theme song in 1988．The lyric contains that the east and the west become one，let's go toward an immortal way hand in hand．However，there are rare people who recognized the song is the development processing of the advent of neohumans and the movement of the new culture．

The reason that one cannot hear the melody and the sound of heaven because they lack spirituality and have an itching palm and ego and have the ignorant thinking structure．People cannot understand the will and secret of mysterious heaven the Bible with the shallow knowledge of men．As the bright light of the east by Tagore，a Indian's poet，predicted，lit again，now is the time when not only Koreans，also all humanity should go toward a new way

thanks to the light of new wisdom. "Gyeoamyourok（格庵遗录）" records，
'时至不知면　节不知　儿이라'. It mean if one does not know that the time comes，they are spiritual babies.

References

Sin Cheul-won，《论语》，《大学》，《中庸》，Seoul，恩光社，2006.

THE BIBLE，「*JPS HEBREW ENGLISH TANAKH*」，（Philadelphia，THE JEWISH PUBLICATION SOCIETY，1999）.

Ariel Han & Angela Kim，*The Secret of New Heaven*（Seoul，GeumSenng Publishing，2012）.

Han Gang-Hyen，*The study of prediction of Gyeokamyourok*（the culture of Korean p rediction and the Victory Altar）.

a master's thesis（Tokyo：Mejiro University Graduate School，2002）.（*Journal of the Korean Academy of New Religions*，April，2011，Vol. 24）"The study for exodus from birth and death & the theory of Eternal life"（On the focus the philosophy of Immortality）.

Han Gang-Hyen，*The Final Issue of NRNs in the World*，Geum-Seong Publishing Company，Seoul，2013. WWW. amazon. com，"The Han-Moum Philosophy（一体）and Neohumans Culture"，*World Culture Development Forum*（*2013*），（湖北大学高等人文研究院主办，社会科学文献出版社，2013），Uhan，中国 www. ssap. com. cn

IANC，"Journal of the Neohumans Culture"，*New Philosophical Movements in Korea to Accomplish Public Philosophy*，Special Edition Vol 1，August，2013.

Kim Young Suk，"*The Hidden Secret of the Bible*"，GuemSeong Publishing，Bucheun，2013. WWW. amazon. com.

Han Gang-Hyen，"The study of prophecy of 'Gyeokamyourok（格庵遗录）'，the culture of prophecy of Korea and the Victory Altar（胜利祭坛））"，（Tokyo：Mejiro University Graduate School，2002）.

The Theme was："The Hidden Manna and the Philosophy of Eternal Life"（Based on the Perspective of Prophecies in Sacred Books）in the 2011 International Conference" by CESNUR，"A New View of the Afterlife and the New Heaven" in the International Conference of the sponsor，CESNUR Morocco in 2012.

"Gyeokamyourok"，which National Jungang Library has，the number of the list nomber of old books：1496 - 4 Ho. 佛法秘传书，"Seonbulgajinsueorok"，which the Academy of Neo-humans and Cultural Archeology has Books of hidden secret，"济众甘露"，which Gyoujanggak，the num-ber of the list：奎 19181，（Hanyang：Gyoujanggak，1878）. International Academy of Neohumans Culture（IANC）Institution of research：The World Institution of Neohumans Culture（WINC）Email：urihana9981@ naver. com.

网络舆情事件传播与社会公平正义的实现

廖声武[*]

摘　要：近年来，网络舆情事件不断发生。热点舆情事件在传播中，往往演化成社会冲突。这是社会转型期的社会矛盾在面对科技进步带来网络传播技术的快速发展而出现的现象。网络舆情事件的传播有其负面的影响，但网络舆情事件的传播是普通民众利用网络媒介技术对自身利益的维护，对社会公平的实现，对社会正义的坚守，是民众自发的生动的民主实践。

关键词：舆情事件　网络传播　公平正义

Internet Public Events and Realization of Social Justice

Liao Shengwu

Abstract：In recent years, Internet public events happen constantly. Hot events are often evolved into social conflicts in the dissemination. It is caused by the social contradictions in the rapid development of network communication technology brought by the advancements of science and technology during the social transformation. The spread of Internet public events has negative effects, while it is the safeguard of common people for their own interests through

---

＊　廖声武，湖北大学新闻传播学院教授。

Internet media technology, the realization of social fairness, the persistence of social justice and people's spontaneous lively democratic practices.

Keywords: Public Events; Internet Dissemination; Justice

网络舆情是指通过互联网传播的公众对现实生活中某些热点、焦点问题表达的态度、情绪等有关的言论和观点，是社会舆论的一种表现形式。

网络舆情具有主体主导、内容多元、群体极化和虚实互动等特点。由于网络传播的快速及其传播的开放性，信息传播范围广、影响大，各种信息交流呈现非理性化、情绪化倾向，流言的传播也十分快速和广泛，其结果就容易导致群体性事件的产生，这就出现了网络舆情事件。

一　网络舆情事件频发

近年来，网络舆情事件不断发生。网络舆情事件中，除了重大突发事件外，社会民生问题是网络舆情事件的重要构成成分。

2011 年热点舆情事件主要在官民关系、贫富分化、房价物价、城管执法、征地拆迁、司法公正、食品药品安全、教育政策等方面，同时，环境污染事件、安全事故、公益慈善信任危机等新问题也呈明显上升趋势。

2012 年，我国舆情事件种类多样，反腐倡廉类舆情事件所占比例最大（28%），其次是社会民生类舆情事件（17%）和公共安全舆情事件（11%），其余较为平均地分散于文化教育、刑事案件、涉外、社会道德、食品卫生、环境保护等舆情事件中。①

2013 年，20 个热点舆情事件中，司法案件突出。9 月继举世瞩目的

---

① 刘鹏飞、齐思慧、周亚琼：《2012 年网络舆情走势和社会舆论格局》，《新闻记者》2013 年第 1 期。

薄熙来案一审宣判之后，陕西"房姐"龚爱爱案、"高铁一姐"丁书苗案陆续开审，北京大兴摔童案、李某某强奸案、河北王书金强奸案等相继宣判，沈阳摊贩杀死城管案主犯夏俊峰被执行死刑，更使得司法公正成为空前集中的网络议题。

2013 年，民生问题和个人权益保护仍然是网络舆情的热点领域。年初的香港奶粉限购令，黄浦江上游的死猪，下半年的延迟退休之争，基层政府和百姓之间、不同社会群体之间的各种摩擦事件，都掀起民众的情感波澜。

2014 年，民生领域的网络舆情依旧位列全年网络舆情总数第一。在环保领域，以"垃圾焚烧、PX 项目、PM2.5、水环境"四大民生矛盾为主，其中"茂名 PX 群体事件"、"博罗垃圾焚烧抗议事件"、"兰州水污染事件"等重大典型舆情被媒体、网络高度关注、大量报道。在食品安全领域，从年初的"云南幼儿园学生群体性中毒"起，到后续曝光的"湖北麻雀死亡"、"福喜过期肉事件"、"惠州 83 名学生集体食物中毒"，都涉及民众的安全感和尊严。在教育领域，主要是针对招生考试、师德师风、教育管理的舆情，如"高考替考事件"、"蓝翔教育模式"等。卫生领域牵涉"H7N9"的舆情信息较多，"四川走廊医生"、"西安医生手术室自拍照"等事件也引起了网民热议。

二 为什么网络舆情事件频发

随着改革在经济、政治、文化等各个领域的发生、发展，中国社会逐渐进入了一个由传统农业社会向现代工业社会，由计划经济社会向市场经济社会过渡的大转型时期。

有学者认为，社会转型是指社会发展过程中发生的一种整体的全面的结构过渡状态，它包括社会结构的转换、社会体制的更新、社会利益的重组与价值观念的嬗变。在这个转型时期，新旧体制转换、利益分化重组、价值取向出现多元与冲突，各种矛盾凸显，整个社会结构发生深刻变革。具体表现如下。

第一，体制发生变化。伴随着计划经济向市场经济的转轨，社会资源配置的方式改变了，以市场经济关系为纽带的社会组织体制代替了以行政关系为纽带的社会组织体制。相伴而行的是新的社会阶层和职业群体出现，所有制成分变得多样。

第二，社会利益重新分配。计划经济体制下，人们的经济活动都服从于国家计划，强调国家利益和集体利益优先，必要时牺牲个人利益；市场经济体制下，市场在资源配置中起基础性作用，个人的利益受到重视，个人的自主性、创造性得到社会的肯定。社会上出现了以按劳分配为主体的多种分配方式并存的新的格局，导致人们利益上的重大差异，使整个社会利益格局出现分化和重组。

第三，价值观念出现多元与冲突。市场经济是自主性经济，市场法则要求平等互利，这种自主性和平等性促使人们摆脱了传统的等级、特权和依附观念，破除了"唯上"意识和依赖心理，自主、自立、平等、自由的主体意识逐步觉醒。人们的生存方式、思维方式和价值观念发生深刻变革，促使社会群体和个人在价值观念上产生出多样的价值追求，表现出多元的价值评价标准和取向上的差异性：强调经济、重视效益、主张权利、期望公平、勇于竞争、肯定个人。一些以前被普遍认可的合理的观念在现如今变得不合时宜，新旧观念之间发生了矛盾和冲突。①

社会转型带来一系列社会问题，比如地区差别、城乡差别、环境恶化、贫富分化、社会保障问题、就业问题以及教育、医疗、交通等问题。而这些问题又不是一夜之间就能解决的，需要一个长期的过程，需要经济的发展和政治改革进行综合治理方能得到缓解。

但恰恰就在这时，科技进步带来网络技术和通信技术的快速发展，互联网一夜之间遍布城市和农村，互联网的普及使得整个世界变成了一个地球村，人们获得信息已经不需要烦琐的工序，而是只需指尖轻轻敲击键盘就可完成的一个简单的活儿。而且互联网的互动性，使得受众不

---

① 糜海燕、符惠明、李佳敏：《我国社会转型的内涵把握及特征解析》，《江南大学学报》（人文社会科学版）2009 年第 2 期。

再仅仅是信息的被动接收者,受众在接收信息的同时他可以立刻转身成为信息的传播者。

这样一来,原先媒体传播的秩序发生了改变。传统媒体的新闻,需要记者采写、编辑审稿方能发布,许多信息可以被有意或无意地遮蔽,有些信息可以被把关者堵截。但互联网的传播颠覆了这种信息传播模式,网民有了媒介接近权,他可以接收媒体的信息传播,同时它又可以成为一个信息传播者。他的这种媒介接近权使他可以对社会上的各种问题发言,他可以对任何问题发表自己的观点,并以此来影响社会舆论。

随着智能手机的普及,手机网民激增。微博、微信等社交媒体的推出,使得传播不再依赖电脑终端,信息传播更为便捷,移动互联网已经成为网络舆情的新磁场。这样一来,以自媒体为草根舆论源头,以网络媒体和传统媒体分属民间和官方的舆论平台的社会舆论架构出现在舆论场上。失去舆论垄断能力的传统媒体已不再具有原先化解矛盾、按自己的意愿引导舆论的力量。

而在社会转型期,由于利益分配的矛盾和价值观念的矛盾不可避免,一旦社会矛盾出现,媒体信息传播失去控制,舆论经过网络传播的发酵,舆情事件便不可避免地发生了。

三 网络传播为网络舆情事件推波助澜

舆情事件的传播得益于网络媒体的出现,网络媒体的发展催生了舆情事件的形成。两者犹如一对孪生兄弟,相互依存。它们在中国的新闻传播史上演绎出一幕幕大戏,也在中国政治史上演绎出辉煌的篇章。

2001年孙志刚事件发生,网络舆论沸腾,推动政府出面终止了《城市流浪乞讨人员收容遣送办法》的实施。从那时开始,互联网十几年来从 BBS、QQ、博客前进到微博、微信,获得持续发展,而网络舆情事件与互联网发展如影随形。

2010年江西宜黄钟家姐妹俩因拆迁纠纷引发自焚事件上访,县委书记带人到机场围堵上访者。《凤凰周刊》记者邓飞在微博中直播该事件的实时进展，引发了全国网友的关注。因此有人将 2010 年称为"微博元年"。这一年，不少标志性网络舆情事件都与微博有关，大多从微博上率先引爆，逐渐影响社会。

中国社会科学院发布的《2011 年中国社会形势分析与预测》蓝皮书中称，微博正在改变着中国互联网舆论载体的格局，成为网络舆论中最具影响力的一种。

2011 年，互联网已经成为热点事件曝光的主要平台和舆论源头。据初步统计，通过网络曝光的热点事件接近 2/3，重大突发事件在事发当天发酵的超过半数。2011 年，互联网话题集聚能力明显增强，虚拟与现实社会互动的影响力提升。网民利用多种方式挖掘事实的主动性增强，形成强大的舆论监督力量。

2012 年，微博逐渐成为我国反腐主战场。网络曝光密切监督社会，尤其是一些贪污腐败的现象，一篇报道、一张图片、一个表情，都可能成为反腐风暴的导火索。网络舆情事件过后，各种公民调查、问询和"行为艺术"也常常大量出现。

2013 年，民生问题和个人权益保护依然是网络舆情的热点领域。年初的香港奶粉限购令，黄浦江上游的死猪，下半年的延迟退休之争，基层政府和百姓之间、不同社会群体之间的各种摩擦事件，都涉及民众的安全感和尊严，掀起情感波澜。

4 月，人民网、新华网等中央重点新闻网站及新浪、腾讯等商业网站均在显要位置推出"欢迎监督，如实举报"的网络举报监督专区。9月 2 日，中央纪委监察部网站正式开通，日均收到网络举报 800 件。这都有利于引导网民利用正规渠道和平台进行合法举报，实现网络反腐与制度反腐的无缝对接。

2014 年，民生领域的网络舆情仍然位列全年网络舆情总数第一。主要集中在环保领域、食品安全领域、教育领域、卫生领域、产品质量领域等。如 3 月 30 日，茂名发生群体性聚集事件，抗议新建 PX 项目，一些媒体、"公知"、网络"大 V"和评论人与多年前的厦门 PX 项目媒体抗议事件一样，再次拿 PX 制造网络舆情事件，进行了大量的舆论动员，引发群众街头抗议。该舆情因网络"大 V"的参与，迅速蔓延为全国关注的网络事件。具有戏剧性的是，3 月 31 日，"演员文章出轨"舆情的爆发，瞬间转移了网络眼球。

四 讨论：网络舆情事件传播的实质与目标

新华社前总编南振中说当前中国存在两个舆论场：一个是党报、国家电视台、国家通讯社等"主流媒体舆论场"，一个是互联网上的"民间舆论场"。[①] 由于中国社会转型期的特点，主流媒体舆论场囿于其官方的背景，其传播角度往往与民众的立场有距离，传播内容有时也与民众的情感相疏离，在重大舆情事件发生时，民众更愿意到网络上寻找信息，或者更愿意相信网上的信息。

网络舆情事件的传播与传统媒体传播相比较，最典型的变化是政府垄断信息源的状况不复存在，传播过程更多地体现出政府、媒介和公众之间的互动，公众在中间的角色往往是独立的、主动的、活跃的。

在民间舆论场上网民在谈论什么呢？网民们在自己掌握的 BBS、QQ、微博、微信等媒体上，议论时事，针砭社会，揭露腐败，品评政府的公共管理。

依托互联网新媒体，社会名人、媒体记者和政务机构积极参与，虚拟社区公共舆论场进一步扩大。自媒体进一步压缩传统媒体的时效空间，并且常常给政府部门、企业和社会组织造成舆情应对压力。

人民网舆情监测室数据显示，2012 年热点舆情事件中，反腐倡廉舆情事件所占比例高达 28%。网络上的毒胶囊事件是网民对食品药品安全问题感到愤怒的一次集中爆发。时任卫生部部长陈竺亲自出来表态之后，毒胶囊事件才逐渐平息。太原市公安局局长李亚力之子醉驾袭警事件也是典型的网络舆情事件。李亚力之子自己作为警察，醉驾不说，被交警拦下却还仗势欺人，打交警。不平则鸣，受害者向舆论讨公道。不料李

---

① 刘华欣：《群体性突发事件网络舆情演变机制的传播学解读》，《新闻知识》2013 年第 3 期。

亚力却动用公权，限制、打击、威胁执法交警，欲操控舆情，压下舆论。不过瞎子点灯白费蜡，李亚力也因滥用公权，被停职调查。

从这些典型案例中，我们可以看出，网络传播就是在与权力阶层、现行体制的摩擦和磨合中，为普通民众寻求公平和正义。

政府权力机构也在寻求与舆情事件主体妥协的路径。人民网舆情监测室舆情分析师胡江春说，在突发事件中，最需要的是政府做出让民众看得见的反应。这些反应包括解决实际问题的具体行为和发出安抚民众情绪的声音。因为一旦没有官方的权威结论，小道消息就会大行其道，其结果就是造成更大范围、更深程度的群众恐慌心理蔓延。想以"维护社会稳定"为由，静悄悄地把具体问题解决掉，在这个互联网时代只会适得其反。①

因此，网络媒体的舆情事件传播是一种社会转型期在互联网络环境下的民主实践。在融合媒体环境下，舆情事件的主体通过微信、微图、微拍、微视、秒拍等网络传播平台的运用对民生问题、公权失范、突发事件、环境事件等发表意见，维护自身权益，揭露腐败，以实现社会公平。由此，社会正义得到维护。同时由于这种网络舆论的传播与应对，达到民众与政府权力机构的妥协与一致。

---

① 《地方舆情报告发布：信息透明是获公众信任第一要素》，《中国青年报》2010 年 11 月 24 日。

The Development of China's Legal Culture in the Perspective of International Rule of Law[*]

Zeng Lijie[**]

Abstract: The interflow of legal culture, a sub-system of culture, is a very important link in the development of human history. International communication among different legal cultures may carry on through borrowing, transplant, etc. In the globalization era, legal cultures communicate at international level by two routines of bidirectional flowing and convergence. The development of international law influences the construction of advanced Chinese legal culture with the legal values of freedom, material equality, humanism, rule of law, peace, co-operation, diversity. Construction of Chinese legal culture advances on the basis of tradition and imports of other legal culture as well as mutual echo between Chinese and international legal culture.

Keywords: International Rule of Law; Chinese Legal Culture; Communication of Culture; Convergence of Culture

---

* 本文是作者主持的湖北大学高等人文研究院"当代中国主流文化研究学科平台建设"项目"国际法治视域下的中国法律文化发展"的最终成果。

** 曾丽洁，女，湖南邵东人，法学博士，湖北大学政法与公共管理学院副教授，研究方向为国际法治。

国际法视域下的中国法律文化发展

曾丽洁

摘　要：作为文化之子系统的法律文化的融通是人类文明发展中的重要一环。不同法律文化之间通过借鉴、移植等多种方式进行国际交流，在全球化时代主要有两种路径：双向互动与趋同。国际法在发展中也以自由、实质正义、人本主义、法治、和平、合作、多元等法律价值推动着中国法律文化的进步。而中国在国际法治进程中，不仅在保持优秀传统文化的同时吸取不同法律文化的优点，也在国内法治建设中对国际法治做出回应。

关键词：国际法治　中国法律文化　文化融通　文化趋同

Legal culture formed and accumulated with the development of human historical change with that of their productive style, living and survival style, and that of social and political system. Under the globalization, the imbalance of legal cultural development caused by economic inequality drives the exports or imports of them, which comes from difference, competiveness, tolerance, expansibility and identification among the nations.

1. Bidirectional Flowing Legal Cultural Communication Comes from Differences and for Complementation

The development of human history is a process of human communication. Generally speaking, in all the communications among countries, economical communication is always the first peer, while that of legal plays crucial role to order the communication and guard the security for it. It directly results the *interflow of legal culture and thus advance the development of law.* ①

Legal culture, as a sub-system of culture, has the common general nature, characteristics and functions as other cultural sub-systems such as religious, moral, and political cultures do. They interact and mutually complement with each other. But as a special cultural phenomena, legal culture has its own particular substitute contents. Lawrence M. Friedman firstly used the term "Legal Culture" in his article *Legal Culture and Social Development* and regarded it as public attitude to law, voluntariness for suit, and the relative significance of law in influence the popularized thoughts and conducts. Generally speaking, legal culture is a set of ideas and value system which has been internalized into legal thoughts, legal systems, and mode of behavior of people, and gives spiritual and principle instruction and limitation on the development of them. On another view, legal culture rooted in the history and culture of particular society, so that directly or indirectly influence the operation effects of legal systems, which on contrast conceal or imply legal culture. So, with the changes in an globalized world, the legal culture subsequently changes a lot not only being interacted among those of different countries but also between international legal culture and domestic legal culture. China is at an era of great social changes and reforms in legal system. The development of China's legal culture in the circumstances of globalization and concurrent development of legal culture of the international law and that of other countries.

I Mode of International Communication among Different Legal Cultures

The imbalance of culture development in different societies of human beings

---

① Mi Jian, "The Communication in Legal Culture and Subjective Awareness of Culture," *China Legal Science*, 2012 (2); 6.

causes the communication among them. Exportation or importation of certain legal culture is the result of both the identities and disparities of legal culture, which created from the common characters and independent nature of human life.

Modern legal culture has some common characters cross different nations or countries. [1] For example, as Friedman described, we all live in a society with strangers, who protect us, sew for us, build houses for us, cook for us, educate our children, store up our property, inform us via media, and even our lives would been controlled by strangers when we go on trip via public transportation... [2] Enhancement of a society of strangers makes an abstract and operational trust mechanism be necessary, and law is the most important one of such abstract trust mechanisms. Countries can indirectly control and regulate the conduct of strangers to prevent such risks. An immigrant country like the United State with so-called "stranger freeman society" thereto has a legal culture with preference to judicial approaches to solve individual or social problems. On the contrast, a so-called "acquaintance society" like China has a traditional sentiment of detesting lawsuit in legal culture.

Different legal cultures influence each other in their communications and bring a harmonious circumstance of side-by-side compatible concurrence. Overall looking the history, at international legal culture level, the communication of different legal cultures proceed bilaterally and multilaterally in the following modes.

1. Borrowing

The legal system of one nation state may intentionally learn some particular rules from another nation state to improve and develop its own. Legal borrowing is

---

[1] Lawrence M. Friedman, "Is There a Modern Legal Culture?" *Ratio Juris*, Vol. 7, No. 2. (July, 1994): 117 – 130.

[2] Lawrence M. Friedman, *American Law: An Introduction* (Revised and Updated Edition), W. W. Norton & Company, 1998, p. 330.

the most basic and common approach of legal advancement, since it's much easier to carry on to find a better way to solve certain practical legal issues with no operation of public power or entities.

In the developing of international law, there is either one nation state borrow specific better approach from the legal system of another state, or adopt the better mechanism of one party in the bilateral relations, or borrow the legal system of one party in creating multilateral rules. For example, The Hague Rules by and large borrowed British Maritime Law. That was not only because the discourse hegemony of great power, but much more for the most perfectness of British Maritime Law rendered by its historical leadership position in shipping industry. In the case *Vita Food Products Inc. V. Unus Shipping Co. Ltd* (Nova Scotia, CA., 1939), the parties chose British Maritime Law, which had no any objective relations with the transaction of international shipping, with meeting of minds through autonomy of will. The court of Nova Scotia initiative recognize the validity of this choice of law, regarding it as a reasonable choice for the parties to select the most perfect maritime law in the world.

2. Transplant

Although American scholar Alan Watson thought that the law of a nation should be distinguishing as the symbol of the nation so that even two closely related legal systems had some obvious differences on some important details, he recognized transplant of a kind of rule or legal system from one nation to another was popular phenomenon in recorded history. [1]

3. Integration

Integration of law may be the most route for legal communication in the level of international law. Out of common benefits and for common goal, different

---

[1] Alan Watson, *Legal Transplant: An Approach to Comparative Law*, second Edit. The University of Georgia Press, Athens and London, 1993, p. 21.

countries and regions seek for unified rules after contact, communication and conflict followed by acceptance, adjustment and confirmation of new, local or overall legal system. In the era of globalization, the preceding integration of economy would be lack of fundamental safeguard if there were no ordering after integration of law. The integration of law can only complicated through the finding or voluntary acceptance of common law by equal subjects.

The most successful integration of law brought by European integration from The Treaty of Rome and The Treaty Establishing the European Economic Community to The Single European Act, The Maastricht Treaty, The Treaty of Nice, and The Treaty of Lisbon, shaping the legal framework of the European Union, was a process of confirming and enlarging the identity under the common sense in the European neighborhood. On the contrary, the integration of law in Europe guarded the integration of Europe in all sphere.

Integration of law happened not only in the Europe but also in other regions and the worldwide.

4. Interflow

Interflow of law is the highest mode of legal culture communication with positive self-adjustment progress of legal culture after the encounter, conflict and the following of interact, infiltration, and acceptance among legal systems and legal cultures in different nation states or regions.

The fundamental condition for interflow of law is the common global culture elements which could be found in any civilization, while the prerequisite is the independent existence of each legal system or culture which would not be eliminate or displaced after the interflow.

Ⅱ Two Routines of Legal Cultural Communication at International Level in the Globalization Era

Legal culture formed and accumulated with the development of human historical change with that of their productive style, living and survival style, and that of social and political system. Under the globalization, the imbalance of legal cultural development caused by economic inequality drives the exports or imports of them, which comes from difference, competiveness, tolerance, expansibility and identification among the nations.

1. Bidirectional Flowing Legal Cultural Communication Comes from Differences and for Complementation

There is no denying that laws has local characteristics. Different regions, nations and countries have their own characteristics or preference in legal culture. Even legal system of US, which has been the model for many countries, still has a lot differences with those of other countries. It is the existence of such difference that form the diversity of legal culture.

Such diversity of domestic laws reversing drives the diversity in international legal system. For example, on the ascertain of the connecting point for lex personalis, there is a lasting insistence on domicile or nationality respectively in common law legal system countries and continental legal system countries. Thus, in private international law (so called the law of conflict of laws in the common law legal system countries), there arose some legal systems, such as renvoi, in some countries to resolve these types of conflict caused by the above difference. With the increasingly frequent foreign connections among people from different countries, all the countries hope to resolve civil and commercial legal disputes involving foreign elements and thus to promote normal transnational communications. So, in some scope of private international law, some countries start to adopt domicile instead of the original nationality, or replace domicile by habitual residency. And at the level of international law, more and more newly international treaties which relate connecting point of *lex personalis*, adopt the much more objective and eclectic connecting point of habitual residence. The creation and popularization of the type of selective conflict rules further provides tools for the diversity of law. A typical example is Hague Convention on the choice of law for mode of testament, which fulfilled a unity in diversity and inclusiveness on the level of international law, reconciled the disputes on domicile or nationality between common law legal system countries and continental legal system countries and on the divergence between the time node of making the will or death of testator, by adopting unconditional choice rules for regulating the conflict of laws with several parallel connecting points.

2. Convergence in the Identity of International Legal Culture Comm-unication

American scholar Lawrence M. Friedman thought modern legal culture had some common characteristics crossing ethnics, nation, or state. ①The essential of legal culture is the relationship and mutual conversion between sollen and sein, locality and universality. As Jeremy Bentham said, the isness of law was quiet different in different countries, while what the law ought to be was same at a great extent in all countries. ②That means the legal culture communications is a routine for locality enhancing to universality, and for human being's pursuing for a maximization and generalization of sollen of law. ③

III The Influence of the Development of International Law to the Construction of Advanced Chinese Legal Culture

The obvious truth is modern international law has developed and thus enhanced its role and influence in the political, economical, social and legal lives in the

---

① Lawrence M. Friedman, "Is There a Modern Legal Culture?" *Ratio Juris.* Vol. 7, No. 2. (July, 1994): 117 – 130.

② Jeremy Bentham, *A Fragment on Government: Being an Examination of Which is Delivered, on the Subject of Government in General*, Shuping Shen (trans.), The Commercial Press, 2009, p. 96.

③ Mi Jian, "The Communication in Legal Culture and Subjective Awareness of Culture," *China Legal Science*, 2012 (2): 7.

worldwide countries. We could find some fundamental principles and spirits of international law integrated into domestic jurisprudence and the legal science and the legal systems per se, thus transferred to a portion of the legal culture of a country.

1. Freedom

Freedom is one of the basic human rights which had been established by international conventions and widely accepted by states. But the concept and scope of freedom is developing, as well as the boundary with the power of government.

The freedom for utilizing private data (especially that cross-national data transferring) is quite differently be treated in EU and other countries. While EU made a series directions to regulate the cross-national data transferring which limit the transferring to a third country which has no adequate legal protection on private data. These regulations made obstacles in international trade especially in cross-national services. Even US, paying the most importance on freedom of individual, still does not match EU criterion of adequateness on legal protection of private data. This is the result of difference in legal culture between EU and US, with the former suffered much disasters from the abuse of private information in the World War II, while the latter prior to the governmental control on private data for it faces more risk in state security. But in order to remove the obstacle to international service trade, US created a Safe Harbor, in which the enterprises who voluntarily choose to give adequate protection on private data in their business could be free in obtaining the transfer of private data from member states of EU.

As surfing the Internet has become a very important means to access information, access to the Internet has been regarded as basic human rights protected by International Covenant on Civil and Political Rights. In July, 2012, UN Human Rights Council passed a Resolution to deem Internet access a basic human rights, a type of freedom of expression. ①But, as the exceptions of Expression Freedom admitted in Article 19 of International Covenant on Civil and Political Rights, international society accepts limitation for state security and public moral, as well as intellectual property protection, on freedom of expression on Internet. Influenced by these international law, governments have to recognize this new type of human right and keep freedom of expression and government censors balanced.

2. Material Equality

One of the remarkable characteristics of late international legal life is material equality, the idea of real equality which requires proper limitation to the strong and special measures of protecting the weak. Thus, equality is not only in the relations between individuals, but also states, the state and individual. The change of idea for equality results a lot reformation in domestic public or private laws.

3. Humanism

Humanism is a remarkable characteristic in modern international law and has influence in wide sphere in domestic law. The former principle of contractual freedom is not regarded as an iron rule anymore, especially in employment contracts and consumer contracts. Much former private legal issues overlap within the scope of public law, the board of public law and private law is not so clear as before.

4. Rule of Law

The most obvious and great change should be the attitude in the relationship between nation and law. The advancing of modern international law from the controlling of law by authority to the reciprocal restraint, manifests the real

---

① See U. N. Human Rights Council, The Promotion, Protection and Enjoyment of Human Rights on The Internet, U. N. Doc. A/HRC/20/L. 13, June 29, 2012, available at http://www. regeringen. se/1/c6/19/64/51/6999c512. pdf.

meaning of rule of law.

5. Peace

Besides restraining war or armed conflict, the fundamental non-force principle asks people seek for judicial means to resolve disputes instead of *lex talionis*.

Furthermore, undue reliance on judiciary or take judiciary as the only way of remedy is not real peaceful condition of the world order. The faith of law may be more reasonable and peaceful mind for the whole society. Governments are more and more self-regulated in international relations. The diversity and flexibility of dispute settlement in modern international law inspires the states not to be so aggressive as before and try to settle conflict peacefully and politically before pursuing legal remedy.

6. Co-operation

Although whether co-operation is a fundamental principle in international law is a controversial issue in academics, it has been regarded a very important and widely adopted principle in modern international activities and has been written into international documents, since people realized co-operation would bring mutual benefits to all parties. The interaction of cooperation among states causes new ideas quite different from the past in governments' consideration for public affairs.

7. Diversity

The international legal cultural communication, no matter borrowing, transplant, integration, or interflow, make the legal culture of one country not to be purely traditional and national anymore, for any legal culture has some imported elements. The bidirectional flowing of different legal culture and the convergence in the identity of international law bring a broad visual field and open-minded legal psychology to the states in construction of their own legal culture.

IV Construction of Chinese Legal Culture and Mutual Echo with International Legal Culture

1. Construction of Chinese Legal Culture on the Basis of Tradition and Imports of Other Legal Culture

It is rare to see any country which has never absorbed experiences of other legal culture or imported legal systems. But the way of absorbing and immigrant always dependents on three conditions. [1]

First, the historical circumstances including objective social conditions and the legal system characteristics of the immigrant country. The real source or vitality of legal system is the outer society, which has the power to make people's value and attitude transferred to desire. No matter import or export of legal system, the construction relates to social power and environment, which decides what are the most important intervene elements and when certain beneficial desire could become requirement.

Secondly, the understanding and recognition of the immigrant country on the legal system of the emigrant country. The application of law needs the operation in conjunction by the objects of it, i. e. the public in a society. People not always merely passively accept laws, but modify or evade them by their conducts so as to revise the operation environment of laws.

Thirdly, the goal pursued by the immigrant country . Modern legal values aforementioned embedded in world-wide legal culture call for more responsibility on governments and public entities. The construction of modern Chinese legal culture could not ignore those modern legal values.

On the other side, any culture is the precipitation of human history. So,

---

[1] Mi Jian, "The Communication in Legal Culture and Subjective Awareness of Culture," *China Legal Science*, 2012 (2): 17.

the construction of modern Chinese legal culture could not abandon the tradition on one side, could not adhere isolated locality on the other side. We should view our legal tradition with a dynamic perspective and positive participant attitude into international legal culture communication, promote the transformation and creation of our traditional legal culture selectively and systematically .

For china's legal modernization, one risk should be avoided is some wrong ideas or actions in the vacuum between the abandonment of tradition and establishment of modern system. So, the most urgent and necessary thing is to cultivate the faith of law which is the most essential and pervasively influential element of legal culture.

2. Mutual Echo between Chinese and International Legal Culture

China not only imports the positive and advanced elements from other international legal culture and international legal culture, but also exports some distinctive Chinese elements of legal culture. Thus echo each other to form a whole world legal culture of multiple modernities.

For china, the arrangement of "one nation, two systems" created a new train of resolve of historical political issues and the co-existence of common law legal system with continental legal system. This was a pioneering work making a contribution to enrich the interflow of international legal culture. And then, the four different territorial legal units, mainland, Taiwan, Hong Kong, Macao, which have some common cultural traditions, interact with each other in all fields of political, economical, social, and legal communications.

On another looking, the mixture of rule by person and rule of law in the process of China's legal advancement fits nicely into international legal culture such as WTO dispute settlement, which requires inevitable due process of consult before going to the panel, and even during the whole periods of following judicial procedural, the competing parties may consult and resolve their disputes by themselves. We could say that international legal culture in not purely western legal culture, but a mixture of advanced, reasonable, efficient elements absorbed from different legal cultures in the world.

Alternatively, it should be pointed out that convergence does not equal to universality.

Law is the mirror of economical structure. While changing with the tendency of economical globalization, the changing of people's living style brought a creasing trend of convergence, which appears the similarity of substantiality and structure, and to certain extend, that of legal idea, attitude, thinking, methodology. These composite the similarity of legal culture.

参考文献

米健：《法律文化交往与文化主体意识》，《中国法学》2012 年第 2 期。

〔英〕边沁：《政府片论》，沈叔平等译，商务印书馆，2009。

Lawrence M. Friedman, "Is There a Modem Legal Culture?" *Ratio Juris.* Vol. 7, No. 2. July 1994.

Lawrence M. Friedman, *American Law: An Introduction* (Revised and Updated Edition), W. W. Norton & Company, 1998.

Alan Watson, *Legal Transplant: An Approach to Comparative Law*, second. Edit. The University of Georgia Press, Athens and London, 1993.

U. N. Human Rights Council, The Promotion, Protection and Enjoyment of Human Rights on The Internet, U. N. Doc. A/HRC/20/L. 13, June 29, 2012.

The "Hope" of Traditions for Human Future

Dr. L. Anthony Savari Raj*

Abstract: In this new contemporary cross-cultural human situation, the author submits, cultures are invited and even expected to perform a double task: to universalize their truth experiences; and to overcome their blind spots in mutual criticism and dialogue. By cultural innovation, I understand the following: Each tradition, inasmuch as it is not stagnant, has to innovate, transform and regenerate itself not only from within but also from without. And also the author would like to explore and examine, very briefly, the value of "hope" as embodied in human traditions by focusing, in a spirit of dialogue, on two myths belonging to two different traditions: the Myth of Development- which is very peculiar and important to the modern-western-technological world-view and the myth of ūzhor destiny which is deeply rooted in the Tamil (Indian) psyche. This paper would like to be a small contribution to the dialogue of cultures which indeed has become a contemporary fact as well as a necessity.

Keywords: Human Future; Tradition; Hope

---

* Dr. L. Anthony Savari Raj, Associate Professor of Philosophy, Faculty of Arts and Law, Manipal University Jaipur, Rajasthan.

人类未来的传统 "希望"

Dr. L. Anthony Savari Raj

摘　要：在新时代文化的背景下，跨文化交际已然成为人类沟通交流不可或缺的一部分。本文认为，各国的文化在跨文化交际中起到了重要的作用，扮演了双重身份：一是对于各国经验的普及有所助益，二是去帮助解决不同文化在相互沟通与指正时所存在的偏差与误解。通过对文化创新的分析，本文指出，每一种传统文化需要的不仅仅是内部的创新与转型，外部的借鉴与再生也是必不可少的。除此之外，本文还将从研究 "希望" 在传统文化中的价值作用入手，分别从现代西方特有的科技的发展的观念与根深蒂固存在于印度泰米尔人灵魂中传统的运气的观念两方面出发，从而为各国间未来的文化发展往来做出贡献。

关键词：人类未来　传统　希望

Introduction

This paper would like to be a small contribution to the dialogue of cultures which indeed has become a contemporary fact as well as a necessity.

Scholars tell us that we presently live in a "second mutation period"[①] -an age in which cultures, religions, world-views, disciplines and people are meeting and mingling on a scale which we have never witnessed before. The boundaries and barriers are breaking and a cross-cultural wind is blowing.

[①] For the notion of the First Axial Age, see Karl Jaspers, *The Origin and Goal of History*, ed. S. N. Eisenstadt (New York: State University of New York Press, 1986), where he points to the emergence and blossoming of some important civilizations of the world.

In this new contemporary cross-cultural human situation, I submit, cultures are invited and even expected to perform a double task: to universalize their truth experiences; and to overcome their blind spots in mutual criticism and dialogue.

Universalizing truth experience does not mean proclaiming one's truth to be universally valid or absolute. But it implies making an effort to present one's heritage and wealth to a wider universe in such a way that a person belonging to another clime, time and tradition might be able to have some kind of resonance of what is being presented, in his or her own tradition.

On the other hand, overcoming the blind spots basically boils down to realizing that no tradition, however ancient, modern, glorious and divine it may claim itself to be, is sufficient in constructing the entire picture of reality all by itself, with a growing conviction that no single culture, tradition, religion, discipline or person is sufficient even to face-let alone solve-any of our human predicaments single handedly. It ultimately boils down to a humbling belief and fact that nobody can claim to possess a 360 degree view of the world. The perspectives of our tradition, therefore, need to be stimulated, provoked, corrected, relativized, and complemented by a tradition other than our own.

I may perhaps introduce here the notion of "*cultural innovation*" which every tradition is invited and even expected to explore, especially in our contemporary cross-cultural human situation.

By cultural innovation, I understand the following: Each tradition, inasmuch as it is not stagnant, has to innovate, transform and regenerate itself not only from *within* but also from *without*, i. e. by accepting inspiration, provocation and even correction from outside. But this external stimulus will become effective, however, only when a tradition is able to find resonance and acceptance in its very heart. [1]

---

[1] Cf. R. Panikkar, "The Dharma of India," *World Affairs*, Jan-Mar 2002, Vol. 6, No. 1, p. 116.

It is in the backdrop of this cultural innovation, I would like to explore and examine, very briefly, the value of "hope" as embodied in human traditions by focusing, in a spirit of dialogue, on twomyths belonging to two different traditions: the *Myth of Development*-which is very peculiar and important to the modern-western-technological world-view and the myth of ūz*hor* destiny which is deeply rooted in the Tamil (Indian) psyche, and which has also been portrayed in the aphorisms of the *Thirukkural.* ①

As it will be elucidated, the myth of Development is based ona particular western understanding of hope, that is, *a hope of the future*, and an Indian understanding represents*a hope in the invisible.* While acknowledging greatly their positive contributions to humanity and for human future, my aim is to show, how in our times, both myths need a revision in the face and light of one another, in mutual criticism and dialogue, in the backdrop of *a hope in the rhythm of reality.*

1. A Western Understanding of Hope: "Hope of the Future"

Let us begin our considerations on the dominant and contemporary idea of development which seems to signal, promise and promote a hope for an ideal future for humanity.

After an initial enthusiasm regarding development, we also now begin to wonder whether it is not a continuation, in disguise, of the previous western colonial attitude and mentality. ②

The essence of colonialism, as we know, is the belief in the monomorphism of culture. It considers everything only in terms of one culture.

---

① The *Thirukkural* (also known asthe Kural) is one of the most important works in the Tamil language. It is a classic *Tamil Sangam Literature* consisting of 1330 couplets. It was authored by Thiruvalluvar, popularly known as Valluvar.

② See Arturo Escobar, *Encountering Development: The Making and Unmaking of the Third World* (Princeton, NJ: Princeton University Press, 1995) Also, Bill Berkeley, *The Graves are not yet Full: Race, Tribe and Power in the Heart of Africa* (New York: Basic Books, 2001) .

Not too long ago, this meant one king, one God, one religion, one empire. Now this is passé-but we go on-one World Bank, one world democracy, one development, one science, one technology, one world market, and one network of everything. [1]

We discern a particular kind of anthropology that seems to operate behind the myth of development.

It has an underlying anthropology, which sees Man as a bundle of potential needs, which require only development in order to make life happy and meaningful. Development, in this sense, seems to be the anthropological counterpart to the biological theory of evolution. Man develops in the same manner as the universe is set on evolution. [2]It vouches for an unquestioned validity and superiority of a single culture involving a kind of "noetic Darwinism" -an ideology of evolutionism in which other cultures and perspectives can be placed on a single evolutionary scale and absorbed within the last, most "progressive" item on that scale. [3]No wonder, development leads to a ruthless competition for the survival of the 'fittest.'

No wonder, too, death is such a tragedy for those who believe in development, because one can never be sufficiently developed. We are "on the way to development," then, death comes so suddenly, shattering all our dreams and ideals. We are almost there, then, it comes like a blow... Can we ever rest and even kiss our child or beloved without getting a guilt complex, because we are not as yet developed, and very incomplete in all that we are and in all that we do? Fulfillment while we have not yet developed, joy while we

---

[1] See Riall Nolan, *Development Anthropology Encounters in the Real World* (Boulder, CO: Westview Press, 2002).

[2] See R. Panikkar, "Ecosophy," *New Gaia*, Vol. 4, No. 1 (Michigan: Eco-Philosophy Centre, Winter 1995), p. 3.

[3] See "RaimonPanikkar on Colonialism and Interculturality," *Harvard University Center for the Study of World Religions*, Fall 1994, Vol. 2, No. 1, p. 3.

are struggling-will not be possible. There is always a mirage to go towards-further and farther.

More basically, behind the myth of progress and development there seems to be a particular understanding of time at work. Here, time is extrinsic to Man which serves as a measure and consequently as an arrow impelling him always to go "somewhere." This can be easily discerned in our "modern" culture in which time has been externalized and simply been put outside ourselves. We are made to believe that our life consists simply in running on the highway, climbing the mountain, or going somewhere-to heaven, *nirvana*, earthly paradise, development, riches, progress, absurdity, or whatever. In other words, one has to be always on the run to achieve something or reaching somewhere. And till one reaches the desired goal, one's life will be "unachieved" and "useless." Consequently, time becomes a scarcity and even a commodity, which ultimately leads to a sense of alienation and fragmentation.

The modern science is an important dimension of western culture and the whole advancement of modern science can be seen in terms of acceleration, that is, modification of time. What the machine ultimately does is to modify time, speed a particle and accelerate. The machine is useful, powerful, and meaningful only because it saves and condenses time, realizes in "less" time something that otherwise would require "more" time. Of course this conception of time is important to Man and even essential to science or western culture, but it is not universal. ①

At this juncture, we may ask, why at all should science and technology place

---

① "In English, a clock runs, but in Spanish, *el relojanda*, he "walks." This simple difference has enormous implication. If clocks run, there isn't minute to lose! If they walk, we can take our time." Stuart Chase, *The Proper Study of Mankind* (London: Phoenix House Ltd., 1957), p. 97. See also, R. Panikkar, "Modern Science and Technology are Neither Neutral nor Universal," *Europe-Asia: Science and Technology for their Future*. ETH Zurich: Forum Engelberg (March 26 – 28, 1996), pp. 205 – 209.

so much emphasis and importance on acceleration and its attendant repetition? A probable answer to this may lead us to reflect on the quantitative and pan-economic vision of life. Once again we may detect here the fragmented notion of time playing a leading role. For the quantitative world-view, the more we have of a thing the better and cheaper it is. Hence the need for acceleration and repletion which would "save" time and also ensure more production so that the "future" will be secure. The hope of the future seems to be the essential characteristic of "modern" Man. He works under the mirage and hope of an historical future to be achieved, a great empire to be built, and so on. Panikkar notes thus:

> And this historical time, called "human" time, is mainly understood as the thrust toward the *future*-in which the fullness of existence or definitive welfare, be this of the individual, the tribe, the nation or all humankind, will be achieved. This human time implies the conviction that we are in bondage, not yet completed, and for that reason we must struggle against Nature, against Fate, against the Earth or Matter. It is a struggle for freedom against anything supposedly antagonistic to Man. Our destiny is (in) the Future. [1]

In a word, the presuppositions behind the hope of the future are: time as an arrow, life as progress, development as goal, etc. "Fulfillment " in life is seen in some future time to come, and not in intensely living out every moment here and now.

2. An Indian Understanding of Hope: "Hope in the Invisible"

Seen cross-culturally, the above vision of life with an ideal of development appears to bemonocultural and is only a particular vision, with a particular meaning. This vision may even be right and beneficial, but is not the only one.

---

[1] R. Panikkar, *The Cosmotheandric Experience. Emerging Religious Consciousness.* Scott Eastham, edited, with Introduction (New York: Orbis Books), p. 100. For short, CE.

The archetype underlying the idea of development implies an anthropology and a cosmology that seem to be not shared universally by all cultures and also proves inadequate for three quarters of the world population.

And we may well affirm that not all cultures operate with a sense of future paradigm and have seen life as a "progression," where the goal or destiny is kept outside of life, to be reached somewhere else. For them, life is not a development-but a constant creation, a constant surprise, which does not go through a highway. Again, not all cultures have the idea that the human being is on a kind of instrumental wheel going towards the New Jerusalem or Heaven or whatever... the quicker, the better with a sense of mastery over destiny. The humansdo not project themselves primarily as actors, but they find themselves asspectators and partakers of life that has been given or allotted to them.

It is here, I would like to situate my reflections on the typical religiosity of the Tamil tradition, embodied in beliefs such as *ūlz* and *ūlzvinai*,[①] which indicate, among other things, that we are ultimately *spectators* in life, despite all our desires, decisions, efforts and actions. Nobody in life can really be held responsible, since what happens is beyond any one's supervision and control.

I shall confine myself to the portrayal and interpretation of this beliefas represented in the Tirukkural *which is also widely diffused in the general mentality of the Tamil (Indian) psyche. Valluvar has devoted an entire chapter to* Ūlz *(371 – 380) — which I prefer to translate as destiny (more in the sense of fate)* .[②]

Valluvar, in the last analysis, seems to believe in the ultimacy of providence and

---

① Scholars do make a distinction between *ūlz* and *vinai*. The latter implies that we are actors who have to face the consequences corresponding to our actions, and the former represents the spectator aspect of the human condition, where nobody can be held really responsible. Cf. Karu. Arumugam, "*ūlz-vinai*," paper presented at theNational Seminar: *Philosophical Insights in Classical Tamil Tradition*, jointly organized by the Central Institute of Classical Tamil, Chennai and St. Joseph's Capuchin Philosophical College at Kotagiri, Tamil Nadu, from 25 – 27 March 2009.

② Fate is from the Latin *fatum* (that which has been spoken and thus determined) . But it also has the connotations of *fame* and *fable*, which open up room for freedom. Destiny, from *de-stanare*, to settle, fix; from *stare*, to stand. Cf. R. Panikkar, *CE*, p. 128.

Man's helplessness in its presence.

   When he says,

தெய்வத்தான்ஆகாதெனினும்முயற்சிதன்

மெய்வருத்தக்கூலிதரும் . ①

   or again,

ஊழையும்உப்பக்கங்காண்பர்உலைவின்றித்

தாழாதுஞற்றுபவர் . ②

Valluvar implies that human effort can circumvent the inexorability of fate and the so-called destiny could be thwarted by constant vigil and tireless effort. But who knows that even these efforts could be part of this overshadowing fate or destiny? The inexorable nature of ūlz and its inevitability are supreme; Valluvar recognizes it like KaniyanPūnkundranar (an influential Tamil philosopher from the Sangam age) who bemoans the inexorability of fate and likensthe hapless soul, operated by destiny, to a tiny boat in a mighty current which rolls away huge rocks.

நீர்வழிப்படூஉம்புணைபோலஆருயிர்

முறைவழிப்படூஉம்என்பதுதிறவோர் . ③

Are human beings then victims of an unescapable fate, or do they really have the power to create their own destiny? This is the age-old question that has plagued philosophers, theologians, and even the common person on the street. Valluvar responds to this question thus:

ஊழிற்பெருவலியாவுளமற்றொன்று

சூழினும்தான்முந்துறும் . ④

---

① *Thirukkural* (619): "Though fate-divine should make your labour vain, effort will yield result, inproportion to bodily exertion. "

② *Thirukkural* (629): "Those who strive hard with unfaltering mind will even make the fate show its back. "

③ *Puram* (192): "We know that precious life makes its waylike a raft riding a powerful huge riverthat roars endlessly, fed by cold rains withbolts of lightning as it crashes against rocks. "

④ *Thirukkural* (380): "What power is stronger than of Destiny? It stands before the very way that tries to overcome it. "

Or again,

நல்லவையெல்லாஅந்தீயவாந்தீயவும்
நல்லவாஞ்செல்வஞ்செயற்கு . ①
ஆகூழால்தோன்றும்அசைவின்மைகைப்பொருள்
போகூழால்தோன்றுமடி . ②

To be sure, there seems to be a kind of ambivalence in Valluvar's thinking on the operation of fate: it can be thwarted as well as it is invincible. What is it then really? The usual compromise is to suggest areas in which fate is unalterable and in which it can be outwitted. But what are these areas? If once it is imagined that fate has been circumvented, who knows if the circumvention itself had not been predestined?③

Valluvar constantly falls back on two sources of correction and iniquity: one, a kindly fate and two, a providentially kind hearted source of authority (a king etc.). The role of fate again is implied in the latter: Whatever is destined to happen, will happen, do what we may to stop it. Whatever happens is due to prārabdha, to borrow a word from another tradition, a man's balance-sheet of destiny actingrigorously accordingto a law of cause and effect.

Hence the acceptance of the given order with changes suggested by an essentially good conscience, plus *a sense of urgent need to stick to it,* plus *a prayerful hope and an ardent wish that nothing will or shall wreck it. This seems to be the attitude of mind and recommendation for life that we may discern from the aphorisms on Ūlz. ④*

In an interesting verse, Valluvar advises the individual distracted by misery to have an inward laugh at it and suggests that there is no better remedy against it:

---

① *Thirukkural* (375): "While acquiring wealth, every favourable thing may become unfavourable, and everyunfavourable thing may become favourable, through the power of fate."
② *Thirukkural* (371): "Perseverance comes from a prosperous fate, and idleness from an adverse fate."
③ Cf. N. Subrahmanian and R. Rajalakshmi, *The Concordance of Tirukkural* (With a Critical Introduction). (Madurai: Ennes Publications, 1984), pp. LXIV-LXVI.
④ Cf. Ibid.

இடுக்கண்வருங்கால்நகுகஅதனை
அடுத்தூர்வத∴தொப்பதில் . ①

There is no advice to face or confront misery but one is asked to ignore it or laugh it away. In fact, adjustment, accommodation and acquiescence are recommended and not efforts to face the challenge. The point is, ūlzis not a challenge which calls for a countervailing response. The humans have to put up with it as gracefully as possible.

Interestingly, the attitude of the Greek Hellenistic philosophers, particularly the stoics, seems to echo Valluvar's stand on this question: Stoicismearns its reputation as a stern way of life with recommendations that we accept whatever destiny brings us without complaint, concern, or feeling of any kind. The stoics show how we should live when circumstances beyond our control seem to render pointless everything we try to accomplish. For Epictetus, for instance, the key is to understand how little of what happens is within our control and since family, friends and material goods are all perishable, he held, we ought never to become attached to them. Instead, we treat everything and everyone we encounter in life as a temporary blessing or curse, knowing that they will all pass away from us one day naturally.

3. An Intercultural Understanding of Hope: "Hope in the Rhythm of Reality"

The above considerationsare adduced not to justify any sense of helplessness/resignment in lifeor to uphold the concept of ūlz, as represented by an Indian tradition. I have only indicated its functional/performative role in society- which in our cross-cultural human situation, however, seems to be exploding and breaking. It remains for us to explore how the myths of development and ūlzneed to be revised, corrected and complemented in the face of one another in mutual criticism and dialogue. And it is here I like to discern and explore the intercultural synergy of hope in the rhythm of realitywhich has indeed become an important cross-cultural value for our times.

From a cross-cultural point of view, if history, progress and development are the

---

① *Thirukkural* (621): "When troubles come, laugh; Laughter alone can drive away sorrow."

measurements of human life and experience, then obviously a greater part of humanity would not be able to fit into this scheme. And yet, for millennia years, cultures do have nourished millions of people, even when they could not "make it" according to the dominant economic, political and developmental paradigm.

We may wonder, what is the meaning of life for that immense majority- the aboriginals, the slaves, the outcastes, the starving, the sick, the hungry, the oppressed, the women- who have not "made it?" Even in the hardest times and in face of greatest survival struggles, people could face life with joy and dignity precisely because they have been sustained by some kind of hope. This hope, however, is not merely of the future, *but perhaps in* the invisible dimension of life and reality.

Of course, as Panikkar reminds us, "*to make out of the necessity a virtue may not be sociologically advisable, but for the oppressed and disadvantaged, it seems to be the only way of upholding and sustaining their human dignity. It is certainly not a vice.* " ①

In this context, Panikkar points to a kind of *transcendental attitude*, which does not necessarily mean an explicit belief in transcendence. It implies an awareness accompanying every action, that life on earth, is only a kind of "comedy" -divine or not-a sort of play, a re-enactment of something bigger than ourselves and yet taking place within ourselves. *Karma*, rebirth, ū*lz* or ū*lzvinai*, transmigration, heaven, moral responsibility and so on, whatever religious or cultural underpinnings they may have, entail a firm sentiment that we are not private proprietors of our life, but actors and spectators of it. Perhaps it is this sort of, what he calls, "cosmic confidence" that does not allow people to be totally crushed by circumstances, however inhuman they may be. ②

In a word, the myth of destiny points to a dimension of hope which is not

---

① Panikkar, "Ecosophy," op. cit. , p. 7.
② Ibid. , pp. 283 – 284.

merely of the future, but in the invisible. It is this hope that allows Man to go beyond the perceptible dimension of reality to what we may call the depth–dimension of reality. It is this depth–dimension that can help face life and life's vicissitudes, especially when Man stands helpless in the face of inexplicable tragedies and sorrows. It is this dimension that could form the basis of optimism that everything has a meaning, though everything need not be perfect and alright in the future.

On the other hand, the myth of development with its thrust and orientation towards future has an important correcting and complimenting value to the myth of destiny. As an external stimulus, itcould inspire, intensify and promote the effort of the traditional cultures to revitalize themselves as they face the new situation of humanity. This inspiration may be seen in the effort of the traditional cultures to take history and progress seriously and to identify and overcome all the traditional notions and elements which have not been so very helpful to a fuller flowering and flourishing of authentic human life.

More concretely, this would mean paying a greater attention to the questions of human right, poverty, appalling conditions of women, a degeneration that has come about in the caste structure and all the conditions that deny a normal human living to millions of people. Pressing problems such as lack of food, housing, healthcare and education would need an immediate attention. In other words, the traditional cultures should do a re-assessment of their traditional values in the light of human welfare, particularly of the oppressed and downtrodden. This re-assessment would be greatly stimulated, complemented and enhanced by the dominant modern culture with its focus on the human dimension.

If the myth of development stands for a *human confidence*, and the myth of destiny for a *cosmic confidence*, then the meeting and synergy between these twoexperiences indeed signal a *rhythmic confidence*. A hope of the future and a hope in the invisible perhaps can meet in a *hope in the rhythm of reality* with a

sense of carefreeness. Synergising the *careful* mentality of human confidence
（development）and a kind of *careless*attitude of cosmic confidence（destiny），
the rhythmic confidence evokes a*carefree* awakening to the dynamism of life. A
participation in the dynamism, freedom or rhythm of being/reality surely
would include a striving and even an expectation for a "better world," but
surely not a "foreseeing." "Rhythm has an 'ever more,' but it does not
have, properly speaking, a future."[1] Human life, in other words, is not to
be seen as a linear progression towards God or some known or unknown
future, but it embodies a rhythm in which every moment is filled with a kind
of eternal/escaping moment in the very temporal moment. Reality is
tempiternal, that is, temporal and eternal in one and the same time in a non-
dualistic relation.[2]Human life, in this sense, implies a striving where the latter
is "neither the dream of an earthly paradise nor the inner self（ *antarātman* ）
alone,"[3] butit is an urge to discover and live in the present the fullness of life
with a struggle for "a world with less hatred and more love, with less violence
and more justice."[4]

Further, the encounter of the myth of destiny and the myth of development in
our cross-cultural human situation indeed signal a transformative process. As
Panikkar notes: "This task of transforming the cosmos is not achieved by a merely
passive attitude nor by sheer activism... The world does not 'go' independently
from us. We are active factors in the destiny of the cosmos. Otherwise, discourse
about the dignity of Man, his 'divinization' or divine character is an illusion."[5]
"What is needed is a 'synergy' in which human beings are seen neither as

---

① Panikkar, *RB*, p. 46.
② Cf. R. Panikkar, "Alternative à la Culture Modèrne（Texte II Dialogue），" Interculture15
（October-December 1982）, p. 25.
③ R. Panikkar, R. Panikkar, *The Rhythm of Being*（New York: Orbis Books, 2010）, p. 351. For
short, Panikkar, *RB*.
④ Ibid.
⑤ Ibid. , p. 350.

designing engineers of development nor victims"[1] of destiny. Theyare creative and active participants in the adventure, dynamismand rhythm of reality.

> To share in that rhythm is our destiny and our responsibility. For this we need purity of heart which will allow us to be attentive to the real rhythms of Being, detectable, first, in the revelation that comes to us from the others, the joys as much as the sufferings of humanity and Nature. It is a dance that is as much ethical as it is metaphysical and cosmic... We are players and chorus, actors, spectators, and co-authors in the rhythm of the real. Paradoxically enough, this openness to the other and the exterior requires a concentration on our interiority.[2]

It's here, Panikkar's concept of the metapoliticalassumesa significance. The experience of the metapolitical allows us to touch the depths of the human being without however being alienated from reality. It does not deny transcendence butonly awakens our consciousness by making us see that to be fully human we must surely insert ourselves into political or developmental activity, but must neither drown in it nor escape to some beyond or even interiority. It is by protesting, rebelling, transforming, failing and even dying to better our situation and that of our own fellow men and the oppressed of the earth, that we shall reach this fullness.

Basically, the hope in the rhythm of being or reality is therefore an affirmation, celebration and flourishing of " Life. " As Panikkar pleads, " plenitude, happiness, creativity, freedom, well-being, achievement etc. , should not be given up but, on the contrary, should be enhanced by this

---

[1] Cf. Fred Dallmayr, "A Secular Age? Reflections on Taylor and Panikkar," *International Journal for Philosophy of Religion* (2012) 71, p. 201.

[2] Panikkar, *RB*, p. 106.

transformative passage from historical to transhistorical M an. "① This transformative passage would surely include and take into account life's contingencies and hardships, but it is important to realize that the uniqueness of a human life has meaning, even under the weight of tragedy. And it is into this life that a synergy of hope in the rhythm of realty inserts itself in order to help discover the fleeting, poor but joyous, meaning of naked existence. It is this hope that can constantly remind us that the meaning of Life is *Life itself*, lived in all its fullness, intensity and depth.

---

① Panikkar, *RB*, p. 359.

The Maoism of *Tel Quel* around May 1968[*]

Xu Kefei[**]

Abstract: The Maoism of *Tel Quel* is an event of May 1968, and an interesting and significant phenomenon capable of revealing the relationship between intellectuals and politics. Seduced by the interpretation that the Cultural Revolution is a movement against any kind of bureaucracy, the Maoists of *Tel Quel* considered Maoism the climax of Marxism, and borrowed insigts from the ancient chinese culture to realize their own cultural revolution of the avant-garde in France. Neverthelss, the China of the Maoist *Tel Quel* is only an imaginary, which, misleading as it is for an understanding of the Cultural Revolution, can nevertheless shed new light on another problem.

Keywords: Maoism; *Tel Quel*; An Event of May 1968

《泰凯尔》知识分子关于中国的想象

徐克飞

摘　要：法国的毛主义是 1968 年五月风暴中一个非常重要的历史事

---

* 本文为教育部人文社科研究青年基金项目（项目编号：15YJCZH192），并受到教育部留学回国人员科研启动基金资助项目（项目编号：213007）的资助。

** 徐克飞（1978—），北京师范大学哲学与社会学学院副教授，研究方向为法国当代哲学与西方马克思主义。

件。《泰凯尔》知识分子曾经以毛主义为旗号进行了激进的政治参与，并且生产了流行于法国知识界的关于中国的想象。在其毛主义时期，《泰凯尔》知识分子将毛主义视为马克思主义的最高峰，认为中国"文化大革命"可以根治官僚制的弊端，还将中国传统文化作为创造新的先锋文化的重要资源。但是，这种想象忽视了中国的现实，他们关于中国的想象是为了解决法国社会问题的一种内向投射，因此具有欧洲中心主义的倾向。对这一现象的分析也是对法国知识分子命运的考察，是对法国六七十年代思想史的断代考古。

关键词：毛主义 《泰凯尔》 1968 年五月风暴

The Maoism of *Tel Quel* is an event of May 1968, and an interesting and significant phenomenon capable of revealing the relationship between intellectuals and politics. Seduced by the interpretation that the Cultural Revolution is a movement against any kind of bureaucracy, the Maoists of *Tel Quel* considered Maoism the climax of Marxism, and borrowed insigts from the ancient Chinese culture to realize their own cultural revolution of the avant-garde in France. Nevarthelss, the China of the Maoist *Tel Quel* is only an imaginary, which, misleading as it is for an understanding of the Cultural Revolution, can nevertheless shed new light on another problem.

Founded by the avant-garde intellectuals, *Tel Quel* is a review advocated for political engagement,[1] and their Maoism is the apex of their political engagement. In the fall of 1966, just after the outbreak of the Cultural Revolution in China, a Maoist group called "Political Committee" was formed around Philippe Sollers and other young intellectuals of *Tel Quel*. In 1972, the magazine rallied openly under Maoist ideology after breaking up with the French Communist Party（PCF）.[2] In 1976, Maoism of *Tel Quel* was finished after the death of Mao.[3] During their Maoist period, we can see three main waves of political engagement. First, in 1971, the Maoists of *Tel Quel* brought into play the "movement of June" . Waving Mao Zedong thought as an essential weapon of ideological and political struggle, the Maoists of *Tel Quel* launched their own cultural revolution on all fronts. [4] Then, in 1972, *Tel Quel* published issues devoted to China in journals 48 and 49. [5] Finally, from April 11 to May 3 1974, a delegation of *Tel Quel* made an official visit to China. The group consisted of five members: Philippe Sollers, Julia Kristeva, Marcelin Pleynet, François Wahl and Roland Barthes. The Maoists of *Tel Quel* wished to observe the Chinese Cultural Revolution on the spot. Another special issue about the Chinese Culture Revolution was published after their return (No. 59, 1974).

Today, the Maoism of *Tel Quel* sounds far away due to the big changes in political and intellectual climate. Yet it is still a shining example for reflecting on the role of intellectuals. Moreover, as a cross-cultural phenomenon, research about the Maoism of *Tel Quel* will reveal the possibility and the necessity to think differently about the relationship with the "Other" .

The Maoism of *Tel Quel* and Marxism

Maoists of *Tel Quel* always considered Maoism in the context of Marxism. It was via Marxism that the "Telquelians" discovered Maoism. What they were interested in was the dialectical materialism developed by Mao in his article "On Contradiction", while contradiction is also a fundamental concept in the dialectical materialism of Lenin. [6] The Maoists of *Tel Quel* believed that they have recovered the living soul of Marxism-dialectical materialism-in the "On contradiction" of Mao. In their eyes, therefore, Mao was the greatest Marxist after Marx, Engels and Lenin. Maoism was thus considered the climax of Marxism by the Maoists of *Tel Quel*.

According to the Maoists of *Tel Quel*, the dialectical materialism of Mao is a remedy against "dogmatism and revisionism" deviated from orthodox Marxism. [7] When Khrushchev became the head of the USSR, a policy of de-Stalinization was initiated by announcing a peaceful coexistence with the imperialism of the United States. For Mao, this kind of socialist imperialism betrayed Marxism-Leninism. Mao also believed that the Soviet Union deviated from its original purpose by taking a revisionist line, and this led him to break up with his former ally. For the Maoists of *Tel Quel*, China then became the new center of world revolution. Thus they engaged openly in an evaluation of the ideas of Mao. By choosing this path, the Maoists of *Tel Quel* wanted to fight against the dogmatic-revisionism of PCF, which supported the policy of the Soviet Union in the 1960s. For them, Maoism was the only way to overcome dogmatism and revisionism.

In fact, for the Maoists of *Tel Quel*, Maoism was more ideology than philosophy. The Maoists of *Tel Quel* were avant-garde writers before becoming Marxist philosophers. They dreamt of an aesthetic and political revolution, and this was why the Chinese Cultural Revolution fascinated them. [8] These Maoists laid their hope in the theoretical basis of the Chinese Revolution, as Maoism was for them both the revolutionary ideology and the philosophy used to tame capitalism.

However, after his withdrawal from the Maoist current, Philippe Sollers, the first Maoist of *Tel Quel*, believed that Mao "killed Marxism."

We can say that perhaps Mao Zedong killed Marxism. (...) The true interpretation, perhaps, of Mao is that he pushed Marxism to the point of incandescence and self-refutation. [9]

So, is Maoism the climax of Marxism Or did Maoism terminate Marxism? And why these two contradictory opinions co-existed in the history of the Maoism of *Tel Quel*? Before we answer these questions, it is necessary to raise a new one. What is Marxism? More specifically, what is the Marxism of *Tel Quel*, and what is the Marxism of Mao? In fact, Marxism of *Tel Quel* is a mixture of materialism, structuralism, Lacanism and other philosophical currents, while the Marxism of Mao is a "sinisation" of Marx's theory, which includes traditional Chinese thought (for example, the dialectic of Taoism). Phillippe Sollers and some other Maoists of *Tel Quel* unconsciously took their own Marxism as the criterion. This probably explains why Philippe Sollers, after the Maoist experience in France, argued that Mao had "killed" the original Marxism, or at least what he thought as the original concept developed by Karl Marx.

Maoism of *Tel Quel* and Anti-bureaucratism

Bureaucracy is a modern mechanism implemented in all forms of administrative and political organization. In the 1960s in France, bureaucracy often meant the political regime of the Soviet Union, where the hierarchy of bureaucracy was designed to serve a ruling class. At the same time, bureaucracy was also spreading rapidly in the camp of the political left in France, especially among the communists. As it was difficult to continue its revolutionary goals after the Second World War, the PCF deviated from a revolutionary party to a party of a sovereign order, with a special relation to the USSR. In the early period of May 68, the PCF was hostile to the student movement. For the younger generation, the PCF was an accomplice of President De Gaulle and of the bureaucracy of the USSR. In fact, the threat of bureaucratization not only concerned USSR and France, but also worried the PRC. Mao believed that his cadres within the Communist Party had lost the revolutionary spirit. They were corrupted by power and "infected" by the "revisionism" of the Soviet Union. In 1966, Mao decided to launch the Cultural Revolution in order to sweep the bureaucrats in the Party and the state institutes.

Due to their dedication to the resistance against any kind of bureaucracy, the Maoists of *Tel Quel* were seduced by the Cultural Revolution in China. "A question was put into my head very quickly, about who were responsible for the uprising of May 68, that is to say, to identify them by their stereotyped habits", says Philippe Sollers. [10]. In their eyes, Mao tried to find solutions to overcome the phenomenon of bureaucracy, and through the Cultural Revolution, China has become, according to them, a great country without bureaucracy.

Mao invented a new form of democracy: the *character posters*（大字报）. During the Cultural Revolution, through the *character posters*, everyone had the right to publish his political views, or to attack any form of authority. Women are entrusted with important political and social positions: "Women hold up half of the heaven"（妇女能顶半边天 *neng ding banbiantian*）. In the cultural field, Confucianism was also the target of attack. As a feudal ideology, Confucianism was the root of a hierarchical social system. Finally, the education revolution in China, through the "open schools"（开门办大学 *Kaimen ban daxue*）, broke the traditional universities——the machine of ideology reproduction. All these measures taken by Mao affected the Maoists of *Tel Quel*, who dreamt of changing the French bureaucratic society in the same way.

Nevertheless, even before the official dissolution of Maoism, some Maoists of *Tel Quel* had already begun to doubt the anti-bureaucracy effect of the Cultural Revolution. During his stay in China in 1974, Marcelin Pleynet strongly disapproved the stereotyped visits presented by the Chinese government. These tours were exclusively directed to him as a "standard business". François Wahl, one of the other participants of the trip to China, published in *Le Monde* a series of articles entitled "China without utopia" (from 15 to 19 June 1974). In these articles, the main feeling was disappointment. In the eyes of Wahl, China "has radically detached from the Soviet model."

The fundamental problem-for the Chinese and the world-is whether, and how successfully, China is radically detached from the Soviet model. (…) [11]

Why such conflicting opinions from the "Telquelians" on the anti-bureaucracy of the Chinese Cultural Revolution? This complex issue can be developed in two ways.

First, from a sociological point of view, this contradiction can be explained by the relationship between bureaucracy and modernity. In fact, bureaucracy is a companion to modernity. On the one hand, the bureaucratic system is necessary because of the division of labor resulting from specialization. On the other hand, bureaucracy also produces inefficient organization and tends to alienate people due to its reliance on a system of hierarchy between superiors and subordinates. Mao did not like bureaucracy. He wanted to eliminate bureaucracy even in the period of Yanan, when Chinese revolution was only in its embryo stage. Yet modernization had always been the goal of the leaders of the new China. In 1954, The Four Modernizations (agriculture, industry, transportation, national defense) as a national long term goal were set forth at the 1st National People's Congress of New China. But how to realize modernization? Mao Zedong at that time decided to use the Soviet Union as China's model, especially the agricultural collectivization. The traces of the soviet bureaucracy were inevitably left on the regime of new China. And it was not a surprise that Francois Whal had the feeling that "China is radically detached from the Soviet model".

It is worth noting that the bureaucracy under Mao and the bureaucracy referred to by *Tel Quel* are different. Mao criticized the deviance of bureaucracy, and "deviance" here is mainly in the sense of oppression and corruption. Even if Mao aimed at the dogmatism of the regime of the Soviet Union, his main target was still the revisionism in the Chinese context. That is to say, Mao worried about the communist cadres losing the revolutionary spirit and degenerating to be the new master of the people. Unlike the French or Soviet bureaucracy, the Chinese bureaucracy was still in the primary stage of development of a modern system of bureaucracy. In this sense, Mao was reflecting on a traditional or pre-modern form of bureaucracy, which was much less developed than the delicate post-modern bureaucracy called by Foucault the "controlled society" with "bio-power". We can also explain Mao's motivation by his different definition of bureaucracy. What Mao pursued was principally "equality", while for the Maoists of *Tel Quel*, "liberty" was the most important goal. They focused their criticism on the alienating effect of all forms of bureaucracy, as represented by the French and the Stalinist bureaucracies. In brief, Mao put forward a model of an egalitarian society devoid of any bureaucratic oppression, while the Maoists of *Tel Quel* claimed total liberation from bureaucratic alienation. Therefore, there was a historical misunderstanding between the Maoists of *Tel Quel* and Mao himself.

Maoism of *Tel Quel* and Chinese Culture (classical)

Maoists of *Tel Quel* have never ceased to be fascinated by Chinese culture (classical). [12] The absorbing interests of "Telquelians" about ancient Chinese culture began before their Maoist era. Some former Maoists of *Tel Quel*, including Philippe Sollers, retain up to this day a real fascination with Chinese culture.

For Maoists of *Tel Quel*, Chinese culture is a part of their avant-garde; they believed that Chinese culture can be helpful for their aesthetic and political revolution. The fascination with Chinese culture of "Telquelians" can be divided into three stages.

Before rallying to Maoism, their fascination with Chinese culture was more aesthetic than political. From its foundation to rallying to Maoism (officially in 1971), *Tel Quel* was not a review of political commitment. During this period, the writers of *Tel Quel* first used Chinese culture to support their aesthetic revolution. As marginal literature writers, the "Telquelians" took

Chinese culture as a new kind of literary and intellectual resource for their opposition to the famous writers in power, for example Jean-Paul Sartre. Philippe Sollers and Marcelin Pleynet both wrote "Chinese novels", the avant-garde novels using Chinese culture. [13] In the eyes of "Telquelians", Chinese culture could play a role equivalent to what the ancient Greek culture did for the Renaissance. As time went by, however, Chinese culture was gradually politicized by the "Telquelians", especially when they rallied to Maoism.

During the Maoist era of *Tel Quel*, the fascination with Chinese culture was more political than aesthetic. Because of the politicization of *Tel Quel*, the avant-garde aesthetics was soon overshadowed by the political "madness". Inspired by the Cultural Revolution of China, the political "revolution" as well as the aesthetic revolution of *Tel Quel* were quickly concentrated into the field of culture, in which Chinese culture was an essential part. At first, knowledge of Chinese culture was first intended to help them better understand the Cultural Revolution of China. Then, the fascination with Chinese culture was politicized and integrated into their desire to pursue their own cultural "revolution" in France.

After the disillusionment with Maoism, however, the fascination with Chinese culture became the way of questioning how the aesthetic ambition of "Telquelians" (or former "Telquelians") had been compromised by a political ambition. [14] Some of the former Maoists, such as Philippe Sollers, converted to Taoism (道家 *Daojia*) and looked for new beliefs (catholic for example). Their disappointment intensified their acts of denial of any political engagement by intellectuals. Consequently, they soon found themselves facing the problem of nihilism, nihilism not only in the political arena but also in the cultural field. Why nihilism? We should know that there is a paradox for the avant-garde. In order to destroy the aesthetic authority of the academics, they realized that a political revolution is necessary, since culture is just a part of the whole social system. But too much political engagement diluted their aesthetic creativity, which is the main domain of intellectuals. And if they forget their cultural mission, they would be no longer intellectuals, but only politicians. Due to this paradox, the avant-garde is usually not durable. Worse, when the fanatic fade away, nihilism is inevitable for the avant-garde, because they deny almost all the aesthetic criteria in the cultural domain. For the same reason, the former Maoists of *Tel Quel* converted to Daoism and took it as a remedy against nihilism.

In parallel with the politicization of Chinese culture through the Maoist ideology, the "Telquelians" discovered Chinese culture through Mao. Mao entered the pantheon of Marxism with Marx, Engels and Lenin. At the same time, Mao Zedong also drew on the sources of Chinese history. Mao was indeed strongly influenced by Chinese philosophy. Maoism differs from other Marxist currents on two key points: the non-determinism and voluntarism. These points are both inherited from the Chinese traditional philosophy. Taoism, for example, gave Maoism more flexibility than the determinism of orthodox Marxism. [15] As to the voluntarism of Mao, it comes from the Neo-Confucianism (Xinxue 心学), which emphasizes the idea that "being" is understood in the heart. [16] For the Maoists, Chinese philosophy has resurrected the issue of dialectical materialism beyond its "Hegelian" influence. By reading the dialectical materialism of Mao, Maoists of *Tel Quel* identified with Chinese philosophy.

Maoism of *Tel Quel* as Imaginary

The same question always haunted the Maoists of *Tel Quel*: why China? Or, does China exist in the Maoism of *Tel Quel*? The answer is "no". China for them is only an imaginary, an imaginary mainly in the sense of illusion.

Marcelin Pleynet admitted later that the Western Maoism is a kind of "introjection."[17] The western Maoists wanted to seek solution from the "outside" (Maoist China) in order to solve the problems of the "inside" (in France). That is to say, even if the Maoism of *Tel Quel* is a phenomenon resulting from Maoist China, it mainly comes from a special French context to solve special social problems of France. Therefore, for "Telquelians", Maoist China becomes an inverted mirror of the French social model, where there are all sorts of serious diseases of alienation of the modernity. Lucien Bianco made the following remark when he spoke of the Maoist phenomenon in France:

China is a solution to our own problems, our problems of the French and Western revolutionaries in the western world. China had no interest in itself; China was a pretext, and there was never the question: whether Maoism is suitable for China's problems and especially those that must be attacked urgently. [18]

Accordingly, the introjection of China in France is mostly an imaginary representation. The discourse of the Maoists of *Tel Quel* does not concern the question of what happened during the Chinese Cultural Revolution. The suffering of millions of Chinese people does not count for many of the Maoists of *Tel Quel*. For the Maoists of *Tel Quel*, China is obviously mythical, and the Maoists of *Tel Quel* are themselves the mythmakers.

Therefore, China in the minds of the Maoists of *Tel Quel* works as an "Other", and the Maoists of *Tel Quel* fell into the trap of ethnocentrism in dealing with an "other". Pleynet has also made the self-criticism on the introjection of Maoism. According to him, this introjection was a mistake, as well as the projection of the Rightists.

Each of these words is in my opinion to be read as a symptom of a disease that would never say its name. It is a paranoid projection, an anxious injection, or an effort to convince himself that class does not disappear. The best way to convince himself is still projecting his own fantasies over the other, or the attempt to fill the gap...[19]

In fact, the common disease of introjection and projection in the case of the Maoists may be named as "ethnocentrism". The recipients of the message from China were the Telquelians in the West. And like the projection of the Rightists, China is only an object in the imagination of the Maoists.

Marcelin Pleynet discovered ethnocentrism in the introjection of Maoism, but he did not find the way to get out. How to get out of this trap? Ironically, the answer perhaps exists in the thought of Mao. The Maoists of *Tel Quel* amputated parts of Mao's thought. Besides "On Contradiction," Mao wrote another philosophical article that interests us in particular, "On practice." The subtitle of "On Practice" is " on the relation between knowledge and practice-between knowing and doing? ". In his article, Mao advanced his opinion on this subject. For him, knowledge depends on social practice. To subjectivism and dogmatism, Mao emphasized knowledge through practice.

If you want knowledge, you must take part in the practice of changing reality. If you want to know the taste of a pear, you must change the pear by eating it yourself. [20]

But in their Maoist era, the Maoists of *Tel Quel* had never attached importance to "On Practice". And they had never tasted the "pear" in China, except the trip to China in 1974. So, the remedy to get out of the ethnocentrism of the imaginary is ultimately simple and clear: to see reality as it is, or as it was in China.

Note

[1] *Tel Quel* (1960 – 1982) is an avant-garde review published in the late 1950s by Philippe Sollers and Jean-Edern Haillier. It has a close coordination with some of the most famous intellectuals at that period, including Roland Barthes, Julia Kristeva, Jaque Derrida, Michele Foucault, Lacan and Louis Althusser.

[2] In 1971, the editing committee received randomly the manuscripts "From China"

from Maria Antoinette Macciocchi (1922 – 2007, member of the Italian Communist Party) .
While the PCF prohibited the circulation of this work at the annual celebration of the party, *Tel Quel* opposed this censorship and broke with the Communist Party in 1972. The review then rallied openly to Maoist ideologies.

[3] In 1976, *Tel Quel* published the article "About 'Maoism'" "(...) therefore specified that if *Tel Quel* has indeed, for some time, been trying to inform the public about China, especially for its opposition to the systematic distortion of the PCF, it can not be the same today. Moreover, our review is subject to attack from the " real Maoists " (...), it must end the myths, all myths. " (Tel Quel " About Maoism, " *Tel Quel*, No. 68, 1976, p. 104) .

[4] According to the Maoists of *Tel Quel*, the movement in June 1971 was born from an internal revolt of *Tel Quel* against the right-wing revisionist line.

[5] In both issues, half of the articles analyzed the Chinese thought and culture, while the rest were fascinated by the descriptions of revolutionary China in order to criticize the PCF. With these two issues, *Tel Quel* reached its sales record (20 000 to 25 000 copies) .

[6] "On Contradiction" (August 1937) and "On Practice" (July 1937), functioned as the hub of the Mao Zedong Thought. Both texts were important for the credibility of Mao as a theorist, and strengthened his claim to lead the party. For the Maoists in the west, these two texts developed dialectical materialism to a higher level. With these philosophical articles, Mao emerged as a new leader of Marxism.

[7] According to the Maoists of *Tel Quel*, the couple of "dogmatism and revisionism" are combined into dogmatic-revisionism.

[8] Although Mao says, like most Marxists, that the infrastructure transformation is accompanied by a broader transformation of the superstructure, he also believes that the transformation of the superstructure can in turn lead to a reset of the infrastructure.

[9] Philippe Sollers, "Why I was Chinese," *Tel Quel*, No. 88, Summer 1981, p. 12.

[10] Philippe Sollers, "Why I was Chinese," *Tel Quel*, No. 88, Summer 1981, p. 13.

[11] François Wahl, "China without Utopia II: Tiananmen or explanation with the Soviet model?" *le monde*, June 16, 1974.

[12] In the (former) Maoist *Tel Quel*, the term "Chinese culture" means the ancient Chinese culture (aesthetics) and not modern Chinese revolutionary culture (political) . For example, *yangbanxi* 样板戏 (revolutionary Peking opera) is not included in the "Chinese culture. " In this article, we follow the concept of "Chinese culture" of *Tel Quel*.

[13] The two "Chinese novels" of Philippe Sollers are *Drama* (1965) and *Number* (1968) . In both "Chinese novels," Philippe Sollers referred to the *Yi-Jing* 易经 . The Chinese novel of Marcelin Pleynet is *Stanze IV*, which borrows a legend-*gold band*-a popular Chinese novel, *Journey to the West*, (*Xiyouji* 西游记) .

[14] The aesthetic revolution will be found later in the same posture.

[15] It may be noted that Mao Zedong borrowed from the dialectic of Yin and Yang, originally an explanation of the nature of the antagonist system. For Mao, the principle of the interdependence of the adversaries is the center of the theory of contradiction. " It is so with all opposites; in given conditions, on the one hand they are opposed to each other, and on the other they are interconnected, interpenetrating, interpermeating and interdependent, and this character is described as identity. " (Mao Zedong, *On Contradiction* " http://www. marxists. org/reference/ archive/mao/selected-works/volume-l/mswvl _17. htm, 20 August 2013) . In Taoism, the permanent action of opposites gives rise to complementarity. " So it is that existence and non - existence give birth the one to (the idea of) the other; that difficulty and ease produce the one (the idea of) the other; that length and shortness fashion out the one the figure of the other; that (the ideas of) height and lowness arise from the contrast of the one with the other; that the musical notes and tones become harmonious through the relation of one with another; and that being before and behind give the idea of one following another. " (Lao Tzu , *The Tao Te Ching*, Translated by James Legge, http://www. taoiststudy. com/content/tao-te-ching-lao-tzu-translated-james-legge, 20 August 2013.)

[16] Before conversion to Marxism, Mao was a disciple of *Xinxue*, a branch of Neo-Confucianism. An article of the young Mao entitled "The power of the mind" (心之力 *xin zhi li*) indicates that the voluntarism of *Xinxue* is deeply rooted in the mentality of Mao: "Men are not the slaves of objective reality. Provided only the consciousness of men is consistent with the objective laws of development of things, the subjective activity of the masses can manifest in full measure, overcome all difficulties, and create the conditions necessary to advance the revolution. In this sense, the subjective creates the objective. " (Stuart Schram, *Mao Tse-tung*, Paris, Armand Colin, 1963, p. 87) .

[17] Upon reflection, Marcelin Pleynet made a conclusion of the various answers to the question "Why China?" To him, most of these responses operate either as introjection- "the subject passed under a fantasy mode, the " outside " to the " inside " objects and qualities inherent in these objects," or as projection- "transaction which is a neurological or psychological

moved and located outside or through the center to the periphery, from subject to subject. " (Marcelin Pleynet "'s speech on China, " *Tel Quel*, No. 60, 1974, p. 12).

[18] Bianco Lucien, "China to the French," *Maté riaux pour l'histoire de notre temps*, January-March 1987, p. 36.

[19] Pleynet Marcelin, "About the discourse on China," *Tel Quel*, No. 60, 1974, p. 12.

[20] Mao Zedong, "On Practice" http://classiques. chez-alice. fr/mao/delapratique. html, last accessed February 12, 2012.

理性机巧与人类自由关系辩证

熊　文 *

摘　要： 黑格尔认为，人类及其活动不过是理性借以实现自身的工具，即所谓理性的机巧，人类自由因此不过是理性的自由。从鲍威尔到马克思，自由从自我意识到现实的人实现了向人自身的回归，理性机巧与人类自由的关系演化成了人类个体与整体的内在关系和矛盾。晚年恩格斯力图用合力论来阐明两者关系的实质，但个体与类、自由与必然的矛盾似仍难解，因为数学模型难免失之于经验与表象，成为单纯量的角力。笔者认为，该问题的最终解答必须回归到马克思所确立的实践唯物主义原则，回归到马克思对类存在、类活动的批判，从思维与存在相统一、对象性活动的角度才能加以阐明，而马克思正是从解决什么是主体、解决什么是天意、解决社会意志与个人意志冲突、解决工具与环节的困惑、解决自由的路径、解决天意是如何产生等六个方面，全面回答了理性机巧与人类自由的关系问题。

关键词： 理性机巧　人类自由　辩证关系

The Dialectical Relationship between Rational Ingenuity and Human Freedom

Xiong Wen

Abstract： Hegel believed that humans and their activities were just tools

---

* 熊文，中南财经政法大学哲学院教师。

used by rationality to achieve its own, which means the so-called rational ingenuity and human freedom were only rational freedom. From Powell to Marx, freedom achieved a return to the people themselves from self-awareness to people in reality. The relationship between rational ingenuity and human has become the internal relationship and contradiction between the individuals and the whole human. In Engels's later years, he tried to use the Joint Forces Theory to clarify the substance of their relationship. However, the contradictions between the individuals and the whole human, between freedom and necessity remain unsolvable because mathematical models are inevitably lost in the experience and representations, becoming the simple number's wrestling. The writer believes that the ultimately answer to this issue must return to the principles of practical materialism established by Marx, to Marx's criticism of human existence and activities. It can only be clarified in terms of the unity of thought and existence and objective activities. And Marx fully answered the issue of the relationship between rational ingenuity and human freedom from six aspects, including the meaning of the subject and the providence, the personal and social conflicts, the puzzles of tools and links, the path of freedom and how the providence generated.

Keywords：Rational Ingenuity；Human Freedom；Dialectical Relationship

人类与自由的关系问题，一直是哲学思想史中的重要课题之一。黑格尔否认人有自由，把人及人的活动看作是理性实现自身的工具，并认为这正是理性的机巧，自由仅属于绝对精神。这种笼罩一切的绝对精神的威严在随后的青年黑格尔运动中遭到质疑。但无论鲍威尔还是费尔巴哈都无力处理黑格尔的这份思想遗产，马克思和恩格斯也对此进行了艰苦的探索，而两人之间也存在一定的差异。

一　自由的主体：绝对精神、自我意识、现实的人

问题缘起于黑格尔，而黑格尔处理任何问题都是逻辑的方式，即按照辩证的方式，自我规定，自我展开，自我深化，自我否定，同时也就是向自我的回归。关于自由问题的处理亦是如此。虽说自由归根结底是绝对精神的本质与属性，也是它的荣誉，但这并不妨碍黑格尔在较低的、不同的层面反复探讨自由问题，因为这也是自由本身自我深化和自我认识的题中之义。因此，黑格尔在处理完必然性与自由的问题之后，在目的性问题上再次深化了对自由的讨论，也就是在这里，他提出了引起争议的观点，所谓理性的机巧。黑格尔说道：

> 作为支配机械和化学过程的主观目的，在这些过程里让客观事物彼此互相消耗，互相扬弃，而它却超脱其自身于它们之外，但同时又保存其自身于它们之内。这就是理性的机巧。
>
> 理性是有机巧的，同时也是有威力的。理性的机巧，一般讲来，表现在一种利用工具的活动里。这种理性的活动一方面让事物按照它们自己的本性，彼此互相影响，互相削弱，而自己并不干预其过程，但同时却正好实现了它自己的目的。在这种意义下，天意对于世界和世界过程可以说是具有绝对机巧。上帝放任人们纵其特殊情欲，谋其个别利益，但所达到的结果，不是完成他们的意图，而是完成他的目的，而他［上帝］的目的与他所利用的人们原来想努力追寻的目的，是大不相同的。①

在这段表述里，自由的主体不仅被归之于绝对精神，而且现实的人们显然成了自由意志的无辜、盲目的工具，供奉于天意的祭品。这一论述乍看起来与传统的天意、命运之类的说法并无不同，了无新意。黑格

---

① 黑格尔：《小逻辑》，贺麟译，商务印书馆，1980，第 394～395 页。

尔的说法之所以让人印象深刻，乃是因为他把天意建立在强大的逻辑基础之上，从本体论、认识论、辩证法同一的角度论证了绝对精神与自由的关系，否认了人的自由。这使得反对这一观点的努力也必须具备同等有力的逻辑力量，而不仅是简单的愤怒和一般意义上的驳斥。

为动摇黑格尔理性机巧的逻辑，各种批判随之展开。青年黑格尔运动率先发起了攻击。他们攻击的目标是自由的主体——绝对精神。绝对精神在黑格尔那里是真正的、唯一的、终极的主体。《精神现象学》回顾了绝对精神诞生的历史，自我意识与实体的矛盾运动，最终导致自我意识对实体的完全占有和实体向自我意识的完全转化，实现的统一就是绝对精神的产生和确立。在这里，实体即主体的原则得到了清楚的展示，实体即是自我意识，实体不过是自我意识的外化、对象化，但主体从自我意识到绝对精神的转化显然只是基于黑格尔那绝对的唯心主义的要求，这种要求在青年黑格尔派看来不过是隐秘的神学而已。用马克思的话说：

> 他重新扬弃了肯定的东西，重新恢复了抽象、无限的东西。宗教和神学的恢复。①

因此，要做的是把主体——绝对精神拉下神坛，恢复自我意识作为主体的地位，从而自由成了自我意识的自由。同时，由于人就是人的自我意识，所以人的自由问题也就转化成了自我意识的自由问题。鲍威尔等人正是这样做的。青年马克思也认同这一点。在其博士论文中，他声称没有任何神能与人的自我意识相并列。他选择研究伊壁鸠鲁的自然哲学也是试图探讨其中所蕴含的自我意识哲学，而自由问题无疑是此项研究的重要方面，这从马克思着力讨论原子偏斜问题可见一斑。

但随着费尔巴哈的出现，自由的主体被进一步从人的自我意识引申为人，现实的人。费尔巴哈平实而富有激情的文字重新唤起了人们对唯物主义的热爱。他严厉批判了黑格尔哲学，认为未来的新的哲学的基础

---

① 《马克思恩格斯文集》第一卷，人民出版社，2009，第200页。

是"以自然为基础的现实的人"。他把被颠倒的主谓重新颠倒了过来。让人成为主词，自我意识回归到了谓词的地位。

马克思对费尔巴哈的观点十分支持，认为以自然为基础的现实的人即是感性的类存在，感性的人是有意识的自由的活动的人。这样的人才是自由的主体，是历史活动的主体。马克思说：

> 因为人和自然界的实在性，即人对人来说作为自然界的存在以及自然界对人来说作为人的存在，已经成为实际的、可以通过感觉直观的，所以关于某种异己的存在物、关于凌驾于自然界和人之上的存在物的问题，即包含着对自然界的和人的非实在性的承认的问题，实际上已经成为不可能的了。①

施蒂纳出版了《唯一者及其所有物》，书中对马克思进行了批判。施蒂纳指责马克思恩格斯把作为类的人抬高到主体的地位，是用新的神取代上帝，类存在的人成了新的神。马克思做了最后的反思，从《关于费尔巴哈的提纲》和《德意志意识形态》等文献来看，当马克思把人放在现实的社会关系和现实的历史前提中时，人才真正回归了现实，现实的人也最终得以确立。自由的主体也最终被找到。

> 这个过程必须有一个承担者、主体；但主体只作为结果出现；因此，这个结果，即知道自己是绝对自我意识的主体，就是神，绝对精神，就是知道自己并且实现自己的观念。现实的人和现实的自然界不过是成为这个隐蔽的非现实的人和这个非现实的自然界的谓语、象征。因此，主语和谓语之间的关系被绝对地相互颠倒了：这就是神秘的主体－客体，或笼罩在客体上的主体性，作为过程的绝对主体，作为使自身外化并且从这种外化返回到自身的、但同时又把外化收回到自身的主体，以及作为这一过程的主体；这就是在自

---

① 《马克思恩格斯文集》第一卷，人民出版社，2009，第196页。

身内部的纯粹的、不停息的旋转。①

这是一些现实的个人，是他们的活动和他们的物质生活条件，包括他们已有的和由他们自己的活动创造出来的物质生活条件。②

二 自由路径的选择：批判与合力

不仅是自由的主体问题，自由如何实现亦是问题。在黑格尔那里，自由的实现之路就是一条辩证之路。绝对精神就是绝对的否定性，推动自由的实现原则就是辩证的否定。当自我意识否定了实体，进而否定了自身，就是绝对精神自由的实现。

以鲍威尔为代表的青年黑格尔派，甚至费尔巴哈，对于辩证法的理解都相当差。同时，他们又把自我意识视为世界的本质，把历史进程视为自我意识的发展，现实成了自我意识的宾词，也就是观念形态的谓词，如此一来，人的活动与实践就成了纯粹观念的斗争。换句话说，推动自由的原则由辩证的否定简化成了观念批判。

即把存在于我身外的现实的、客观的链条转变成只是纯观念的、纯主观的、只存在于我身内的链条，因而也就把一切外在的感性的斗争都转变成了纯粹的思想斗争。③

可见自由实现的方式不过是主体活动的方式，是主体自我实现的方式。如果主体仅仅只是实现了从精神到精神的转化，那么从绝对精神到自我意识并没有什么实质的转变。鲍威尔片面发展黑格尔哲学，将自我意识因素推至极端，成为独立的绝对。他把自我意识与实体绝对对立，

①《马克思恩格斯文集》第一卷，人民出版社，2009，第217页。
②《马克思恩格斯选集》第一卷，人民出版社，1995，第67页。
③《马克思恩格斯文集》第一卷，人民出版社，2009，第288页。

把自我意识看成不依赖于感性具体世界的精神活动，一方面否定了存在于人之外的自然界，另一方面否定了作为自然存在物的人。自我意识成了创造的主体。在马克思看来，鲍威尔对黑格尔存在着双重不彻底性的克服：

> 第一，黑格尔虽然承认作为世界发展基础的绝对精神的存在，但还没有直截了当地说，我就是绝对精神。第二，绝对精神作为现实的创造主，只是到最后才认识到自己的这种创造主的地位和作用，所以黑格尔只是事后才来撰造过去的历史。①

鲍威尔取消了这两个不彻底性，宣布批判就是绝对精神，他就是批判。因此，总体看来，鲍威尔既没有真正理解黑格尔的自我意识，也没真正掌握黑格尔的辩证法，作为批判的批判的原则只能沦为空谈。

至于费尔巴哈爱的原则，甚至连批判还具有的一点否定性原则的残影都没有，只能是孤芳自赏的一道残阳。这一点，恩格斯在《路德维希·费尔巴哈和德国古典哲学的终结》一书中曾给予了无情的讽刺。

如果不是思想的路径，那么现实的路径呢？值得注意的是，在讨论人的自由与必然性问题上，恩格斯的合力论有着很大的影响。它仿佛是对黑格尔理性机巧的唯物主义的说明。

但历史的真实过程是怎样的呢？人的自由与历史是什么关系呢？恩格斯提出社会历史发展是人作为历史主体及其合力的结果：

> 无论历史的结局如何，人们总是通过每一个人追求他自己的、自觉预期的目的来创造他们的历史，而这许多按不同方向活动的愿望及其对外部世界的各种各样作用的合力，就是历史。②

---

① 《马克思恩格斯全集》第二卷，人民出版社，1957，第182页。
② 《马克思恩格斯文集》第四卷，人民出版社，2009，第302页。

　　历史是这样创造的：最终的结果总是从许多单个的意志的相互冲突中产生出来的，而其中每一个意志，又是由于许多特殊的生活条件，才成为它所成为的那样。这样就有无数互相交错的力量，有无数个力的平行四边形，由此就产生出一个合力，即历史结果，而这个结果又可以看做一个作为整体的、不自觉地和不自主地起着作用的力量的产物。……每个意志都对合力有所贡献，因而是包括在这个合力里面的。①

　　可见，恩格斯把天意转换成了合力，同时也保留了个人的自由，而正是在合力中，历史的自由意志得到了实现。这似乎是一个完满的解答。现实的人按照自己的自由意志在活动，彼此互相消耗，形成合力，推动着历史朝着合力所指的方向走。这里没有任何神秘色彩，超越个人的力量和规律不是天意，而是人们的行为所造成的，历史既是人们自由的创造，又不以任何个人的意志为转移。

　　但合力论不是无可指摘的。第一，它用数学模型来解决哲学问题，这似乎是原则性的方向错误。人文学科的方法早已自觉，难道辩证法不比力学更适合解决历史自由的问题？第二，自然科学的方法恰恰是无主体、去质化的。人能代入平行四边形，显然这样的人不再是生动的、历史中的感性的、充满个性的现实的人，而是抽掉了特质、作为原子式的量的存在的人。试问个性、特点等等全然不同的两个人如何能简化成力矩，更不要说合并了。不同的质之间根本不可能实现同一，世界上并不存在木制的铁。第三，在历史发展的实际过程中，是转化为否，否转化为是是常态，对立双方均被扬弃更是常态。哪有什么合力可言？

　　因此，批判的道路非现实，合力之路看似现实实际也只停留在理论层面，仍非现实。那么现实之路呢？我们必须回头看马克思的解答。

---

① 《马克思恩格斯文集》第十卷，人民出版社，2009，第592页。

三 自由的实现：自由与实践关系辩证

马克思显然认为自己已经知悉历史自由之谜的答案。一个明显的标志是，马克思在《资本论》第一卷中说道：

> 劳动资料是劳动者置于自己和劳动对象之间、用来把自己的活动传导到劳动对象上去的物或物的综合体。劳动者利用物的机械的、物理的和化学的属性，以便把这些物当作发挥力量的手段，依照自己的目的作用于其他的物。①

在作出这番论述之后，马克思马上自信地引用了黑格尔关于理性机巧的相关段落。可见，马克思已然超越了黑格尔，如此才能信手拈来。

实践在马克思那里是自由的有意识的感性的对象性活动。实践之所以能成为解决自由问题的关键，是因为它解决了六个问题。

第一，解决了什么是主体。自由的主体如上所述，是现实的感性的活在一定历史条件下的人。并不是什么非人的事物或神。自由总是人类的自由。

第二，解决了什么是天意。天意不是什么神意，也不是什么宿命，亦不是合力。天意只是历史的自身的规律，而历史的主体是人，历史不外是人的活动，所以天意不过是人的自身规律。更确切地说，天意是社会历史发展的规律和原则。这个原则当然不是抽象的、永恒的，但不可否认，它依然是普遍性的规律。

第三，解决了社会意志与个人意志冲突的问题。这里似乎出现了个人意志与社会意志的冲突，人类自由与个人自由的对立。可问题是，什么是个人意志？我们总认为存在特殊的个人独有的意识和意志，但语言是思想的直接现实，而语言只能表达普遍，因此，所谓的特殊意识与意

---

① 《马克思恩格斯全集》第四十四卷，人民出版社，2001，第209页。

志其实仍是普遍意识和意志，是社会意识和意志的自为存在，个人的特殊意识和意志只是特殊化的普遍的社会意识和意志而已。个人意识和意志固然与社会意识和意志有矛盾之处，但这并不能否认两者的同一。个人意识和意志统一于社会意识和意志之中。正如印度宗教的比喻，譬如瓶等破，瓶等合空。情命归自我，于是亦如是。瓶中之空与瓶外的空本质是一样的。同样，任何感性的实践行为，既是特殊的，也带有普遍性。

第四，解决了工具与环节的困惑。如果个人的意识与行为既是特殊的，也是普遍的，那么也就不难理解，人在历史中既是主体也是环节是工具。人在历史实践中，既是主体，是编剧，也是演员和观众。而人之所以能做到这一点，只是因为实践是有意识的自由的活动，因此，人作为意识和行为的主体，也始终把自己的意识和行为当作自己的对象。

> 动物和自己的生命活动是直接同一的。动物不把自己同自己的生命活动区别开来。它就是自己的生命活动。人则使自己的生命活动本身变成自己意志的和自己意识的对象。他具有有意识的生命活动。这不是人与之直接融为一体的那种规定性。有意识的生命活动把人同动物的生命活动直接区别开来。正是由于这一点，人才是类存在物。或者说，正因为人是类存在物，他才是有意识的存在物，就是说，他自己的生活对他来说是对象。仅仅由于这一点，他的活动才是自由的活动。①

第五，解决了自由的路径。通往自由的路径正是人的感性实践。这不再是绝对精神自我设定，自我克服，回复自身的过程。

> 作为推动原则和创造原则的否定性——的伟大之处首先在于，黑格尔把人的自我产生看做一个过程，把对象化看做非对象化，看做外化和这种外化的扬弃；他抓住了劳动的本质，把对象性的人、

---

① 《马克思恩格斯文集》第一卷，人民出版社，2009，第62页。

现实的因而是真正的人理解为人自己的劳动的成果。①

黑格尔的错误在于，他把自我对象化的内容丰富的、活生生的、感性的、具体的活动，转变成为：

> 这种活动的纯粹抽象，成为绝对的否定性，而这种抽象又作为抽象固定下来，并且被想象为独立的活动，或者干脆被想象为活动。因为这种所谓否定性无非是上述现实的、活生生的行动的抽象的无内容的形式，所以它的内容也只能是形式的、抽去一切内容而产生的内容。②

第六，解决了天意是如何产生的。对于天意通常的解释是来自先验的原则，要么是自在的，要么是神赋的。或者，如恩格斯所主张，是合力。其实如果是合力，那就比拳头好了，因为这只是量的比较与综合。

思维和存在是同一的。马克思观察、研究、分析资本主义社会，写下了资本的逻辑。这个逻辑并不是若干简单的原理或范畴，而是充满辩证联系的范畴的体系。逻辑从最简单的商品开始，从价值分析入手，逐步深入，从抽象到具体，辩证展开，最后在逻辑的整体上再现了资本主义社会的全貌。不同质、不同层面的范畴之间相互转化，扬弃前行，构成了整个资本的运动。在整个运动中，在整个体系中，那作为实体的方面，那本质的方面，规定了历史的方向，构成了天意。这是由质而非由量的综合决定的。

马克思说：

> 在一切社会形式中都有一种一定的生产决定其他一切生产的地位和影响，因而它的关系也决定其他一切关系的地位和影响。这是

---

① 《马克思恩格斯文集》第一卷，人民出版社，2009，第205页。
② 《马克思恩格斯文集》第一卷，人民出版社，2009，第218页。

一种普照之光，它掩盖了一切其他色彩，改变着它们的特点。这是一种特殊的以太，它决定着它里面显露出来的一切存在的比重。①

天意其实就是唯物史观所说明的：

> 每一历史时代主要的经济生产方式和交换方式以及必然由此产生的社会结构，是该时代政治的和精神的历史所赖以确立的基础，并且只有从这一基础出发，这一历史才能得到说明。②

虽然历史的构成是具体的，包括生产力、生产关系、意识形态等等，但历史的走向、历史的必然性却是确定的。正如马克思所言：

> 人们在自己生活的社会生产中发生一定的、必然的、不以他们的意志为转移的关系，即同他们的物质生产力的一定发展阶段相适合的生产关系。这些生产关系的总和构成社会的经济结构，即有法律的和政治的上层建筑竖立其上并有一定的社会意识形式与之相适应的现实基础。物质生活的生产方式制约着整个社会生活、政治生活和精神生活的过程。不是人们的意识决定人们的存在，相反，是人们的社会存在决定人们的意识。社会的物质生产力发展到一定阶段，便同它们一直在其中运动的现存生产关系或财产关系（这只是生产关系的法律用语）发生矛盾。于是这些关系便由生产力的发展形式变成生产力的桎梏。那时社会革命的时代就到来了。随着经济基础的变更，全部庞大的上层建筑也或慢或快地发生变革。③

也许有人会重提自由与必然的冲突，但这个问题在黑格尔那里就已

① 《马克思恩格斯选集》第二卷，人民出版社，1995，第24页。
② 《马克思恩格斯选集》第一卷，人民出版社，1995，第257页。
③ 《马克思恩格斯选集》第二卷，人民出版社，1995，第32～33页。

经不是问题。自由并不排斥必然性，而是扬弃必然性于自身之内。必然不必自由，但自由却必然包含必然性。

> "历史"并不是把人当作达到自己的目的的工具来利用的某种特殊的人格，历史不过是追求着自己的目的的人的活动而已。①

这句针对性极强的话，说明马克思在理性机巧与人类自由的关系问题上已经有了自己的确定答案。马克思一生追求自由，热爱自由，从推崇自我意识，到类存在，直到把"能动的方面"贯注到唯物主义中，在现实的人的感性实践中得到了最终的解答。马克思说：

> 社会生活在本质上是实践的。凡是把理论导致神秘主义的神秘东西，都能在人的实践中以及对这个实践的理解中得到合理的解决。②

因此，对自由的解答只是其中之一。

---

① 《马克思恩格斯全集》第二卷，人民出版社，1957，第118页。
② 《马克思恩格斯选集》第一卷，人民出版社，1995，第60页。

杰文斯悖论的价值论根源

李白鹤[*]

摘 要：从根本上讲，在人类社会发展中真正消除杰文斯悖论，有赖于建立符合正义原则的社会制度，在此前提下才可能实现人与自然、人与人之间的和谐，建立真正的生态文明。但是，制度的变革有赖于人类自身觉悟指导下的实践，在能源—环境问题日益严峻威胁着人类的生存和发展的紧迫时刻，对杰文斯悖论的价值论根源的考察，有助于人们更深刻地认识技术的社会功能，也有助于推动人类合理地改造人与自然以及人与人关系的实践。技术是人类认识和改造自然的重要中介和工具，由此也形成了技术与人之间的重要价值关系。从价值论上探寻杰文斯悖论的形成原因，我们会发现，在技术实践中所出现的价值目的的偏离、衡量技术发展的片面的技术进步观、仅将操作规范作为约束技术实践的技术规范，这些都是导致杰文斯悖论的重要原因。杰文斯悖论的价值论根源昭示出技术的发展和应用要以人类整体的生存和持续发展作为最高的价值目标，经济的发展不能代替人的发展，人类局部的暂时的利益不能代替人类整体的利益。这也要求人们相应地树立包含着"人的尺度"的技术进步观，确立包含着价值规范的技术规范。在利益分化广泛存在的社会里，以人类整体的生存和持续发展作为技术实践的最高价值目标，以相互尊重和求同存异为原则就实现这一目标的途径和方式逐渐形成不

---

* 李白鹤，中南财经政法大学哲学院教师。

同范围的价值共识，并将其融入技术实践的具体目标和技术规范之中，以此指导和约束人类的技术实践，这是在现时代合理地利用技术为人类的共同利益而努力的现实路径。

关键词： 杰文斯悖论　技术　价值

Exploring the Causes of Jevons Paradox from the Perspective of the Theory of Value

Li Baihe

Abstract： Fundamentally, to virtually eliminate the Jevons paradox during the development of human society, it depends on the establishment of a social system in line with the principles of justice. It is possible to achieve the harmony between human and nature, between people and people, to establish a genuine ecological civilization only in this context. However, the reform of the system depends on the practice of human under the guidance of self-consciousness. As the energy-environmental problems have become an increasingly serious threat to human's survival and development, the investigation of the Jevons Paradox's axiology source helps people have a deeper understanding of the social function of technology, and also helps promote the rational reconstruction practice of the relationship between man and nature as well as the interpersonal relationship. Technology is an important intermediary and tool for people to understand and transform the nature, which also forms a significant value relationship between technology and people. To explore the causes of Jevons Paradox in terms of the value theory, we will find that the deviation of value objects in the technology practice, the one-sided view of technology advances in the measurement of technological development and techniques specifications which only use operation specifications to constrain the technology practice are all major causes of Jevons Paradox. The Jevons Paradox's axiology source reveals that the development and application of technology should consider the survival and sustainable development of human as the highest value targets. The economic development can not replace human's development and the local temporary interests of humanity can not replace the interests of the human as a whole. It also requires people to build up a view of technology advances containing "human scale" and to establish technical specifications containing the criteria of value accordingly. In the society where the social differentiation widely exists, we should consider human's survival and sustainable development as the highest value targets of technology practices, the mutual respect and the seeking of common ground as the principles. We should also gradually form the value consensus of different ranges on the ways and means to achieve this goal. Meanwhile, we should integrate the value consensus into the specific objectives and technical specifications of technology practices so as to guide and constrain people's technology practices. That's the realistic way for us to work for people's common interests by using technology rationally in the current era.

Keywords: Jevons Paradox; Technology; Value

　　2009 年，来自美国、英国、日本、西班牙的几位学者写的《杰文斯悖论：技术进步能解决资源难题吗》[1] 一书以严密的理论研究和数据分析再次论证了杰文斯悖论在当代世界各个地区的普遍存在。19 世纪经济学家杰文斯针对当时人们致力于在技术上提高煤炭的利用效率以满足人们的煤炭需求的努力指出，实际上，煤炭的使用效率越高，人们将会消耗更多的煤炭能源，煤炭能源的耗竭速度将会加快。这意味着，技术的进步并不能解决人类社会发展所面临的资源难题。《杰文斯悖论：技术进步能解决资源难题吗》一书的作者们指出，在当前的 21 世纪，尽管煤炭已非人们使用的唯一重要能源，然而人们通过技术创新以提高能源的使用效率的努力仍然无法真正解决资源难题，相反却会刺激能源的使用、带来排放的增加。在书中，作者们不但以具体的实证研究揭示了杰文斯悖论在美国、欧盟等地的存在，也以详尽的数据模型说明了杰文斯悖论在亚太地区包括中国、印度等国家的存在。人们致力于技术的创新发展以期节约能源、减少排放，然而杰文斯悖论在当今世界范围内的广泛存在却再次表明技术的进步不但无法应对能源危机、解决环境问题，而且甚至会刺激能源消耗和增加排放。从这一角度看，无疑，杰文斯悖论是当前人们共同关注的技术悖论的重要组成部分。作为人类认识和改造自然的重要中介和工具，技术是人类开发和利用能源、改造环境的重要手段，然而技术的进步却无法解决反而会加深当代人类社会所迫切面临的能源－环境问题。为什么会出现这一悖论？如何消解这一悖论？这是当前人类社会在积极推动技术进步的同时急切探寻答案的重要问题。

一

在对杰文斯悖论的形成原因和消解途径的探讨中，杰文斯悖论的认识根源和社会根源受到学者们的关注。

从人类认识的发展过程来看，在某个具体阶段，人们的认识能力会有其局限，人们对技术应用可能带来的后果的认识也会有局限，这种认识上的局限是杰文斯悖论形成的重要原因。比如，杰文斯悖论的提出本身就是人们逐渐在实践中认识到，煤炭利用技术的进步虽然能够提高煤炭的利用率，但是也会带来生产规模的扩大并因此增加煤炭的消耗而不是减少煤炭的需求，这显示出人们对于技术应用的影响的全面认识不是一蹴而就的，技术在应用中可能会出现的背离人们初衷的影响可能是在其应用中渐渐被人们认识的。

社会制度是导致技术悖论包括杰文斯悖论的最深刻的社会根源。杰文斯悖论的出现与技术使用的资本主义方式是分不开的。在资本主义的制度下，资本家为了最大限度地追求利润，在对技术的运用中不可能会牺牲自己的私利而真正遵循生态原则。西方马克思主义理论家对此曾有明确的揭示，"典型的资本主义把任何危机的原因都归咎于影响资本扩张的障碍，而不是资本扩张本身。解决办法就是扩大资本领域，把自然也作为理性的商品交换体系的一部分"[2]，而资本的私人占有，意味着自然的私有化，资本家对于最大利润的追求，将会耗尽自然资源。因此，"资本主义对生态问题的终极解决方案——因其制度自身的根本变化是有限的——也只能表现在技术性意义上"[3]，而资本主义制度本身决定了这种制度下技术的使用无法解决生态问题。

实际上，在对杰文斯悖论的认识根源和社会根源的考察中，可以看到杰文斯悖论的形成所涉及的重要价值问题。在当前理论界关于人类中心主义和非人类中心主义的争论中，在处理人与自然的关系问题上是否应当把人看作唯一的价值中心和价值主体是两种立场的论争焦点。非人类中心主义认为正是传统的人类中心主义将人视为唯一的价值主体和价值中心，而导致人们使用科学技术对自然无限制地开发和利用，因而在他们看来，人类中心主义这种以人作为唯一的价值主体和价值中心的价值观是导致环境问题、生态问题的重要价值根源。面对非人类中心主义的批判，现代人类中心主义强调运用科学技术开发和利用自然应当关注全人类可持续的发展，应当以全人类包括子孙后代作为价值主体和价值中心。从认识的角度来看，在技术的使用中，对于传统人类中心主义带来的消极影响缺乏足够的认识，这是导致杰文斯悖论的重要认识根源。而从社会制度的角度来看，在私有制占主导地位的社会中，技术的使用所指向的价值中心往往是在经济、政治上占统治地位的那些阶级或利益集团。然而，认识的发展源自人类自身的探索思考，制度的变革有赖于人类自身觉悟指导下的实践，因而对杰文斯悖论的认识根源、社会根源的探讨并不能替代关于其价值论根源的思索，对杰文斯悖论的价值论根源的考察，有助于人们更深刻地认识技术的社会功能，也有助于推动人类合理地改造人与自然以及人与人关系的实践。

二

技术是人类认识和改造自然的重要中介和工具，由此也形成了技术与人之间的重要价值关系。在这一价值关系中，人是价值主体，认识和改造自然以满足人的需要是价值目的，技术是价值对象。杰文斯悖论却显示出，尽管技术是人类认识和改造自然、开发和利用能源的重要手段，然而技术的进步却无法解决反而会加深当代人类所急需解决的能源－环境问题。在杰文斯悖论中，价值对象是否真的无法满足价值主体的需要？价值对象究竟为何无法满足价值主体的需要？

实际上，从价值论上探寻杰文斯悖论的形成原因时，我们首先会发现，在人类运用技术的实践中出现了价值目的的偏离。人们运用技术的价值目的从根本上说是为了满足人的需要。然而，一方面，人的需要多种多样。在杰文斯悖论中，技术的发展之所以被称为进步，就是因为它符合一定的技术进步标准，满足人们某些方面的需要。这种技术进步标准更多地与生产力的提高、经济效益的增加相联系。它所满足的需要，也是人们希望凭借节能技术的应用、新能源的开发利用等带来生产成本的减少、生产规模的扩大、经济利益的增加等需要。按照这样的技术进步观和需要观，我们所看到的将只会是"社会被经济层面上激增的财富与个人层面上的匮乏的体验之间的永恒矛盾所困扰。无论多么勤勉地或多么成功地寻找到不断增长的资源和能源的供应，也不能解决这一矛盾"[4]。另一方面，在存在利益分化的现实社会中，进行具体实践活动的个体总是隶属于一定的阶级、群体和利益集团，不同阶级、群体和利益集团之间可能会有利益的冲突，不同个体、群体与人类的利益并不能总是保持一致。2009年，来自192个国家的代表参加了在丹麦首都哥本哈根召开的世界气候大会，并协商达成了2012年至2020年的全球减排协议——《哥本哈根协议》。这显示出环境问题在当今世界范围受到广泛的重视。然而，在会议上所出现的关于"责任共担"的争论，却显示出不同地区和国家作为不同的利益主体，在关注各自的利益时而造成的彼此间的利益冲突。对于气候学家们强调的必须在全球范围内减少温室气体的排放以防止全球平均气温的上升，由于事关全球人类的生存和发展，参会各国都予以认同，然而，究竟各国在减排问题上应当承担怎样的责任，却引发了会议中激烈的争论，发达国家是否应当承担更多的责任？像中国、印度这样的主要发展中国家又如何处理经济发展与节能减排的平衡问题？就杰文斯悖论而言，不同国家不同地区在节能技术的应用时以各自国家、地区作为价值主体，那些对本国本地区有利的实践带来的可能是从总体上阻滞人类整体发展、妨碍人类整体利益的后果。因此，不同的价值主体指向是导致杰文斯悖论的重要原因。正是由于不同个体、群体与人类的利益并不能总是保持一致，因此，在人们使用技术改造自然的现实实践中可能会出现为了追求某些个人或群体的利益而损害他人、其他群体的利益，或者是为了人类局部、某些个人或群体的暂时利益而损害人类整体的、长远的利益的情况。由此，我们可以看到，人们运用技术的价值目的从根本上说是为了满足人的需要，但是人的需要多种多样，而且个人、群体、人类的需要之间还可能存在着冲突。就杰文斯悖论而言，能源－环境问题之所以是人类急需解决的问题，不仅仅在于这类问题限制着生产规模的扩大、影响着经济利润的增长，更为重要的是这类问题影响着人类未来的生存和发展。人类关注节能技术的研发，注重绿色能源的开发等，实际上也包含着对人类整体的长远利益的考虑，但是在应用这类技术的现实实践中，当经济利益、眼前利益更为现实、更为直接时，当个人利益、集团的利益与人类整体的长远利益存在矛盾时，人们倾向于满足的是眼前的、局部的、暂时的经济利益，由此使得节能技术的应用带来的是能源消耗的增加、环境破坏的加速。在这一意义上，这些技术实践不但没有真正满足人们的需要，反而给人类未来的生存和发展带来更大的威胁。由此可见，在运用技术的实践中出现了价值目的的偏离是杰文斯悖论形成的重要原因。

在技术与人的价值关系中，当我们从价值对象的角度探寻杰文斯悖论的形成原因时，我们可以看到，片面的技术进步观、新技术的传播和推广中所使用的技术规范的价值中立性也是导致杰文斯悖论的重要原因。一方面，前文已经提到，在技术的发展中，人们通常使用的技术进步标准往往更多地与生产效率的提高、经济效益的增加相联系。按照这样的进步标准，节能技术的研发、新能源的开发利用，它们的发展方向、研究规模都会受到经济指标的影响，那些暂时地需要增加生产投入的新节能技术或是在一定时期内需要加大生产成本的新能源的利用就可能会因为这样的影响而被人为地忽视。另一方面，技术规范是技术实践中新技术的传播和推广最重要的载体。所谓技术规范，是指一定时期由于某种成功的技术成果的典型示范作用而形成的为技术共同体认可的关于这种技术开发利用的原理、规则、途径和方法等，是技术实践的重要约束条件。可以看到，在现实的技术实践中，人们所强调的技术规范更多地涉及保证产品质量和施工质量的规定、标准，这些主要属于操作规范。实际上，技术在社会中的应用不可避免地会涉及对人、对社会的价值作用，技术的不同方式的运用也会带来不同的价值后果。因此，仅仅只是限于从技术知识和技术方法、工艺流程和规程、操作准则等操作规范上来约束人们的技术实践，这也是技术发展不能真正解决能源——环境问题的重要原因。

三

尽管杰文斯悖论的重要社会根源在于技术的资本主义使用方式，杰文斯悖论的根本消除有赖于建立符合人类普遍利益的社会制度，但是，在揭示杰文斯悖论的价值论根源的基础上，确立合理的技术价值观，对于指导人们发展和应用技术的实践、推动人们合理地改造人与人关系的实践有着重要的积极作用。

杰文斯悖论的价值论根源昭示出技术的研发使用应确立合理的价值目标。非人类中心主义批判传统人类中心主义仅将人作为唯一的价值中心，因而带来了人与自然的对立，也导致了人类对被视为仅具有工具价值的自然的过度开发和索取。在这些批判中，一些批判者提出以自然中心主义、动物中心主义或生态中心主义代替人类中心主义。他们指出自然界的各种组成部分对于维持生态系统的平衡都有不可替代的重要作用，认为自然界的其他组成部分与人一样都具有与生俱来的内在价值，因而他们强调人们的实践活动应当重视自然的内在价值，应当把自然、生态而不仅仅是人视为价值中心。实际上，正如人类中心主义的辩护者们所指出的，价值关系的形成本身就源自人类改造对象的实践，正是在人与对象的改造与被改造的关系的基础上形成了对象对人的需要的满足关系，即价值关系。因而，价值的主体或中心是人，这是价值的重要特征。自然、生态的重要价值并不是因为它们的客观存在，而是因为它们对于人的生存和发展所具有的重要意义。进而，我们还可以看到，人们对生态环境问题的关注，对人类中心主义问题的反思，其根本目的还是为了人类更好地生存和发展。因而，技术的研发使用，其根本的价值目标应当在人而不在物。还应当看到，尽管在运用技术利用和改造自然时，价值中心是人，但是需要注意的是，正如现代人类中心主义对传统人类中心主义的修正那样，这里的价值中心并不是某些时期的某些特定群体或特殊集团，而是全人类。全人类包括子孙后代的存在和发展是技术的研发使用的最高价值目标。因此，任何技术的研发和应用，都应当以有利于人类整体的、长远的利益为准则。

技术的研发使用应当以人类整体的生存和持续发展为目标，这也要求人们相应地树立正确的技术进步观。以往在衡量技术的进步时，经济指标、生产力标准被给予更多的关注，因而也就会出现在技术的研发和使用中为最大限度地追求经济利益和生产发展而不惜牺牲环境资源的情况，这也是杰文斯悖论出现的重要原因。事实上，环境－资源问题的恶化，最终仍会对社会生产造成阻碍，影响社会经济的增长。应当看到，人作为社会生产力的首要因素，是社会生产力、社会经济发展的主体力量，但同时，人更好地生存和发展又是社会生产力、社会经济发展的根本目的。这样，技术的进步应当意味着人类自身正在为人的生存和发展创造着更为美好的未来而不是相反。因此，经济指标或生产力标准不是技术进步的唯一标准，技术的进步，其落脚点在于人，"人的尺度"是技术实践的根本尺度。

强调以有利于人类整体的生存和持续发展作为技术研发使用的最高目标和基本准则，这就要求作为技术研发使用的约束条件的技术规范不应当仅仅只是涉及技术方法、工艺流程和规程、操作准则和技能等操作规范，还应当涉及控制技术的合理应用的价值规范。技术规范应当包含着有利于人类整体生存和持续发展的价值导向。从杰文斯悖论的形成来看，能源利用技术的提高却会带来能源的更多消费，这也源自人们对技术的社会后果缺乏充分的认识和考察，并对于技术的应用缺少必要的控制。因此，就技术的研发、应用、转化和推广而言，无论是技术专家还是技术应用者都应当具有高度的责任感，要尽量充分全面地探究和预测技术应用的社会后果，要以有利于人类整体的生存和发展为价值准则来选择技术的发展方向、发展途径以及转化为现实生产力的途径和手段。依据技术规范中所包含的价值规范，社会应当建立相应的管理机制，对于技术的研发和应用进行相应的调控，调节人类的技术实践，以引导技术的研发和应用朝着更有利于人类生存和发展的方向发展。当前，在关于技术的反思中，人们所提出的关于"技术发展应走向技术生态化"等论断所反映的正是对技术的应用和发展中的价值取向和价值规范的强调，即强调技术的应用和发展带来的应是经济效益、生态效益和社会效益的综合统一，强调人与自然、人与社会、自然与社会的协调发展应是技术生态化的应有之义。

不难发现，以人类的整体利益作为技术实践的根本价值目标和价值准则，在现实生活中会遭遇到众多困难。因为自从原始公社瓦解，人类社会进入私有制社会之后，利益冲突成为一种普遍的社会现象，不同的个人、阶级、民族、国家等之间存在着各种各样的利益冲突，因此在私有制占主导地位的社会中，要求不同的个人、阶级、民族、国家的技术实践时时处处以全人类的整体长远利益作为价值准则，这似乎只能是一种奢谈。但是，这并不意味着人们应当放弃对人类整体利益的倡导，也并不意味着人们只能在利益分化消失的社会中才能开始消除杰文斯悖论的努力。实际上，哥本哈根世界气候大会的召开所引发的全球瞩目，反映的正是不同国家的人们对人类整体利益的重视。当前，全球的环境、生态、资源、安全等问题引发的世界关注，正是折射出人类共同的生存和发展所面临的危险的紧迫性。尽管在当今世界，不同的个体之间、群体之间存在着种种利益的分化，但是人们共同生活于同一个地球之上，共同的生存环境和生存方式决定了人类在共同的地球生活中有着众多共同的利益。这些共同利益的损害最终会威胁每一个人的生存和发展，无论阶级、民族、地域或国别。在全球化的今天，不同国家、民族、地区间的联系日益紧密，一衰俱衰、一荣俱荣的全球效应在时间上不断缩短、在空间上不断扩展，更是促使不同国家、民族、地区的人们必须在实践中共同紧密关注人类整体的利益。共同关注人类的整体利益并不意味着对不同个体、群体利益的抹杀，《哥本哈根协议》所遵循的"共同但有区别的责任"原则就显示出在关注人类共同利益的前提下对不同国家的合理利益要求的尊重和承认。实际上，以人类整体的生存和持续发展作为技术实践的最高价值目标，以相互尊重和求同存异为原则就实现这一目标的途径和方式逐渐形成不同范围的价值共识，并不断将其融入技术实践的具体目标和技术规范之中，以此指导和约束人类的技术实践，这是在利益分化普遍存在的现时代合理地利用技术为人类的共同利益而努力的现实路径。

参考文献

［1］〔美〕约翰·M. 波利梅尼等：《杰文斯悖论：技术进步能解决资源难题吗》，许洁译，上海科学技术出版社，2014。

［2］〔美〕约翰·贝拉米·福斯特：《生态危机与资本主义》，耿建新译，上海译文出版社，2006，第 28 页。

［3］John Bellamy Foster, "A Failed System: The World Crisis of Capitalist Globalization and Its Impact on China", *Monthly Review*, 2009, 60 (10): 16.

［4］William Leiss, *The Limits to Satisfaction*, McGill-Queen's University Press, 1988, p. 32.

比较研究

东西方伦理文化差异比较

葛晨虹[*]

摘 要：不同的历史发展道路造就了不同的文化特质。东西方伦理文化在理性思维模式、社会治理模式、价值取向等方面，都存在一些不同。探讨东西方文化到底存在那些重大差异，研究形成这些差异的深层的背后的现实理由和历史原因，对于理解东西方文化差异，理解中国文化、韩国文化、西方文化，融通东西方文化，更好地发展人类文化，都具有重要意义。

关键词：东西方伦理文化　差异　比较

The Comparative Study of Eastern and Western Ethical Cultural Difference

Ge Chenhong

Abstract：Different historical development roads produce different characteristics of culture. Western and eastern ethical culture are different from each other in the mode of rationality，the methods of social management and

---

* 葛晨虹，中国人民大学哲学院教授。

value orientation. To explore the difference and find the realistic reasons and historical origins behind is siginificant for us to better understand the cultures of China, South Korea and West, build a bridge between east and west to make a better development of human culture.

Keywords：Eastern and Western Ethical Culture；Difference；Comparison

东西方文化存在着差异。在理性思维模式、社会治理模式、价值取向等方面，都存在一些不同。不同的历史发展道路造就了不同的文化特质。探讨东西方文化到底存在哪些重大差异，研究形成这些差异的深层的背后的现实理由和历史原因，对于理解东西方文化差异，理解中国文化、韩国文化、西方文化，融通东西方文化，更好地发展人类文化，都具有重要意义。

一 东西方不同历史道路的比较

社会物质生产条件决定社会生活方式，也决定一定社会生活方式的思想文化，我们要理解东西方历史、东西方思想文化，就必须首先深入到产生东西方文化的社会历史背景中去，去分析那些特殊的社会历史条件。

许多经典作家在论及人类由原始社会进入文明社会的历史进程时，认为东、西方曾走了两条不同的道路，即以古代希腊为代表的"古典的古代"，和以古代东方国家为代表的"亚细亚的古代"。

具体说来，"古典的古代"发展道路是从氏族到私产再到国家，个体私有制冲破了氏族组织，国家代替了氏族。"亚细亚的古代"则是在没有摧毁原始氏族组织的情况下直接进入奴隶制国家，血缘氏族制同国家的组织形式相结合。对这两种不同历史途径，中国著名思想史家侯外庐先生解释说，"古典的古代"是"革命的路径"，"亚细亚的古代"是

"改良的道路"。^① 古代东方从氏族直接过渡到国家的历史道路，使整个社会结构有了以血缘为纽带的氏族遗制。这是理解古代东方生产方式、社会制度、思想文化的关键，尤其是研究东方文化形成及其特点的直接历史根据。

古代东方氏族血缘组织何以没有如西方那样被个体私有制所冲破，这需要到历史背景即当时物质生产条件中寻找答案。

第一，商品经济没有发展起来。亚洲自给自足的农业经济是与商品经济相对而言的，指产品不为交换而是为满足生产者本身的需要而生产。《老子》中对古代东方社会作了描述："甘其食，美其服，安其居，乐其俗，邻国相望，鸡犬之声相闻，民至老死不相往来。"^② 自给自足的农业经济特性阻滞了商品经济发展及私有制的产生。

第二，土地（因水利）公有制的牢固存在。除商品经济没发展起来外，使古代东方社会氏族纽带未经私有制冲破而直接进入国家的，还有一个重要历史条件，即古代土地公有的牢固存在。在自然农业生产条件下，农业劳动的方式是集体耕作土地，由此土地也就以氏族公有方式存在着。特别是水利事业，须依赖共同体的力量。如中国古代从大禹治水始，兴修水利一直是国家的一项重要职能。据计，自公元前722年至公元1911年，前后2600多年间，共有治水活动7000余次。^③ 古代东方农业对水的依赖，水利对共同体的依赖，强化了氏族社会共同体的存在。

西方"古典的古代"走了不同于东方的历史道路。古希腊的雅典城邦国家是在打破血缘氏族体制后建立的。如雅典在克利斯提尼改革中，用划分地区的原则取代了氏族制度的血缘关系原则，这一划分打破了氏族社会的血缘组织关系。按地区划分城邦是一次改革，改革背后有复杂的历史原因，其中最根本的原因，是相对发达的古希腊商品经济。氏族

---

① 侯外庐：《中国古代社会史论》，河北教育出版社，2003，第2页。
② 见《老子》第八十章。
③ 冀朝鼎：《中国历史上的基本经济区与水利事业的发展》，朱诗鳌译，中国社会科学出版社，1981，第36页。

部落中越是发展起商品经济，氏族组织也就越加迅速地被瓦解。商品经济使氏族成员彼此间不再受制于血缘关系制约，成为相对平等自由的经济个体。而商品交换也使人们有了最初的平等观念。

血缘氏族的彻底解体和历史性的保存，使东西方走上了"古典的古代"和"亚细亚的古代"不同的历史文明之路。由此，东西方社会的治理模式和文化内容，也形成了很多不同的取向和特点。

二　东方宗法（氏族）国家的特点

"亚细亚"历史道路表明，古代东方所处的自给自足的小农经济、土地公有制，以及特定的社会组织形式，使国家职能在没完全分化解体的氏族组织基础上产生出来，国家的社会结构自然就落在了天然的血缘组织上。对此侯外庐先生曾分析："古典的古代"是从家庭到私产再到国家。国家代替了家族。"亚细亚的古代"是由家族到国家，国家混合在家族里面，叫做"社稷"。① 西人的"country"在汉语叫做"国家"，实缘于指称家族的血缘关系和国家的政治关系一体化的宗法性社会政治组织，国家政治体制中带有深刻的氏族遗制烙印，使得古代东方的社会结构、文化精神、历史进程获得了极大的特殊性。

氏族对于国家是作为原型组织而存在，国家所能借鉴和模仿的统治模式也直接源于氏族统治模式。氏族首领及其机构的对内作用，主要就是亲睦协调氏族内部成员、各部落关系。这样，带有氏族遗制血缘组织的"国家"，就不可避免地在统治方式上沿用氏族组织的伦理治理方式。比如中国周朝在社会管理方式中，就既需要体现新的政治关系的"忠"与"尊"，同时也需要体现旧的血缘关系的"孝"与"亲"。诸侯们既要把自己同周天子的关系当成臣君的关系，同时也要当成子父关系。而各诸侯间则既有臣臣关系，同时也有兄弟关系。如此，"惟忠惟孝"，"忠孝合一"，便可维护治理这种政治关系与血缘关

---

① 侯外庐：《中国思想通史》第1卷，人民出版社，1956，第11页。

系相合为一的社会。

儒家感悟到了当时社会关系的血缘宗法性质，看到了仁礼德治对于国家秩序稳定的重要，把"齐家"与"治国"提到同等地位。[①] 儒家认为如同以伦理维护宗族一样也应以伦理维持国家。儒家引发出一整套天人合德、德性天赋，以及仁礼治世的思想，形成了儒家独特的仁义道德为价值核心的德性思想体系。可以说，孔子创立的学说并不是儒家思想家杜撰的一种政治理想，而是对古代东方氏族（宗法）国家现实存在的一种理论反映，是"亚细亚"的历史道路在思想领域的另一种延展。古代东方以血缘为根基的"亚细亚"历史道路，是理解古代东方氏族国家宗法社会的关键，也是解开儒家德性思想产生及在东方社会有强大生命力之谜的钥匙。

三 东西方两种理性文化取向比较

人与自然的关系，在东方儒学文化中和西方希腊文化中，呈现不同的架构。在古代东方天人合德意识系统中，自然物理之学多置于人道心性之学之下。而古希腊人往往自然主义地理解道德。两种不同的意识系统，使研究自然为中心的科学认识理性文化，和研究社会伦理为中心的德性价值理性文化，在东西方构成了不同的思维模式，从而，科学理性和人文价值理性在东西方各自施展了自己的魅力。

理性是人的能动力量。认识世界探究自然，是人的一种理性能力，研究社会认识自己，给社会设定理想目的并给自己立法，也是人的理性能力。在此，相对于二者所研究的对象的区别，我们把以自然科学为对象的理性称作"科学理性"，把以伦理道德等社会人文为对象的理性称作"价值理性"。科学认知理性，主要回答世界"是什么"的问题，它探究自然规律，能动运用这些规律，创造出为人类服务的科学技术及物质财富。相对而言，科学理性所驾驭的世界，是一个"真"的领域。这

---

① 见《易经·家人》。

是一个不以人类意志为转移的领域。① 人文价值理性，主要回答世界"应当是什么"的问题。它主要给认识、征服、利用自然的活动合理的计划。另外，人要认识控制自然对象，也要把握自己的命运，让人类发展得更完善，生活得更美好。没有价值理性，人类的科学理性将是盲目的力量。人类世界本应具有真善美合一、科学与价值统一的特性。

在人类早期朴素思维中，科学理性和价值理性往往结合在一起。然而西方在从古代走向现代的历史中，科学理性更突出地发展起来，人文价值理性没有得到应有重视。科学理性证实了人类的能力，给人类带来了极大的物质解放。但与此同时，缺少价值理性指引的科学技术，在有些情况下成为一种盲目力量，破坏了人与自然的关系，也破坏了人之所以为人的高贵。20 世纪的人们开始对科学理性带来的文明进行重估和反思。在反思这一问题时，许多西方学者不约而同地把目光投向了东方。研究科技史方面成就斐然的李约瑟，对儒学有很高评价。② 儒学将天人看作整体的观念，以德性理性统领真、善、美的文化价值体系，给陷入唯物质文化和唯科学文化怪圈中的西方世界提供了一种古老而又现代的智慧。1988 年，全世界诸奖得主聚会巴黎，他们发表宣言说："如果人类要在 21 世纪活下去，必须回顾 2500 年，去吸取孔夫子的智慧。"③ 东方真善美统一的智慧使儒学在高扬德性主体价值理性的同时，包容了科学理性发展的空间和可能。李约瑟博士认为孔夫子的哲学智慧像是现代科学的一种先觉。④

四 比较视野下东方伦理法与社会德治模式

以德性手段作为管理国家调控社会的主要手段，是德治文化重要特

① 葛晨虹：《道德是什么及其在社会中的功能体现》，《西北师范大学学报》2004 年第 6 期，第 7 页。
② 参见李约瑟《中国科学技术史》第 1 卷，科学出版社，1990，序言。
③ 转引自董光璧《传统与后现代》，山东教育出版社，1996，第 175 页。
④ 参见李约瑟《中国科学技术史》第 1 卷，科学出版社，1990，序言。

征。但"德治"不在于没有法治，而在于它所动用的法的手段里也充满了伦理道德内涵。这种伦理内涵和法形式的结合体一般被称作伦理法。相对来说，西方社会治理传统具有比较独立的法制特点，而东方社会治理传统则具有德主刑辅的特点。

人类历史都是由道德走向法律的，东方何以没有像西方那样由伦理法走向成熟形式的独立法？又是怎样在"德主刑辅"模式中发生法的德化？这需要讨论促使西方法律走向独立形态、东方长期没走出伦理法形态的历史因素。

第一个因素即东方社会缺少深植于西方传统中的"契约精神"。古希腊在氏族关系冲破后，就用契约来解释社会规范。在智者文化中，在苏格拉底、伊壁鸠鲁等人思想中，都能感受到西方较早存在的契约意识。在作为西方文化重要源流的《圣经》中，神圣契约是一项重要内容。在《旧约》《新约》中，"立约"之举随处可见，不仅上帝与人之间立约，人与人之间也不断立约。《圣经》通过事件记载和寓言，明确传达：违约者必遭报应。

西方契约精神并不仅仅停留在古代法和宗教中，还运用到政治制度和社会管理手段中。17、18 世纪的西方政治思想中，社会契约思想几乎占据了主导地位。而东方传统法律则相对缺乏这种文化特点。契约精神的重要特点是：规则由多方主体约定。而古代东方的法，少有出自众人共约的。礼法要么是"天道"天定，要么是"圣人作法"。如孔子认定"礼乐征伐自天子出"。《礼记》也称，"非天子不议礼，不制度不考文"。法家代表作《管子》也主张，"法制独制于君而不从臣出"。这一切完全不同于契约精神所要求的共立约共守约的原则。

第二个因素是"平等"观念的历史差异。西方"古典的古代"历史道路，使雅典公民按地区划分进行他们的政治、宗教活动。雅典的奴隶主民主制以及西方的哲学、宗教文化中已产生了后世"平等"观念的种子。在古代东方宗法社会文化中，上下尊卑是"天道"安排好的。在这种社会组织基础上，一方面形成了东方式家族本位文化，一切人与人的关系，包括行业关系和其他社会团体关系，都只有纳入宗法人伦关系，或类似的亲缘、地缘等人伦关系，才觉可靠并被有序治理。另一方面，在文化心态中，又形成了宗法等级观念，论辈分、分亲疏。

法不同于道德的最主要一点，即法的普遍性原则。这个原则不允许个体或团体具有法律以外的特殊身份和权利。"法律面前人人平等"，表达的正是这种原则特性。东方古代传统法律更多以伦理法性质而不是契约法性质而存在，深层缘由在于古代东方社会没有提供一种平等自由的法律人际关系。在伦理法中，处处可见渗透着亲亲尊尊现实和观念的内容。如宗法伦理注重伦理亲情，所以在法理中往往兼顾情理。如"子为父隐"是"孝"道主张。这一伦理主张明显表现在关于"亲隐"的立法之中。中国古代秦律对"亲隐"的规定很直接："子告父母，臣妾告主，非公室，勿听。而行告，告者罪。"① 在这里，"亲隐"直接成了法律规定，告父母、主人者反而要定罪，因为它违反了忠孝伦理要义。法律判案中对尽忠孝而复仇的行为的宽容，也反映出东方式法律的伦理倾向。另如，出于尊卑伦理的影响，传统法中规定了允许某部分人具有特权的"八议"程序。八议包括议亲、议故、议贤、议能、议功、议贵、议勤、议宾。② 根据"八议"制，没有皇帝批准，一定级别的官吏及亲属可不受法办，此谓"刑不上大夫"。对同一罪行给予不同刑罚规定的，还有根据"动机"裁决的"原心定罪"原则。这种对道德情理和身份等级的容纳，直接排斥了法治所要求的技术化、形式化、普遍化要求。

纵观整个人类法制发展史，存在过的法律形态无非属于"混沌法"、"伦理法"、"独立法"三大类。"混沌法"作为人类早期不完全自觉的规范系统，是纳道德、宗教、法律、风俗、习惯为一体的混沌状态。"伦理法"则是人类觉醒和社会经济基础发展处在农业社会的产物。随着人类文明向工业社会、商品经济社会的发展，法律也必然要向更独立更完

---

① 参见睡虎地秦墓竹简整理小组编《睡虎地秦墓竹简》，文物出版社，1990。
② "亲"指皇室一定范围的亲属；"故"指皇帝的某些故旧；"贤"指朝廷认为"有大德行"的贤人君子；"能"指"有大才业"，能整军旅、莅政事，为帝王之辅佐、人伦之师范者；"功"指"有大功勋"者；"贵"指职事官三品以上、散官二品以上及爵一品者；"勤"指"有大勤劳"者；"宾"指"承先代之后为国宾者"（见《唐律疏议·名例》）。

善的形态发展。

对于今天的东方国家来说，有一个如何对待德治传统和伦理法传统的问题。在现代建设中，许多东方国家早已建立起一套有别于伦理道德的独立法体系，但仍面临在制度上、实践上进一步完善法制的任务。一方面要使法律在规范形式和程序技术手段层面更多地发挥独立的作用；另一方面，应建立起既出自人类价值理想，又符合社会现实的道德价值体系的法制体系。总之，应该使法律和伦理道德既保持内在契合，又保持外在张力，既有彼此的独立形式，又有相互的内在联系。建立起法治和德治共同发挥调控作用的社会治理模式。

综上，我们探讨了东西方存在的两种不同道路和文化差异。但无论东方还是西方，任何民族在其走向现代化的过程中，都不能忽视"民族自我"，不能忽视自己文化传统的传承和弘扬。对自我、对自己文化传统和民族精神缺乏自信心的民族，是无法从过去走向未来的。任何一个民族都应从民族文化的特质及历史根基的现实出发，才可能更好地使自己的民族文化及整个民族走向现代化，走向世界，走向未来。

参考文献

侯外庐：《中国思想通史》，人民出版社，1980。

田昌五：《中国古代社会发展史论》，齐鲁书社，1992。

严耀中：《中国宗教与生存哲学》，学林出版社，2006。

〔俄〕科瓦略夫：《古代罗马史》，王以铸译，上海书店出版社，2007。

〔美〕D. 布迪、C. 莫里斯：《中华帝国的法律》，朱勇译，江苏人民出版社，2003。

《论语》，《诸子集成》（一），上海书店出版社，1986。

《孟子》，《诸子集成》（一），上海书店出版社，1986。

《管子校正》，《诸子集成》（五），上海书店出版社，1986。

（汉）孔安国：《尚书正义》，上海古籍出版社，1990。

陈澔注：《礼记》，上海古籍出版社，1987。

葛晨虹：《德化的视野——儒家德性思想研究》，同心出版社，1998。

朱贻庭等：《当代中国道德价值道向》，华东师范大学出版社，1994。

Different Methodologies of Life Indicated in Eastern and Western Classical Works

Li Jialian[*]

Abstract: Eastern and west culture are different from each other, from which different ethical spirits are produced. All ethical spirits are aimed to direct methodology of life. Taking Daoism and Bible as classical works in East and West, the paper make a comparison between different methodology of life between East and West.

Keywords: Classic Works; Methodology of Life; Daoism; Bible

东西方经典著作中的不同处世方法之比较

李家莲

摘　要：东西方文化不同的文化特质孕育了不同的伦理精神。一切伦理精神最终都要落脚于处世技巧，本文以《道德经》和《圣经》为经典文本，考察了东西方伦理精神所暗示的不同处世技巧。

关键词：经典文本　处世技巧　道德经　圣经

---

* 李家莲，土家族，湖北建始人，浙江大学博士后，湖北大学哲学学院副教授、高等人文研究院副院长。

Common supreme beings of philosophy are illustrated in Taoism and Genesis although they are presented in different names, namely "God" and "Tao" (with the meaning of "way", "path" or "principle", reflecting something that is not only the source of, but also the force behind everything that exists. Laozi's Tao is extremely identical to God of Christianity. Tao refers to non-personified and non-theistic God, while God belongs to personalized and sacred Tao" (Gong Zhebing, 2004: 77). The Western concept of "God" is identical to Chinese "Tao" in some aspects......; according to Laozi's philosophy, "Tao" is a supreme ontological rule, with several meanings such as ontology, cosmology and value theory, so its concept is similar to the definition of "God" in this respect (Liu Zhijing, 2006; 18). In fact, apart from *Taoism*, other Chinese schools of philosophy also considers "Tao" as research focus, for which it has been argued that "pursuit for going beyond the real world is one of inborn desires of human beings, which isn't an exception for Chinese people" either (Feng Youlan, 1996: 4).

However, great changes have occurred since Chinese and Western philosophers began to connect supreme beings of universe with "people". As a result, such differences of cultural origins have gradually evolved into distinctive philosophical connotations and cultural traditions between China and Western countries. Concerning ethical thoughts, "De" is a requirement for people ad defined by the same supreme beings of philosophy in *Taoism*, while people are required by the supreme beings to be "moral" in *Genesis*. Although "De" and "moral" have nearly identical meanings when they are translated into Chinese, their cultural connotations are completely different, which just reflects different ethical requirements for people in *Taoism* and *Genesis*. Ethically, people are required by "De" of *Taoism* to know unchanged rules, whilst they are asked by Genesis to following rules by signing covenants. By comparing different ethical thoughts and practices between these two classical works, different methodologies of life implied from Taoism and Genesis are found to not only reflect different attitudes of Chinese and Western nations toward supreme beings of philosophy, but also reveal different positions of Chinese and Western "beings" in philosophy, especially differences in basic thinking models between Chinese and Western philosophy.

1. Different Theoretical Ethical Requirements of "De" and "moral": Knowing Unchanged Rules and Covenant-kepping

It is commonly advocated in *Taoism* and *Genesis* that people shall obey moral principles, whereas the principles greatly differ. In *Taoism*, "De" has double implications, including ontological and ethical meanings which are different. Ontologically, a general ethical requirement, namely to know unchanged rules, has been defined by "De" by people. To analyze "De" in *Genesis*, it is firstly necessary to understand specific meaning of "De" in English. In English, "De" means moral, which is interpreted in the Webster Dictionary to be "concerned with principles of right and wrong behavior". In brief, what is concerned and discussed by "moral" are just codes and principles for judging if people's acts are right or not. This definitions reveals that "moral" isn't only concerned about people's codes of conduct, but also includes criteria for judging value of the standards of conduct. Based on definition of moral, people's conducts are considered to be right if they obey orders of God, as defined in *Genesis*. Therefore, "covenant-keeping" may be suitable for summing up main ethical concent and requirements of "De" in *Genesis*.

In *Taoism* (*Dao De Jing*), Tao is the general principle for generation of the universe and De is a principle for generation of certain things, which belongs to an ontological meaning of "De". "The grandest forms of active force From Tao come, their only source. Who can of Tao the nature tell?" (Chapter 22, p. 20). All things are produced by the Tao, and nourished by its outflowing operation. They receive their forms according to the nature of each, and are completed according to the circumstances of their condition (Chapter 51, p. 16). Therefore all things without exception honor the Tao and exalt its outflowing operation. Tao is just the general principle for generation of the universe. It is just because of this that things have come into being for the same virtues. Hence, Tao and De are used and exemplified together in books like *Laozi* and *Zhuangzi* (Feng Youlan, 2000: 172). Relations between "Tao" and "De", discussed in *Taoism*, are concerned about associations between supreme beings of the universe and specific things. On the whole, such relationships refer to connections between "Tao" of supreme beings of the universe and "De" that is closely related to people. Based on relations between "Tao" and "De", virtues concerning people are revealed in *Taoism* to put forward an overall ethical requirement, namely knowing unchanged rules, for people. Laws generated from universal Tao may be called laws or general rules, while the requirement for "knowing unchanged rules" may be met as long as the rules are unified (Feng Youlan, 2000: 138). One may be judged if he or she is moral or has a right methodology of life based on whether he or she could do things based on "knowing unchanged rules".

In *Genesis*, differences between "moral" in *Genesis* and "De" in *Taoism* are reflected from following two aspects. On one hand, Western languages are inherently exact. From above analysis of "moral", it may be known that it only a concept that matters if people's codes of conducts are right or not. In this respect, the greatest difference between "moral" and "De" consists in that their relationships aren't discussed from the perspective of ontology, while people are the only objects of "moral". On the other hand, in *Genesis*, "moral" reveals that people's correct methodology of life is to be absolutely submissive to Jehovah. The god returned home to people after the work of the 6th day's genesis was created by Jehovah. "And the LORD God formed man of the dust of the ground, and breathed into his nostrils the breath of life; and man became a living soul. And the LORD God planted a garden eastward in Eden; and there he put the man whom he had formed." (*Genesis*, 2: 7 − 8). The LORD God was considerate and considered that "it is not good that the man should be alone" (*Genesis*, 2: 18) . Thus, he created a woman to be Adam's partner. Nevertheless, all of the God's good purposes were conditional. To be exact, men were not allowed to eat fruits in the tree of the knowledge of good and evil. "And the LORD God commanded the man, saying, Of every tree of the garden thou mayest freely eat: But of the tree of the knowledge of good and evil, thou shall not eat of it: for in the day that thou eatest thereof thou shalt surely die. " (*Genesis*, 2: 15) .

Before eating fruits in the tree of the knowledge of good and evil in the garden, people were works of Jehovah, received infinite love from Jehovah and could survive permanently like Jehovah. However, tempted by snake and impacted by free wills, people finally went against God's orders, was exiled out of Eden and began to lead a secular life by exchanging food for life with hard work. From that moment on, they weren't immortal any longer, but could only survive for limited years. Except for obedience and submission, people had no other choices. As to " Tao " represented by Jehovah, people were only works of Jehovah even if " people " in the Eden could never have " Tao " or " De", as they could never be as omniscient or almighty as the God. They would be considered to be immoral, suffering from punishment and expiating themselves for ever if they broke any rules.

For people, different interpretations of virtues in *Taoism* and *Genesis* have reflected their distinct value. In *Taoism*, "Tao" may be used as tools and people have ultimate value. Based on "Tao", it may be discovered that people have found how to survive by keeping physically healthy, namely " knowing unchanged rules", in order to realize ideal of Taoist philosophy for maintaining physical health in the history of Chinese philosophy. In *Genesis*, Jehovah or "Tao" had no value of tools, whereas men were works of the God. In other words, men had value of tools and were shadows of the God, who ruled the world through men.

2. Different Methodologies of Life in *Taoism* and *Genesis*: Nonaction and Covenant-keeping

Theoretically, different ethical requirements, including knowing unchanged rules and covenant-keeping, are illustrated in *Taoism* and *Genesis*. As two different ethical thoughts are integrated with realities, these two classical works have offered people different methodologies of life. Methodology of nonaction is implied in *Taoism*, while covenant-keeping methodology of life is revealed in *Genesis*.

In practical and vivid worldly life, a specific methodology of life, namely nonaction, has been put forward in *Taoism*. People without action know regular rules. As mentioned in Taoism, "not to know it leads to wild movements and evil issues". People knowing regular rules follow "De (virtues)" and they shall try to lead a "simple" life as possible as they can. How to lead such a life? For this purpose, it is necessary to follow "Tao" that "having arrived at this point of non-action, there is nothing which he does not do". How can people follow Tao? Striving to be close to "Tao", which aspects shall be concerned? Major efforts shall be made to copy roles of "Tao" positively and negatively. First of all, "Tao" has two positive roles, including without wills and names. "Man takes his law from the Earth; the Earth takes its law from Heaven; Heaven takes its law from the Tao. The law of the Tao is its being what it is.". There are no wills belonging to people, and all things are products of natural laws. Therefore, men shall renounce their wills and discard redundant desires. If we could renounce our sageness and discard our wisdom, it would be better for the people a hundredfold. If we could renounce our benevolence and discard our righteousness, the people would again become filial and kindly. "If we could renounce our artful contrivances and discard our (scheming for) gain, there would be no thieves nor robbers. Those three methods (of government). Thought olden ways in elegance did fail And made these names their want of worth to veil; But simple views, and courses plain and true Would selfish ends and many lusts eschew. " For fewer desires, men shall discard their wisdom and thus shall not acquire knowledge. " (Then) appeared wisdom and shrewdness, and there ensued great hypocrisy" . Knowledge may broaden men's horizons and stimulate their desires. " The difficulty in governing the people arises from their having much knowledge. He who (tries to) govern a state by his wisdom is a scourge to it; while he who does not (try to) do so is a blessing" . For the positive role of Tao that it has no name, Tao means nothing. " The Tao, considered as unchanging, has no name. " " The Tao is hidden, and has no name. " It is considered to have no name as compared with existence of specific things. All of the universe is considered as beings, while Tao is the general rule generating the universe and has no name. " All things have been generated from beings, which have originated from nothingness" . According to ethical requirements of *Taoism*, it is improper for men to seek fame and honor in life. Thus, based on the Tao of being " sagely within and kingly without" of Confucianism, passive methodologies of life may be found from *Taoism* from personal perspectives to discard fame. Hence, as one suffers failure in the course of seeking fame and fortune, " Taoist theory may ease Chinese people's minds and give them comfort...This is just why each Chinese person is a Confucianist during success and become a Taoist over again in suffering failure. " (Dai Maotang, Jiang Chang, 2001: 112) . To simulate reverse acting mechanism of Taoism, " The movement of the Tao By contraries proceeds" , which implies people shall do all things from the opposite aspects. " When one is about to take an inspiration, he is sure to make a (previous) expiration; when he is going to weaken another, he will first strengthen him; when he is going to overthrow another, he will first have raised him up; when he is going to despoil another, he will first have made gifts to him. " " He is free from self-display, and therefore he shines; from self-assertion, and therefore he is distinguished; from self-boasting, and therefore his merit is acknowledged; from self-complacency, and therefore he acquires superiority. It is because he is thus free from striving that therefore no one in the world is able to strive with him. " Based on above analysis, it may be concluded that there is always a general requirement for men no matter they follow "Tao" from the right or opposite sides, namely to discard all things of men such as body, consciousness and desires. In a word, men shall abandon all of their acts to realize the ideal of "nonaction" .

For finite worldly life, a practical methodology of life, namely covenant-keeping, was proposed in *Genesis*. For people, two aspects were involved about covenant-keeping. On one hand, covenant-keepers thoroughly followed orders of the God, living in Eden without any worries and leading a life infinitely long like God. Although they are pure without any guilt, they are limited, so it was impossible for them to follow laws of God all the time. They violated rules and were punished over and over again. On the other hand, although these men lived on the earth and called "human beings" , they had no free wills and were known as single-sided people without personalities or love, on the grounds that the partners were distributed to men as special gifts, in order to discard disadvantages of living alone just like the fruits in the Eden. What's worse, they didn't have pleasure, anger, sorrow, joy, seven passions or six desires. Likewise, two sides are covered by breaking rules and violating covenants. On one hand, these men went against orders of the Lord and lost the garden of Eden where they could be immortal. Instead, they lost the worry-free life and began to strive for living with sweat, only having limited time to survive. Free wills brought people sins and punishments. On the other hand, men exiled out of the garden had really begun to lead their own lives from that moment on. After Adam and Eve left the Eden and came to the earth, Eve was immediately pregnant and gave birth to children. With lots of offspring, they became ancestors of all human beings. People walked in the earth with free wills at the price of not being immortal by breaking covenants. As a result, they had become beings in the earth rather than those in Eden without free wills.

Nevertheless, people were just works of the Lord. Although people could compose a wonderful song of worldly life for themselves with free wills during their limited survival, they would never forget the father who created the earth, because that was the earliest home and hometown of human beings. Due to sin, men lost their previous homes, whereas the Lord didn't forget establishing covenants with men over again and marked tokens of establishing covenants in spite of worldly life for his endless life to people. In this way, men could aways return to the home they were exiled from by establishing covenants with the Lord and keeping them even if they were sinful. Therefore, it may be found that covenant-keeping is the most important methodology of life as proposed by the Lord in *Genesis*, all parts of *Bible* and particularly *The Old Treatment*, while men's obedience to and violation of "covenants" became inner motive forces of their fate.

Different practical methodologies of life in *Taoism* and *Genesis* imply different roles of Tao and God in various cultures. In Taoism, "Tao" loses its mystery due to people's imitation. Thanks to their imitation of "Tao", people have finally developed into saints "experiencing life and death" throughout the development of Zhuangzi's philosophy. As regards God, men offended God for their free wills in *Genesis*, and were punished over and over again. The God became increasingly more authoritative in the course of punishing men, whose positions were increasingly weakened. Men gradually fell into sins and sufferings, finally was enslaved by Egyptians. Only if they could further establish covenants with men and keep them could they escape away from their sufferings. In fact, God established covenants with men for the third time through Moses and saved people out of sufferings through their covenants. All in all, God gets increasingly more mysterious and powerful as the text goes on in Genesis, finally becoming the king of kings respected by everyone.

3. Conclusion

Above comparisons suggest that in spite of different names, supreme beings are covered in *Taoism* and *Genesis* from the perspective of ontology in the philosophical sense. However, completely different methodologies of life are implied in these two books once aforementioned supreme beings are connected with men, because Laozi and author of *Bible* treated supreme beings and people with different attitudes and gave them totally different positions. Nevertheless, it may be discovered after deeper mediation that the underlying cause of the differences consists in two strikingly different ways of thinking between China and Western countries: namely subject-object dichotomy and harmony between men and nature. It is just because of such different ways of thinking that has led to the formation of apparently different methodologies of life in *Taoism* and *Genesis.*

Firstly, different methodologies of life reflect distinct attitudes of Chinese and Western nations toward supreme beings: namely imitation and worship.

In Taoism, supreme beings are endowed with prophecy, and their actions have greatly inspired people. People attempt to realize their pursuits by simulating "Taoist" actions, while their most perfect imitation is to make themselves become beings identical to "Tao" through "nonaction". Actually, such imitation has become an unbroken tradition in Chinese history of philosophy. Compared with Chinese people's pragmatism, "Genesis" has presented completely different attitudes, namely admiration and worship. The supreme beings are granted apparently different roles in *Genesis* from those in *Taoism*. Their roles in *Genesis* are far higher beyond their "instrumental" ones in *Taoism*, whereas they have evolved into an omnipotent, omniscient and almighty god, being a "king of kings" in the whole universe. Thereby, they were admired and worshiped by all human beings. In *Genesis*, Westerners admire and worship the supreme beings and they never have any wide wishes for simulating the supreme beings. They may consider that it is enough as long as such supreme beings can save their souls with their infinite benignancy. In fact, Christianity plays an important role in Western cultures, so for Western philosophy and literature impacted by Christianity, the humble attitudes towards the supreme beings have been always implied from words of all prominent philosophers and litterateurs, being transformed into a unique Western collective unconsciousness.

Secondly, Chinese and Westerners' different attitudes toward themselves are reflected. For supreme beings, "people" enjoy far higher positions in *Taoism* than those in *Genesis*.

People are considered to have higher positions in *Taoism* than those in *Genesis*. One of the important reasons consist in that there are no "gods" with higher power than people for punishing them in Taoism. The "Tao" and "De" are implied in *Taoism* for reminding people that wise people should be good at copying acting model of "Tao" and grasp correct methods for doing things, or else they will go through disasters. In this sense, the supreme beings in Taoism may be considered to be affiliated to people, whose being is above everything, and "Tao" is subordinate to existence of "beings", existing for the existence of people. Comparatively, "people" enjoy much lower positions in *Genesis*, where people aren't special beings and just created by supreme beings. For such supreme beings, people are humble, because except for respect, admission, obedience and submission, none of their wills are useful, as they can only bring them sins and punishments. Additionally, "people" are freer in *Taoism* than those in *Genesis*, on the grounds that the former people won't be punished or examined by supreme beings. Meanwhile, they can do everything as they like, getting happiness and achieving success as long as they known unchanged rules revealed from *Taoism*. It is impossible for them to face any hazards, let alone sins. If only people consider that they are conscient, there will be no sins in this world. According to this thinking, unique aesthetic cultures and psychology have developed in Chinese cultures.

Thirdly, different ways of thinking between Chinese and Western nations are reflected, including subject-object dichotomy and harmony between men and nature.

Basic characteristics of thinking of Chinese philosophy are reflected from methodologies of life in *Taoism*, namely the covenants may be established between men and nature, because "nature" may be simulated, existing within visions and interests of people. This reflects the way of thinking about "harmony between men and nature" from the perspective of Taoist philosophy. As Laozi said, "Man takes his law from the Earth; the Earth takes its law from Heaven; Heaven takes its law from the Tao. The law of the Tao is its being what it is. " Men can live in harmony with nature, while heaven, earth and men can be integrated. People can follow natural laws to finally associate subjects with objects. The methodology of life delivered by *Genesis* shows a characteristic of basic thinking of traditional Western philosophy, namely subject-object dichotomy. Although "nature" and "men" were in the same universe, they have distinctive roles. "Men" shall act dutifully and be prohibited from trespassing the fields of "nature", or else they will have no choices but to suffer eternal punishments from "nature" and step onto an endless road for expiating themselves. It is just because of subject-object dichotomy that "people" would violate rules for free wills, because people have taken precedence over the fields of "nature" and committed crimes since they stealthily ate fruits in the tree of the knowledge of good and evil, thereby suffering punishments. " And unto Adam he said, Because thou has hearkened unto the voice of thy wife, and hast eaten of the tree, of which I commanded thee, saying, Thou shalt not eat of it: cursed is the ground for thy sake; in sorrow shalt thou eat of it all the days of thy life; Thorns also and thistles shall it bring forth to thee; and thou shalt eat the herb of the field; In the sweat of thy face shalt thou eat bread, till thou return unto the ground; for out of it wast thou taken; for dust thou art, and unto dust shalt thou return. " (*Genesis*, 3: 17 – 19). According to traditional Christian ideas, men were exiled out of the Eden for their original sins and began to lead a worldly life opposite to the

Lord's. Thereafter, men could only be saved with the grace of the God, find the holy land flown with milk and honey and finally return to their lost home.

References

Gong Zhebing, "Laozi and Taoism," *Taoist Studies*, 2004.

Liu Zhijing, "Theories about Unspeakable 'God' and 'Tao'", *Journal of Yanan University* (Natural Science Edition), 2006.

Feng Youlan, *Short History of Chinese Philosophy*, Beijing: Peking University Press, 1996.

Feng Youlan, *History of Chinese Philosophy*, Shanghai: East China Normal University Press, 2000.

Dai Maotang, Jiang Chang, *Traditional Values and Contemporary China*, Wuhan: Hubei People's Press, 2001.

Dai Maotang, Jiang Chang, *Western Values and Contemporary China*, Wuhan: Hubei People's Press, 2002.

Dai Maotang, *Western Ethics*, Wuhan: Hubei People's Press, 2002.

Zhao Hongmei, Dai Maotang, *About Ethics of Literature and Art*, Beijing: China Social Sciences Press, 2004.

Deng Xiaomang, Zhao Lin, *A History of Western Philosophy*, Beijing: China Higher Education Press, 2005.

Does Wisdom of Eastern and Western Cultures Respond to the Question: What is Human Dignity?

Hortensia Cuéllar[*]

> Confucius said:
> "With wisdom, there is no delusion;
> with benevolence, there is no worry;
> with courage, there is no fear"
> The Lun Yü, 9 – 28

Abstract: What I hereby submit-as it seems to me-is a review of the outstanding views in the West and the East regarding dignity of persons. From these, I will endeavor to describe some of their specific axiological paradigms which, even though they have arisen asynchronously and at regionally located environments-Asia, Europe, America-have a universal projection. They are proposals arising from the wisdom of different people and civilizations, which all of us can nurture from. Why not attempting it? An open mind and an offered hand are symbolic expressions of acceptance, recognition and respect to the

* Hortensia Cuéllar, TEC de Monterrey-Campus Ciudad de México.

others, towards the whole humanity. My approach is necessarily a synthetic one.

Keywords: Wisdom; Human Dignity; Legacy of Humanity; Outstanding Traditions

东方智慧和西方文化可以回答"何谓人类尊严"这一问题吗?

Hortensia Cuéllar

摘　要: 此处我提出的—在我看来—是对中西方就人类尊严优秀观点的一个回顾。我会努力阐述其中一些观点特定的价值论范式，它们异步出现于——亚洲，欧洲，美国——在区域环境上具有普遍映射。这些建议来自不同的人类与文明智慧，所有人都可以培养获得。为什么不尝试呢? 豁达的心胸，伸出的双手都是接受、认可、尊重他人和人类整体的象征。我的研究必然是一种综合研究。

关键词: 智慧　人类尊严　人类遗产　优良传统

When I received the invitation to participate at the World Cultural Development Forum, 2015, here at Assam Don Bosco University (India), in collaboration with the Institute for Advanced Humanistic Studies (IAHS) of Hubei University (China), and read the title of the Forum, "Asian Values and Human Future", I recalled the outstanding article by Prof. Thomas Menamparampil (nominated to Nobel Prize for Peace in 2011), with the title "*Asia's Future: Profiting from the Ethical Wisdom of the World*" (2014). After reading it, I found it programmatic for the subject of this International Forum, since in its pages, the interest is discovered to get us closer to the cultural wealth of the great Asiatic continent and, in a parallel way, it warns about the pressure coming from Western modern and post-modern trends, whose influence may seriously erode the cultural foundations of ancient Asian civilizations. Is Prof. Menamparampil right? Does he pose a *Clash of Civilizations* on Samuel Phillips Huntington's fashion? (1993).

I do not believe this was Prof. Menamparampil's intention, but rather the opposite: showing the world that East, in its genuine sources immersed in multiculturalism-Asia is a huge continent integrated by various nations and cultures-possesses a matchless life wisdom which, when shared, it enriches the wisdom of the great Western cultures, and not only that, but it also enriches the wisdom of the rest of the humanity, because its vitality and message are part of humanity's legacy.

Menamparampil's proposal is not rival but complementary in the immense field of present day civilizations and cultures, because he endeavors to show how valuable it is what has been cultivated and experienced in the East, in its history, traditions, philosophical and social thought, religious beliefs, art and appreciation of nature, as well as peaceful revolutions through its great wise persons, philosophers, writers, poets, social leaders, but also among common people in those lands.

What he aims for-I and wholly adhere to it-is finding coincidental principles and values-universal values-enabling us to construct a more human world where-rather than confrontation-harmonious and free coexistence, sustainable development, justice and peace prevail (Cuéllar-Pérez, 2009). This is so because "in spite of many differences in worldviews and ethical codes, convergences of moral principles are evident" (Menamparampil, 2014: 315).

Showing evidence of the convergence of such principles on a global level is not an easy task, because of the wide cultural, ethnic, linguistic and religious diversity we live in, linked to diverse histories and traditions, to particular worldviews and lifeways, and to moral codes occasionally seeming antagonistic.

Does this mean that the battle is lost when trying to show that there are ethical principles which are common for all? Not at all, because such differences have a coincidental core: the fact that we *are* human beings.

This is undeniable. Hence the natural inclination all of us have to pursue truth, good, justice, solidarity, happiness, harmony, friendship, peace, etc. , which has been sufficiently studied-from antiquity to our days-by great teachers of humanity. For instance, from the East: Confucius, Lao-Tzu, Buddha (Siddharta Gautama), Mohamed, Gandhi, Mother Teresa of Calcutta; from the West: Socrates, Plato, Aristotle, St. Augustine, St. Thomas Aquinas, Kant, Hegel, Max Scheler, Nelson Mandela, John Paul II, and currently ruling Pope Francis.

But the search and cultivation of those principles that render us better persons at an individual and at a collective level, is not exclusive of such distinguished personalities, but-as Menamparampil puts it- "People search for moral norms and ethical principles at the first instance from the insights provided by their own culture and civilization; i. e. , what they have learnt from their parents, relatives, teachers, elders; from the wise men of their society, including (…) writers, poets, artists" (Menamparampil, 2014: 322) .

In this context, the classic Socratic question, "what is living well and how this should be achieved?" *is common* to any human being. Therefore, the ethical aspiration of the *search for good life*-mutual understanding, work in favor of common good, promotion of public policies favoring protection and custody of family, priority in quality education for children and young people, and the construction of strategic alliances in favor of the socio-economic and cultural development of peoples and nations- (Jiang Chang, 2013), is a universal aspiration.

Then…Why does it seem that there has been a small progress about such aspirations? Why so much violence and so much abuse against the dignity of persons? Why so much cruelty, not only against human beings but against other living species as well, and why the destruction of our planet? Why so much corruption and so many crimes, including crimes against humanity? Why forgetfulness about the others–our neighbors–and endless injustices and evil doing? Is it perhaps that the desire of being better is just a delusion, a utopia for a few dreamers? ...

I don't think so. The history of humanity has proceeded in its way, and advances in multiple fields of human action are visible: true civilizing processes in the fields of science, art, technology; universal recognition of human rights, rising of living standards as compared to past times, associations for knowledge and information, democratic life, citizen awareness, etc. This enables us to assert that it is possible to reasonably talk about wisdom of East and wisdom of West, as humanity's heritage.

But it is not an inert heritage to be admired as a cultural legacy of bygone times, but as a living source which, as centuries pass by, has shown its vitality and profile: despite adversities, conflicts, injustices and wars, its influence is perceived in the cultural identity it confers to those who have nursed from its sap and projection, as well as in the configuration of some of the greatest civilizations and cultures of humanity, including Chinese, Indian, Egyptian, Hebraic, Roman and Christian. This does not exclude other cultures, such as the Pre-Hispanic ones in America, and the very ancient cultures in Mesopotamia (Sumerians, Chaldeans, Assyrians, etc.), which are not contemplated in this discussion.

The way I have chosen to develop this approach is through a concept that is unquestionably linked to the cultural legacy of humanity: the notion of human dignity and the values derived therefrom, which are neither East's nor West's property, neither South's nor North's, but are the whole humanity's wealth. However, and consistent with our objective, it is legitimate to wonder: Which ways of recognition about dignity of persons are found in East and West? Are some of these ways outstanding? This is the question, and hence, it is doubtlessly necessary to *reconsider* this question, because the ignorance about it is the root of multiple violations to human dignity in our days.

The approach is not univocal or performed through one single way, but much more open, *analogical* and-if I may use the expression-*multicultural*, meaning that the notion of dignity may be appreciated and expressed from different perspectives, depending on the civilizing tradition it has stemmed from, but always referred to the value of human being *per se*, arising from its substance, from its very existence, and this is applicable in all cases to persons in either the East or the West, either the North or the South, from…anywhere in the world!

Because recognition of the dignity of women and men, with its lights and shadows, is humanity's heritage, and has been patiently forged, as though by chisel strokes, along history, even though-this is life experience-it has been and continues to be trodden on, abused or even ignored in our days, due to diverse schemes of human shrewdness in different spheres of life; for instance, tyrannical and perverse powers outraging citizens without giving heed to their condition of persons; the violation and/or ignorance of fundamental human rights; unfair legislations favoring a few while ignoring the majority; impunity and non-combated corruption; programmed permissiveness aimed at eroding basic communities of the social weave such as the family, or publicity campaigns of any kind against several human groups aimed at excluding them and even murdering them, as it happened in times of Apartheid in South Africa before its independence was achieve by Nelson Mandela, or with the massive annihilation of Jews in Hitler's time, or, more recently, the ethnic "cleaning" in the Balkan conflict in times of Slobodan Milosevic, and other linked to terrorism in Central Asia (Afghanistan, Pakistan, …), or the persecution of Christian groups in some African countries such as Kenya, Chad, Tanzania (Burgos, 2014). It is for these and many other reasons in favor of the human being, that I have chosen this subject.

How will I proceed, considering that this is a very relevant, but a very complex question? The way is inevitably a synthetic one, highlighting some of the essential features of the cultural traditions I have chosen about this matter.

The structure I will follow from now in this contribution is: I–Human nature, self-knowledge and transcendence. II–Outstanding traditions about dignity of persons: West and East. III–Final comments. IV–Sources.

I   Human Nature, Self-knowledge and Transcendence

"What is the dignity of persons?"① It is not an easy task to give a simple question to a complex question, maybe due, among other reasons, to the fact that the process of knowledge about the human being and what its dignity implies has been very slow at the historical and philosophical levels. I mean by this that this question and the answers to it presuppose *self-knowledge*, i. e. self-reflection about what we are, which is a *gnoseological attitude*, having as an object of study *the same human being from the human being*, this attitude resulting therefore much more elaborate than the attitude implying–as expressed by Nicolai Hartmann (1965) –the *intentio recta*, which is the natural direction at a cognitive level followed by man in ordinary life, in his approach to the physical nature, to the knowledge of the surrounding world and the starry sky above his head, different from the self-reflection or *intentio oblique* we may have when knowing ourselves, not only in the psychological or social sense, but mainly in

---

① I use as equivalent the terms "human dignity" and "dignity of persons", with a universal applicability horizon, always referred to any human being in any part of the world, at any time and in any place. This is a substantive notion, always referred to our personal being, but with huge repercussions in different spheres of human existence. I have worked on this subject in two former articles, "Ripensando la dignità umana" (2015a), and "The Question About Human Dignity and the Value of Education" (2015b), both under way of publishing. This contribution at Assam, India is a part of this triad about the subject.

our own ontological contexture, which is the root of our dignity.

Not that such natural inclination is out of focus in this sense. Not at all. Referred to appreciation for human dignity-looking after the others, regretting the injustices we see against our neighbors, or applauding actions taken in their favor-it is *intentio recta*, *rational observation*, not installed inside rational process proper, but indeed very worthy because it connects us intelligently with experience. In fact, it was thanks to such spontaneous, natural inclination, that Aristotle wrote: "All men, by nature, wish to know" (Meth. 980^a), which, along with the classical question: "Why?" (Agazzi, 2011), have given rise to philosophy and sciences, but also to the craving for art and culture, civilization, technology, as well as preoccupation about education and integral human development, all of these supremely useful advances for any man or woman, where we unquestionably project what we are: human beings.

This is why, regarding *appreciation* for the dignity of persons, *knowing the physical nature is not enough*; *it is necessary to know human nature* which, by itself, is complex and full of a vital dynamism making us unique and original in the universe (Cuéllar-Perez, 2011: 7) . Knowing or researching about *macrocosm*-the whole universe if it were possible-*is not enough*, but *it is necessary to inquire* what *the human microcosm* is, *who are we* and *what is the reason for our value as persons*.

It is not a simple task, at the gnoseological and conceptual levels, because it implies the search of *truth* about ourselves, and this attitude demands humility and courage, it demands knowing and admitting the root of the value we have as human beings, i. e. our own *dignity as persons*. Carlos Llano, Mexican philosopher, refers to this intellectual adventure as a "trip to the center of man" (Llano, 2002) . The metaphor is relevant because, as I see it, an expression with such a style can lead us to the encounter with our proper, intimate and spiritual ontological structure, i. e. , it attempts to give an answer to the questions: who are we? ..., what is our origin and what is our destination? ..., what can we do to be better, to help others, to build a secure present and a secure future and a world that is much more inhabitable than our present day world?

In the Western world, the first great step about self-knowledge was taken by Socrates, with his celebrated expression: "I just know that I know nothing", followed up, from the Christian perspective, by Saint Augustine of Hippo and his doctrine on the interiority of truth: "Do not go outside; it is in the inner man where truth dwells. In your interior you will find God" (Augustine, 2002); both instances show a huge life wisdom meriting a permanent meditation: in the case of Socrates, at a philosophical level; in the case of Augustine of Hippo, from the theological and religious perspectives.

In the East, the teachings of Confucius, the great teacher of Chinese wisdom (Confucius, 1986), of Buddha and his search for illumination through the way of asceticism, of Gandhi, India's liberator from his pacifism, and from Teresa of Calcutta with his essential love toward the poorest of the poor, have been exemplary in this sense. All of them, in their thoughts and teachings, have shown in a theoretical and practical manner, concrete ways to know ourselves and looking after others.

But... do those ways respond to the great question, "what is the dignity of persons"? It seems to me they do, but from different angles. In some cases, that was their specific intentionality, and they contribute luminous ideas about it in the fields of philosophy, religious revelation and enlightening, and the law. In other cases, they respond to that question with their message and with practical concretization at the ethical, political or religious levels, because they are interested in treating the human beings according to their dignity, and to devote themselves to them; for instance, Confucius, Gandhi, Teresa of Calcutta. This is a fact that cannot be put aside.

Once we have reviewed the need to know our own ontological contexture, as a *non-dodgeable* foundation regarding dignity of persons, we will proceed with some of the most outstanding traditions about this topic, and the wisdom arising from them.

II Outstanding Traditions about the Dignity of Persons

The traditions hereby presented are invaluable contributions to the great treasure of humanity about the dignity of persons. They rise-I insist-*not* in a solution of continuity, but in different times, cultures and environments, but they have an enormous influence in our days. From these traditions, I think, an answer can be given to the question our interest is centered upon.

I will begin with the West to continue with the East. Regarding West, I explore three approaches: the juridical-social approach, the theological-religious approach and the philosophical-humanistic approach; as to the East, I will focus on two of their great representatives: Confucius and Gandhi, who, as live wisdom teachers, are out of any question. All this will be developed in a synthetic way.

West

In the West, a plausible response about dignity of persons is found from three different, asynchronously risen sources: at a *juridical-social* level, among ancient Romans and, from the *theological-religious* perspective, in the Judeo-Christian Revelation. The philosophical question about human dignity rises at the Italian Renaissance (15th Century), and is later retaken by other philosophers, from different angles, Kant among them, from whom I recall some relevant arguments.

Juridical-Social Positivism

According to Daniel Vidart, the issue about dignity of man rose at

Classical Antiquity, mainly among Sophists and Stoics (Vidart, 2012).
His contention, however, requires a textual support to render it plausible.
From other sources, I found *the use of the term* in the Roman Empire,
where it was usual to talk about the dignity of free men, but never about
slaves. Free men were Roman citizens, or those to whom this honor was
granted, as in the case of Ben Hur, the principal character in the great
novel from Lew Wallace (1880), or those-as Cicero says-who *having it*
(*the citizenship*) *by birth, it was highlighted* by their participation in political
action or in war (as the case was with members of the Senate and
conquerors), or those who, because of their spotless moral integrity,
were an example for citizens, as it is told about Seneca. In this sense, it
was possible to praise somebody because of his dignity (*laudare aliquem pro
dignitate*).

For slaves, such recognition and such condition were impossible;
i. e., human dignity among Romans was *selective and attributed only to their
citizens*, because of the political power coming from the Empire, of to
those who had a social recognition because of their life integrity. This
shows-as Antonio Pelé says-that there were " different dignities and
inequalities", even within a context of citizen dignity.

This vision is not archaic as it may seem; we find it, with a different look, in
all countries and political organizations where the foundation for human dignity
is installed, *as though it were its legitimate source*, in such social recognition or in
the juridical positivism. That is to say, only if such dignity is recognized by
their respective laws, or if the subjects are successful, rich and famous, if they
are esteemed in the political-social sphere, and if it can be defended in their
customary law or in their *internal legislation*, and their expressed subscription or
rejection of international treaties demanding an integral respect to the dignity of
persons and their rights.

This feature, however, does not destroy the rule of law in those nations, and their defense, custody or protection of the dignity of persons from their own legislation is always praiseworthy. (García González, 2007) . In fact, this is one of the great achievements of modern and contemporaneous thought where in democratic societies-at least *de iure*-all of us citizens are equal in dignity and rights. A different matter is the practical concretization of these principles, and what happens in daily life.

What is clear is that this approach-with all its relevance-contains several elements of *fragility*, because law enforcement may depend on the letter of the law and its hermeneutics, rather than on what we human beings deserve because of our own worth as persons. Its acceptance or defense is subject to the political will of those in power, or to the legal *loopholes* to which law enforcement is subject. We find current instances of such de facto fragility in the day-by-day law enforcement in most countries in the world, but mainly in nations where law is not integrally respected, but rather its application is "adapted" depending on circumstances. This is more clearly found in countries that are ruled in an authoritarian way by tyrants or dictators, for instance, North Korea, Venezuela and different African countries.

Judeo-Christian Thought

The Judeo-Christian thought, considering its authentic sources, the Holy Scripture and the Tradition, culminating with Jesus Christ and his teaching, 2000 years ago, does not make such a kind of distinctions when talking about the dignity of persons. In its high spirituality, it tells us that the human beings and their dignity have a transcendent origin, and this is found in God, the Creator; hence, all of us human beings have such dignity, either we are women or men, slaves or free, rich or poor, impaired or in full use of our human capabilities, independently or race, sex, social-economic status and condition. The reason: all of us are children of God, created at his image and likeness.

The Holy Book-the *Bible*-tells this as follows: "And God said: Let us make man in our image, after our likeness (...) So God created man in his own image, in the image of God created He him; male and female created He them. And God blessed them, and God said unto them: Be fruitful and multiply, and replenish the earth and subdue it" (*Genesis* 1: 26 – 28).

This shows that the origin of our dignity-strongly expressed by Christianity-is in God. This is why it is possible to talk about "the dignity of the children of God", where all of us human beings are included, believers or not believers, atheists or agnostics, of any race, origin or condition, and at any time or place in history. This approach is theological and with a universal impact, if its message is comprehended: all of us are children of God, either we are aware of this fact or not. This is why it is possible to call God, in Jesus Christ's words, "Our Father", and not only Creator of all that exists. And this, independently of the religion we believe in. As Gandhi said: "All of us are children of God" (Harijan, February 11, 1933).

A different subject, linked to what has been said, is the question about the meaning of God making us "in his own image and likeness". It does not mean that we are equal to God, i. e. "divine beings", as Roman Caesars or gods in Greek mythology were believed to be. No. What it means is that, by constitutively creating us, as body and soul in the unity of our own being-matter and spirituality in our genetic and ontological dotation-, each human being is unique and original, but also originated and originating (Cuéllar, 2011) of everything the human being is capable of creating and recreating, as in the outstanding fields of culture, education, industry, philosophy, sciences and arts, generated in a given space and at a given historical time, where what is looked for-as a consequence of the social message-is not only abating ignorance, but achieving an integral education and the social, economic and cultural progress and development of the different people and nations (cfr. Declaration "*Gravissimum Educationis*"). All this is said without forgetting its deep message, which is its salvation doctrine through love and care for the other, whose original source is God.

Because of this, the Judeo-Christian message states that we human beings are children of God, with an *infinite*, *non-negotiable*, *non-transferable value*, due to our transcendent origin, the deepest foundation for the dignity of any woman or man, anywhere in the world.

But human dignity is not only to be recognized and to be lived in solitude. Any man or woman-social beings par excellence-needs the others for his or her self-fulfillment, which means living in the society, which is our common home, our fittest *habitat*, at the historical, educational and cultural levels.

This idea, a legacy of humanity and thoroughly diverse cultures such as Chinese and Hindu cultures, is also found in the *Bible*: "And the Lord God said: "It is not good that the man should be alone" (Genesis 2: 18), thus making present the great theme of sociability (*sociabilitas*) and complementarity (*complementum*). At an educational level, and at the practical and cultural levels, that aspect is very relevant, and is linked to a multiplicity of values, among them familiar values, life defense, ethical and social values of coexistence and looking after the others (Cuellar-Pérez, 2009).

Philosophical Humanism

Another relevant milestone about the question about human dignity, even though interconnected with the Biblical text and an original exegesis installed in philosophical modernity, comes from the Humanistic thought from the Italian Renaissance. In 1486, Giovanni Pico della Mirandola wrote his outstanding "*Oratio de hominis dignitate*" ("Discourse about Human Dignity") (Della Mirandola, 2004), where he proposes that the origin of our dignity lies on *the liberality with which God created us when endowing us with an identity of our own*-that of human beings-*and the personal freedom with which we can forge our own destiny*, expressed in the following beautiful manner:

"I have placed you at the very center of the world, so that from that vantage point you may with greater ease glance round about you on all that the world contains. I have made you a creature neither of heaven nor of earth, (…), in order that you may, as the free and proud shaper of your own being, fashion yourself in the form you may prefer. It will be in your power to descend to the lower, brutish forms of life; you will be able, through your own decision, to rise again to the superior orders whose life is divine. " (Della Mirandola, 2004: 4).

This humanist, in his interpretation of the Biblical text he refers to (Genesis 1: 26 – 28), shows that our ontological structure comes from God, who is the Creator ("I have made you a creature neither of heaven nor of earth…"). But this is not a static structure, but always in a vital dynamism making us "…free and proud shapers of our own being…", i. e. rational and free. It is on this amalgamation, *created by God but intelligent and free*, *where dignity human lies*, to the extent that we, with our free actions can force His will: "..It will be in your power to descend to the lower, brutish forms of life; you will be able to rise again to the superior orders whose life is divine".

Because of these reflections, Della Mirandola's contribution, at a philosophical level is taken as the necessary background of the question: "What is human dignity?"

Three centuries later, in 1785, Kant takes a further step when he writes, in one of his most significant texts, *Groundwork for the Metaphysics of Morals*, where he explicitly asserts that we human beings are *ends in ourselves*, and never *means.* Hence, *we are not subject* to the discretionary use of this or that will. He expresses this as follows:

"… But suppose there something *whose existence in itself* had an absolute worth, something that, as *an end in itself*, could be a ground of determinate laws; then in it, and only in it alone, would lie the ground of a possible categorical imperative, i. e. , of a practical law.

Now, I say that the human being, and in general every rational being, *exists* as an end in itself, *not merely as means* to the discretionary use of this or that will. (Kant, 2002: 45).

And he continues:

"The beings whose existence rests not on our will but on nature, nevertheless have, if they are beings without reason, only a relative worth as means, and are called *things*; rational beings, by contrast, are called *persons*, because their nature already marks them out as ends in themselves, i. e. , as something that may not be used merely as means" (Kant, 2002: 46).

Kant, starting from transcendental philosophy, re-formulates in an original way our condition of persons, when stating that *the human being*, because it is rational, has *an absolute value*, never a price. His practical background leads us to the idea that we have no reason for being manipulated by anybody, or used as instruments, because we are ends in ourselves, never means; *we are persons, never things.* Put it in a contemporary way and using a relative pronoun, we are *somebody*, never *something*. We have a *per se* value, never a price. Hannah Arendt would pose the question as: "Who are you"?

This approach-as the previous ones-is very outstanding, and it implies important consequences at the anthropological, ethic, juridical, religious, and political-social.

The East

From Asia, I have selected the wisdom, full of spirituality, of two of its great representatives: Confucius and Gandhi, whose teachings and the impact of whose works are out of question. I present some minimal ideas from them enabling us to appreciate the wisdom of the East and its theoretical-practical preoccupation about the dignity of persons.

Confucius (551 – 479 B. C.)

The great philosopher and teacher of Chinese wisdom lived 2500 years ago. His teachings and thought are not only influential at the East, but serve as model for humanity because of the wisdom of his words. It is regarded as the founder of an ethical system in force up to our days, where order, virtue, peace and trust are the rules for living (Confucius, 1986). These principles turn Confucius into a great social theoretician, and are discovered in the millenary tradition of present China and its cultural values.

Confucius, in his teachings, shows that mutual respect among all, love to family care of children and old persons, veneration to wise persons and teachers, are precepts for a spotless behavior forming virtuous and worthy citizens to be elected to public functions and be able of governing. Is this not perchance having in mind the dignity of persons?

This is shown in the following wonderful text, from *The Record of Rites*, Book IX, "*The Commonwealth State*".

"When the perfect order prevails, the world is like a home shared by all. Virtuous and worthy men are elected to public office, and capable men hold posts of gainful employment in society; peace and trust among all men are the maxims of living. All men love and respect their own parents and children, as well as the parents and children of others. There is caring for the old; there are jobs for the adults; there are nourishment and education for the children. There is a means of support for the widow, and the widowers; for all who find themselves alone in the world; and for the disabled. Every man and woman has an appropriate role to play in the family and society. A sense of sharing displaces the effects of selfishness and materialism. A devotion to public leaves no room for idleness. Intrigues and conniving for ill gain are unknown (...). The door to every home need never be locked and bolted by day or night"

For him "these are the characteristics of an ideal world, the commonwealth state".

In such an orderly, peaceful and ideal state, all work for common good, with effort, discipline and wisdom, perseverance and honesty, kidness and politeness. In this regard, education coming from home and that given in schools must have a high quality, where all are taught how to live well, how to be a good citizen who loves and respects his/her family and friends, but always directs his actions towards the good of the community. This is the source of his/her conviction about the need to educate persons in solid values and principles where tradition, Chinese wisdom and new things are contemplated.

At the *Lun Yü*, Confucius expresses this as follows: (Chapter 4, p. 25)

"With virtue there is no solitude: there is always company" (Chapter 4, p. 25)

Regarding family:

"Are not filial piety and brotherly love the roots of benevolence?" (Chapter 1, p. 2).

"In the home, the young should behave with filial piety, and out in the world, with brotherly love. They should be prudent and trustworthy" (Chapter 1, p. 6).

Regarding teachers:

"Exploring the old and deducing the new makes a teacher" (Chapter 2, p. 11).

"The Master learns by being gentle, kind, courteous, modest and deferential" (Chapter 1, p. 10)

Regarding friends:

"To live among the benevolent is good. To choose not to be with the benevolent.... of this I know not! (Chapter 4, p. 1)

Appreciation for tradition:

"I was not born knowledgeable. I am devoted to antiquity and am quick to seek knowledge" (Chapter 7, p. 19)

Regarding Government and State:

"In leading a state of thousand chariots (meaning a large state), respect the office and be trustworthy; and love the people" (Chapter 1, p. 5).

The message and the ideas herein presented show clearly the moral and human temper of this great Chinese philosopher, who devoted his life to the edification of his nation by way of his conversations, discourses and legacy. His principles, having risen at the East, are a part of the humanity's treasure. This is why Confucius can be portrayed in the following words, taken from the Lun Yü:

" A man of supreme dignity of bearing, graceful in movements, formal in his conduct, stern yet compassionate. Confucius was a man of formidable eloquence, enlightened beyond his time" (Confucius, 1986) .

Gandhi (1869 – 1948)

The figure of Mahatma Gandhi is that of the leader of " *non-violence and pacific resistance*" . His fight without weapons in favor of justice, non-oppression and freedom render him not only a holy man to Hindus, but a model of integrity for all, centered in "truth, purity, human dignity and national independence" (Gandhi, M. , 2001) . For him, a different behavior was deeply unjust and contrary to the dignity of persons, and "war is the law of the jungle" .

Gandhi was a deeply spiritual man, capable of leading a whole nation to independence from England in 1947, avoiding violence and promoting peace. This is shown not only by his intense political activity and his life, but also the numerous confessions made through his books: it is shown–among other–in his peerless *An Autobiography-The Story of my Experiments with Truth* (1927 – 1929), and one of his most celebrated books, *Words for Peace* (Gandhi M. , 2007) . Regarding his *Autobiography*, he tells how he was reluctant to write it, but he was gradually convinced about the fact that in it he could simply narrate the "story of his numerous experiments with truth" , but not any kind of truth, but above all that linked to his *spiritual, particularly moral* experiences.

He says it as follows: these experiences "will of course include experiments with non-violence, celibacy and other principles of conduct believed to be distinct from truth. But for me, truth is the sovereign principle, which include numerous other principles" (Gandhi, 2001) . Such as which principles? ...

Sanctity, justice, humility, compassion, generosity, social inclusion, equality, etc. This is why for Gandhi, in the political field, "non-violence was truth in action".

In *The Story of my Experiments with Truth*, he tells that, when he lived in London (1888 – 1891), his reading of the *Bible*, particularly the New Testament, impressed him strongly the *Sermon on the Mount*, which "...reached directly my heart" (Gandhi M.) . Why do I recall this anecdote? Because Gandhi is inspired on that sermon when writing *Words for Peace*, and when he develops-jointly with Eastern wisdom and the cosmopolitan spirit moving him, a series of thoughts and advices about non-violence and peace. For instance, he says: "Blessed are the non-violent", "Blessed are those who hunger and thirst for righteousness", "Blessed are the pure in heart", which is another way of praising the human being and its dignity.

He nurtured his spirit as well from other books of the Eastern wisdom. He expresses this as follows:

"They have instructions to arrest me...I took with me a breech, two blankets and five books: the Bhagavad Gita, the Ashram Song Book, the Ramayana, the Coran's translation by Rodwells and an edition of the Sermon on the Mount..."

From Prison

Much more can be expressed about this great man, regarded as hero by Muslims, and perhaps a criminal by some British. His fight, however, yielded its fruits because, since the times of his South African experience, he realized that he should fight in favor of his people and their dignity, and against everything that was oppression, injustice and colonialism for any good will person. What was his strength?: His deep interior life and prayer. "From prayer I have obtained the strength I have for my action in the political field" .

"I have known persons who used to envy my interior peace, but this peace, I can assure it, comes from prayer" (Gandhi, 2001).

Doubtlessly, Gandhi is a figure that is full of inspiration for the 20th Century.

Final Comments

We now connect with the great subject-debate of this International Forum: How values from Asia can contribute to the future of humanity? ... In many ways: We only have to get close, to know and to admire the contribution of their millenary cultures, full of spirituality, cultural, artistic and religious richness, love for nature, and the wisdom of *known or unknown* women and men, who have forged, with their lives and example, the profile of what we know as the East, where the intermingling, and at the same time mutual distinction takes place of histories of peoples and nations, varied traditions, races, values and principles, political affiliations, beliefs leading to the search or love of God, science and art, technological advances making out that immense *culturally plural* mosaic which, in what it has of worthy and universal, becomes *transcultural*, i. e. a legacy of humanity.

How can we illustrate in this review the moral, social and spiritual richness of the East and its link with the respect to the dignity of persons? Perhaps we can do it by recalling the nine virtues which, according to Indian sage Yajnavalkia, are common to all: non-violence, truth, refraining from theft, purity, control of senses, generosity, self-control, compassion and patience" (Metamparampil, 2014: 322).

Or perhaps we can do it by mentioning the five fields of social action recommended by Confucius, which are *fully up to date*, in order to favor good government (relationship between ruler and subject), love, harmony and familiar coexistence (husband and wife, parents and children, brothers and sisters) and appreciation for friends (Shicheng, 2013).

There is not only that, but also "a few values cherished among Asians of various origins: Altruism, a sense of community, social virtues, respect for nature, uprightness in public life, and religiosity". (Menamparampil, 2014: 323)

That legacy-because it is such-is a live richness, profitable for any citizen, any community or any nation in the planet, who can reciprocally offer what they have forged from their culture as a wealth of their own. In this case, we talk about West's cultural heritage, linked to a great number of nations and cultures that can be *more or less* developed, or *under way* of development, where there is a strife to combat poverty, disease, famine, violence, and social cancers such as drug traffic, organized crime and trade of persons (even in societies in the so-called "First World"), where sustainable development, education, justice, welfare and comfort for all, in a climate of peace, is one of its goals.

There are, however, in our pluralistic world, vital experiences we could deem *counter-value pressures*, because they obscure or cause the loss of the sense of good, truth, justice, solidarity, peace, or they can even lead to banality of evil Hanna Arendt referred to. We talk about exacerbated relativism, hedonism and consumerism *per se*, materialism, blind to spiritual values, or existential nihilism, leading almost always to the lack of meaning of world and life, to the lack of appreciation for values and contributions from either our own culture or other cultures, having as a center what is fleeting or insubstantial, a superficiality that renders persons and societies insensitive about other people's needs and problems, and anesthetizes not only persons but whole communities, depleting them from ethical, cultural and social dynamism. Thus, the question 'how should we live?' becomes problematic.

Those threats *are combatable* via education and culture, by nurturing ourselves from the wisdom of humanity that is transmitted and forged in families, school and good quality educational policies promoted by good rulers and private initiative, transcendent beliefs that prevent fanaticism, and appraisal and esteem of scientific, artistic and technological advances in the time when we happen to live, with a sustainable, prospective, innovative and creative vision, where all of us can be better human beings. This way of behaving is an evident expression of care and respect to the dignity of persons.

References

Agazzi, E. (2011) . *La ciencia y el alma de Occidente.* (J. A. Casanova, Trad.) Madrid, España: Tecnos.

Agustín, S. (2002) . *Las Confesiones.* Buenos Aires, Argentina: Gaia.

Burgos, B. (2014) . "Persecuciones religiosas: los cristianos en Africa". *Revista Arvbil* (47)

Confucius. (1986) . *The Lun Yü in English.* (W. Cheung, Ed.) Hong Kong, China: Confucius Publishing Co Ltd.

Cuéllar Pérez, H. (2009) . *El ser y la esencia de los valores. Una axiología para el siglo XXI.* México D. F. , México: Trillas.

Cuéllar Pérez, H. (2011) . Persona. Núcleo del tejido social. 7. México, México: Enlace.

Cuéllar, H. (n. d.) . Ripensando la dignitá umana (In ricerca dei fundamenti) .

Chang, J. (2013), *World Culture Development Forum (2013) .* En AAVV, & J. A. Chang (Ed.) Beijing, China: Social Sciences Academic Press.

Chang, J. (2014) . "Building a World with Economic Justice Address at World Cultural Development Forum (2014)". En AA. VV, & J. Chang (Ed.) , *World Culture Develpment (2014) .* Saint Paul Minessota: Hubei University Press.

Della Mirandola, P. (2004) . *Discurso sobre la dignidad del hombre.* (h. 11/num11/art102/ art102. pdf, Ed. , & A. R. Díaz, Trans.) México, México: Revista Digital Universitaria.

Gandhi, M. *An Autobiography or An experiment with Truth.* In: http://www. columbia. edu/itc/ mealac/pritchett/00litlinks/gandhi/#part1.

Gandhi, M. (2001) . *Palabras para la paz* (María Otto ed.) . Santander, España: Sal Terrae.

García González, A. (2007) . La dignidad humana: núcleo duro de los derechos humanos. *IUS Revista Jurídica* (28) .

Hartmann, N. (1965) . Zur Grundelung der Ontologie. Berlín, German: Walter de Gruyter & Co.

Huntington, S. (1993) . The Clash of Civilizations. *Foreing Effairs*, 72 (3) .

Reuter, A. (2015, April 17) . La ONU investiga si el régimen sirio bombardea con gas cloro. *El País* 22 – 49.

Kant, I. (2002) . *Groundwork for the Metaphysics of Morals.* (A. W. Wood, Trans.) New Haven and London, USA: Yale University Press.

Llano, C. (2002). *Viaje al centro del hombrfe*. México D. F. , México: Diana.

Menamparampil, T. (2014). Asia's Future: Profiting from Ethical Wisdom of the World. In AAVV, & J. A. Chang (Ed.), *World Culture Development Forum (2013)*. Beijing, China: Social Sciences Academic Press.

Shicheng, W. (2013). Confucio y el Confucionismo. *Observatorio Virtual del Asia y el Pacífico*, 1 – 5.

Vidart, D. (2012, June). *Sobre la dignidad humana*. (www. filosofía. mx, Editor) Retrieved March 19, 2015.

Reuter, A. (2015, April 17). La ONU investiga si el régimen sirio bombardea con gas cloro. *El País*.

文化发展论丛（世界卷）稿约

　　《文化发展论丛》是由湖北大学高等人文研究院和中华文化发展湖北省协同创新中心共同主办的探讨中国、世界和湖北文化发展的大型丛刊，分为"中国卷"、"世界卷"和"湖北卷"三个部分（分三本书），每年出版一期。湖北大学高等人文研究院成立于 2013 年 6 月 6 日，是湖北大学汇集文科学术骨干和国内外相关高校和研究机构的著名专家为主要成员的专业研究机构，主要围绕中国文化发展、世界文化发展、湖北省文化发展三个领域展开研究，研创出版《文化建设蓝皮书·中国文化发展》（蓝皮书）、《世界文化发展蓝皮书》和《湖北省文化发展蓝皮书》，已经多次成功举办了"中国文化发展论坛"、"世界文化发展论坛"、"湖北省文化发展论坛"，并且在社会科学文献出版社结集出版了相关集刊《中国文化发展论丛》（2013）、《世界文化发展论丛》（2013）、《湖北省文化发展论丛》（2013），以及《文化发展论丛》（中国卷、世界卷、湖北卷）（2014）。同时，以上各卷的 2015 版也正在出版中。

　　《文化发展论丛》（世界卷）作为探讨世界文化发展的专业论丛，每年拟定一个主题（2016 年的主题是"和平、发展和人类的共同价值"），并分为"理论前沿"、"论坛专题"、"问题探讨"、"学术争鸣"和"比较研究"栏目。论丛将在湖北大学高等人文研究院网站每年年初公布来年主题，欢迎关心世界文化事业的广大学者赐稿，本刊将择优刊用；同时，对于研究世界文化具有前沿意义的稿件，将不受主题限制，常年接受赐稿。

　　论文要求具有一定新意、结构严谨、论证清晰，具有较高学术水准，入选论文将在社会科学文献出版社结集出版，稿酬从优。

来稿要求：作者简介采用脚注（与一般论文发表格式同）；注释采用脚注（每页重新编号，编号数字采用①、②、③……），其中引用的著作必须加以详细注释（包括作者、文献名称、出版社、年代日期、页码），若是翻译著作，在文献名称后加入译者；文后列出参考文献；同时附中英文题目、中英文内容摘要和中英文关键词（内容摘要一般控制在200字以内）；正文字数一般控制在1万字以内。此外，引用报刊文章请参照引用著作，出版社和年代日期改为报纸日期和刊物批次。

论文后请附告知详细通信地址，以便联系。

本刊聘请专家客观公正评审稿件，尊重作者观点，但必要时也可能作相应技术处理，凡不愿修改者请事先说明。

本集刊接受电子版投稿，投稿请寄李家莲博士邮箱：lijialian@126.com。

《文化发展论丛》（世界卷）编辑部

2016 年 4 月

图书在版编目（CIP）数据

文化发展论丛. 世界卷. 2015 / 江畅主编. —— 北京：
社会科学文献出版社，2016.9
ISBN 978 - 7 - 5097 - 9181 - 3

Ⅰ. ①文… Ⅱ. ①江… Ⅲ. ①文化发展 - 文集②文化
发展 - 世界 - 文集 Ⅳ. ①G0 - 53②G11 - 53

中国版本图书馆 CIP 数据核字（2016）第 196710 号

文化发展论丛（世界卷）2015

主 编／江 畅
执行主编／强以华
副 主 编／李家莲

出 版 人／谢寿光
项目统筹／周 琼
责任编辑／黄金平

出 版／社会科学文献出版社·社会政法分社（010）59367156
地址：北京市北三环中路甲 29 号院华龙大厦 邮编：100029
网址：www. ssap. com. cn
发 行／市场营销中心（010）59367081 59367018
印 装／三河市尚艺印装有限公司

规 格／开 本：787mm × 1092mm 1/16
印 张：21 字 数：305 千字
版 次／2016 年 9 月第 1 版 2016 年 9 月第 1 次印刷
书 号／ISBN 978 - 7 - 5097 - 9181 - 3
定 价／95. 00 元